TWENTIETH CENTURY VIEWS

The aim of this series is to present the best in contemporary critical opinion on major authors, providing a twentieth century perspective on their changing status in an era of profound revaluation.

Maynard Mack, *Series Editor*
Yale University

TENNESSEE WILLIAMS

TENNESSEE WILLIAMS

A COLLECTION OF CRITICAL ESSAYS

Edited by
Stephen S. Stanton

Prentice-Hall, Inc. *Englewood Cliffs, N.J.*

A SPECTRUM BOOK

Library of Congress Cataloging in Publication Data
Main entry under title:

Tennessee Williams: a collection of critical essays.

(A Spectrum Book)
Bibliography: p.
1. Williams, Tennessee, 1911- —Criticism
and interpretation—Addresses, essays, lectures.
I, Stanton, Stephen Sadler (date)
PS3545.I5365Z845   812'.5'2   77-24463
ISBN 0-13-903625-3
ISBN 0-13-903617-2

For Eric Bentley, Jac Tharpe, Charles Carpenter,
Ruby Cohn, Nancy Tischler, and Esther Jackson,
whose suggestions and comments
have helped shape this book.

10 9 8 7 6 5 4 3 2 1

PRENTICE-HALL INTERNATIONAL, INC., *London*
PRENTICE-HALL OF AUSTRALIA PTY. LIMITED, *Sydney*
PRENTICE-HALL OF CANADA, LTD., *Toronto*
PRENTICE-HALL OF INDIA PRIVATE LIMITED, *New Delhi*
PRENTICE-HALL OF JAPAN, INC., *Tokyo*
PRENTICE-HALL OF SOUTHEAST ASIA PTE. LTD., *Singapore*
WHITEHALL BOOKS LIMITED, *Wellington, New Zealand*

Acknowledgments

Acknowledgment is gratefully made to Random House, Inc. for permission to reprint excerpts from *The Glass Menagerie* by Tennessee Williams (© 1945 by Random House, Inc.) and to New Directions Publishing Corporation (for the Authors) for permission to reprint the following:

Baby Doll, © 1945, 1946, 1953, 1956 by Tennessee Williams
Battle of Angels, © 1940 by Tennessee Williams
Camino Real, © 1948, 1953 by Tennessee Williams
Cat on a Hot Tin Roof, © 1955, 1975 by Tennessee Williams
Dragon Country (all contents), © 1970 by Tennessee Williams
The Eccentricities of a Nightingale, © 1964 by Tennessee Williams
Hard Candy, © 1948, 1950, 1952, 1954 by Tennessee Williams
Eight Mortal Ladies Possessed, © 1971, 1973, 1974 by Tennessee Williams
I Rise in Flames Cried the Phoenix, © 1951 by Tennessee Williams
The Kingdom of Earth, © 1967, 1968 by Two Rivers Enterprises
The Nightly Quest, © 1954, 1964, 1966, 1967 by Tennessee Williams; © 1959 by Two Rivers Enterprises, Inc.
The Milk Train Doesn't Stop Here Any More, © 1963, 1964 by Two Rivers Enterprises, Inc.
The Night of the Iguana, © 1961 by Two Rivers Enterprises, Inc.
Orpheus Descending, © 1955, 1958 by Tennessee Williams
One Arm and Other Stories, © 1939, 1945, 1947, 1948 by Tennessee Williams
Out Cry, © 1969, 1973 by Tennessee Williams
Period of Adjustment, © 1960 by Two Rivers Enterprises, Inc.
The Roman Spring of Mrs. Stone, © 1950 by Tennessee Williams
The Rose Tattoo, © 1950, 1951 by Tennessee Williams
Small Craft Warnings, © 1970, 1972 by Tennessee Williams
A Streetcar Named Desire, © 1947 by Tennessee Williams; Introduction to *Streetcar,* © 1947 by *The New York Times*
Suddenly Last Summer, © 1958 by Tennessee Williams
Summer and Smoke, © 1948 by Tennessee Williams
Sweet Bird of Youth, © 1959 by Two Rivers Enterprises, Inc.
27 Wagons Full of Cotton, © 1945, 1953 by Tennessee Williams

Contents

III. Work in Progress

Introduction

by Stephen S. Stanton

I

The publication in November, 1975, of Tennessee Williams' *Memoirs* climaxed a series of revelations made earlier in several magazine interviews *(Esquire, The Atlantic, Playboy)* that, together with more than a dozen plays published or produced since 1966, have brought about a rejuvenation of interest in one of America's most gifted dramatists. The disclosure in the *Memoirs* of Williams' private life did not, of course, come altogether as a surprise. When he was asked by David Frost on television in 1970 whether he was homosexual, the playwright, though hesitating for a moment, replied, "I cover the waterfront." The audience applauded his courage.

This first public confession indicated not only a new tolerance of homosexuality on the airwaves, but marked the start of a new understanding of Williams, who has been widely discussed but often misjudged and misunderstood. "It is hard now to realize what a bad time of it Tennessee used to have from the American press," Gore Vidal wrote recently in *The New York Review of Books*.[1] "During the Forties and Fifties, the anti-fag battalions were everywhere on the march. From the high lands of *Partisan Review* to the middle ground of *Time* magazine, envenomed attacks on real or suspected fags never let up. ... From 1945 to 1961 *Time* attacked with unusual ferocity everything produced or published by Tennessee Williams. 'Fetid swamp' was the phrase most used to describe his work." Many critics were exasperated, too, by his increasingly violent—some said depraved—plays, from *The Glass Menagerie* (1945) to *Sweet Bird of Youth* (1959). George Jean Nathan found even the language of *A Streetcar*

---

[1] "Selected Memories of the Glorious Bird and the Golden Age" (comments on Williams' published *Memoirs*), February 5, 1976, p. 14. Another quotation in Part III of this introduction will be identified by page number.

Named Desire (1947) shocking, and Mary McCarthy called his favorite kinds of decadent situation peep-shows for the vulgar. After *The Night of the Iguana* (1961), his career seemed over.

True enough, Williams has his shortcomings. There is much lyrical excess in the earlier long plays, accompanied by occasional sentimental lapses and unresolved ambiguities of characterization. These faults stem from his unfortunate compulsion to invest a play with more "meaning" than its plot and characters can support—to strive pretentiously for deep significance through the complex use of myth and private symbol. But his virtues and strengths have also begun to stand out.[2] He has a genius for portraiture, particularly of women, a sensitive ear for dialogue and the rhythms of natural speech, a comic talent often manifesting itself in "black comedy," and a genuine theatrical flair exhibited in telling stage effects attained through lighting, costume, music, and movement. More than many writers, he seems to have been obsessed by a need to write for his own survival, and he has continued through the years (except for a brief period in the late sixties when he suffered a mental breakdown) to complete or revise on the average a play a year. This too, however, has its price: recent plays like *Out Cry* (1973)—called in earlier and later versions *The Two-Character Play*—and some of the pieces in his *Dragon Country* collection of 1970 are deeply marred by his personal involvement in the desperate situations of his characters. This involvement may reflect his own growing despair during the late sixties, but if it is to become drama, it must be better distanced and universalized.

One valuable contribution of the recent *Memoirs* (Catharine Hughes' review is reprinted in this volume) is Williams' attempt, through uncompromising honesty and a graphic, though chronologically disjointed, narrative of the particulars of his life, to make clear, as a recent critic has phrased it, "a continuing preoccupation with the relationship and interdependence of life and art."[3] For Williams, sexual powers (the uninhibited drives of the Lawrencian life-force) are equated with artistic powers. Perceptive critics have realized—though without specific proof until

[2]At this writing, *Tennessee Williams: A Tribute,* an important volume of critical essays on many aspects of Williams' life and work, is being edited by Professor Jac L. Tharpe of the English department, University of Southern Mississippi. See the *Selected Bibliography.*

[3]Albert E. Kalson, "Tennessee Williams Enters *Dragon Country,*" *Modern Drama,* 16 (June, 1973), 61.

the appearance of the *Memoirs*—that Williams, like all authors, recreates his personal life in his works. His early plays reflect a joyous confidence in the assertion of the life-force; later ones show increasing doubt, verging at times on despair, about its effects. Nancy M. Tischler, for example, writes:

> In *Streetcar* the key to Blanche's problem was a homosexual husband. We suspect, however, that in her case and in others, the puritanical, idealistic, confused females are really only female impersonators. ... Williams, apparently, has been discussing his own situation in most of his plays. The female who claims his sympathy is an expression of many of his own needs and blocks. ...[4]

Tischler draws here on Stanley Edgar Hyman's perceptive discussion of the homosexual element in the work of Williams and several other authors.[5] Hyman gives numerous examples from stories and plays of the substitution of women for men as "symbolic vehicles for homosexual love," and he names this metamorphosis the "Albertine strategy," because Marcel Proust employed it in his cyclic novel, *Remembrance of Things Past*, changing Albert into Albertine. Among works by Williams that contain these homosexual switches, according to Hyman, are the story *Rubio Y Morena* (1948), the novel *The Roman Spring of Mrs. Stone* (1950), and *Streetcar*.

In the foreword to his *Memoirs*, Williams says that he became more and more entranced with what for him was a new form, "undisguised self-revelation." The unusual preoccupation in the book itself with his homosexual loves, ranging in depth and intensity from "cruising" and one-night stands to extended sexual partnerships (the one with Frank Merlo lasted many years, and Williams entered a long period of mental depression after Merlo's death in 1963), makes one thing clear: his stories, novels, and plays are metaphors for his own life, just as the women in his works are metaphors for their creator. In one sense they are a literary device, a camouflage; in another, a confession. He identifies himself with the women in his works, just as throughout the *Memoirs* he shows an unusual affinity with the female sex, as in his adolescent propensity to blush and his learning to follow at male dances. There is no living person who "doesn't contain both

---

[4]*Tennessee Williams: Rebellious Puritan* (New York: Citadel Press, 1961), p. 213.

[5]"Some Trends in the Novel," *College English*, 20 (October, 1958), 2-9.

sexes," he remarked in an interview with Mel Gussow of *The New York Times* before the publication of the *Memoirs* (see footnote 10). "Mine could have been either one. Truly, I have two sides to my nature." Later in the interview Williams inadvertently let slip: "I suspect that I will end my life as a woman"—"with a woman," he corrected. This disclosure means at least two things: his plays are frequently transvestite since they substitute women for men in the sexual relationships; and the best of them succeed in transforming homosexual into heterosexual relationships. Louise Blackwell's article sees the latter from an unusual angle. This is an important part of Williams' achievement: in drawing on his private experience, he has universalized it. When the author of a homosexual play proclaimed, in *The New York Times,* the existence of a "gay theatre" and accused Williams of betraying homosexual culture by his "vile art of substituting women for men as characters in plays," the critic Eric Bentley retorted: "...Williams' nature is quite well expressed in his works. If he does not write 'homosexual plays' it is, one can be fairly sure, because he is a human being first and a homosexual second, and not because he is afraid."[6] In the interview quoted above, Williams himself remarked, "It's bad criticism to say I can't put an authentic female character on stage. A true faggot does not like my women. I do not have a faggot, a homosexual, a gay audience. I write for an audience."

Another aspect of Williams' preoccupation with his own androgynous nature is his extraordinary ability to portray the psychology of prostitutes. His most memorable creations of this kind can be found in short plays like *This Property Is Condemned, The Lady of Larkspur Lotion, Hello from Bertha* (all 1945), *A Perfect Analysis Given by a Parrot* (1958), *The Mutilated* (1966), and *Confessional* (1969)—revised as *Small Craft Warnings* (1972), as well as in the long plays *Streetcar, Summer and Smoke* (1948), *Sweet Bird,* and *This Is (An Entertainment)* (1976). At least one psychoanalytic study has been made of this aspect of his work.[7]

[6]Lee Barton, "Why Do Homosexual Playwrights Hide Their Homosexuality?" *The New York Times,* January 23, 1972: II, 1,3. Bentley's letter appeared in the *Times,* February 13, 1972: II, 5.

[7]Phillip Weissman, "A Trio of Tennessee Williams' Heroines: The Psychology of Prostitution," in *Creativity in the Theater* (New York: Basic Books, Inc., 1965). Reprinted in *Twentieth Century Interpretations of "A Streetcar Named Desire,"* edited by J. Y. Miller (Englewood Cliffs: N.J.: Prentice-Hall, 1971).

So we encounter a paradox in Williams. A homosexual, he not only sympathizes with women but strongly identifies with them. As Eric Bentley has written of Albee's *Who's Afraid of Virginia Woolf,* the confusions of sexual identity (are Martha and George simply surrogates in a homosexual marriage?) suggest our own myriad confusions of identity in the modern world.[8] Gordon Rogoff has contended that Williams' exploitation of lurid sexual situations in his plays only serves to titillate the men and women in his audience and, by making them hunt for clues to his sex life, turns them into voyeurs seeking homosexual innuendos (in a time when such things were to remain hidden). In *Streetcar,* for example, they would see Blanche DuBois simply as a man in drag.[9] But the *Memoirs* makes it clear that she is more.[10] We can look beneath that surface and see her as a psychological extension of her creator, a sensitive specimen of the "fugitive kind," lost in a broken world and haunted by the same illusions, guilts, and fears, seeking to find God ("Sometimes—there's God—so quickly!") in intimate personal relationships ("intimacies with strangers was all I seemed able to fill my empty heart with"). We no longer need to puzzle over the mystifications of sexual identity that so troubled Williams' critics before 1975.

II

In the nearly forty years that Tennessee Williams has been writing for the theatre, how has his style of writing changed?

[8]*What Is Theatre? Incorporating The Dramatic Event and Other Reviews: 1944-1967* (New York: Atheneum, 1968), p. 413.

[9]"The Restless Intelligence of Tennessee Williams," *Tulane Drama Review,* 10 (Summer, 1966), 78-92. Quotations from this essay will be identified in Part II of this introduction by page number.

[10]*Memoirs* (Garden City, N.Y.: Doubleday, 1975). See, for example, pp. 131, 231. In the interview with Mel Gussow quoted above, Williams said: "All my relationships with women are very, very important to me. The most stupid thing said about my writing is that my heroines are disguised transvestites. Absolutely and totally none of them are anything but women. It's true about my work, and it's true about Albee's in 'Virginia Woolf.' I understand women, and I can write about them.

"It's true my heroines often speak for me. That doesn't make them transvestites. Playwrights always have somebody speak for them. I think that more often I have used a woman rather than a man to articulate my feelings. ..." "Tennessee Williams on Art and Sex," *The New York Times,* November 3, 1975, p. 49. More than two years before, in "Let Me Hang It All Out," *The New York Times,* March 4, 1973: II, 1, 3, Williams had protested that Blanche DuBois is not a drag queen.

Since 1960, considerably. What about dramatic structure? Gordon Rogoff sees most of the major plays through *The Milk Train Doesn't Stop Here Anymore* (1962) as impossible quests for release from the prison of the self; endless, futile searchings for an exit; turbulent studies in groping motion but with "no shape,... no interior logic, no place to go" (91). But despite their lack of overall structure, they contain for Rogoff excellently constructed individual scenes. "Williams was never so much an expert *play*-wright as he was a superlative *scene*wright" (89). However, in the two plays of *Slapstick Tragedy (The Mutilated* and *The Gnädiges Fräulein* [1966]), Rogoff finds signs of change: though they are "plotless tales...more remembered than dramatized," the protagonists "are where they are to stay. It isn't necessary for them to move anywhere in order to feel the force of dislocation. Life... sits at a jerking standstill..." (91). One supposes that Rogoff has perceived this same structural simplicity, inevitability, and lack of pretense in certain later plays like *Kingdom of Earth* (1968)— also called *The Seven Descents of Myrtle*—and *Out Cry.*

It is unfortunate that space limitations do not permit an essay to be included in this volume on Williams' short stories as the genesis for many of his plays. Although Ruby Cohn, in her chapter reprinted in this collection, touches on the debt of *Streetcar, Camino Real* (1953), and *Cat on a Hot Tin Roof* (1955) to early stories or plays, other dramas evolved from such experiments, among them *Glass Menagerie, Summer and Smoke, Orpheus Descending* (1957), *Suddenly Last Summer* (1958), *Iguana, Milk Train, Small Craft Warnings,* and *Out Cry.* Two essays on this subject are listed in the bibliography.

Although Williams has often been called a realist, everyone has noted his many departures from realism. He is more poetic, more lyrical, probably more symbolical than Arthur Miller. He is a disciple of the earlier avant garde playwrights, particularly the surrealists and expressionists. Creator of "plastic theatre" (a synthesis of the theatre arts), he first used the form to advantage in *Glass Menagerie,* with its cinematic techniques and symbolic imagery. Here were manifested those characteristics which have become his trademark: the poetic, nostalgic mood; realistic action filtered and slightly distorted through the narrator's memory; elaborate production notes; the use of scrim, slide projections, and music; the visual symbolism of the glass menagerie itself; and the subtler religious symbolism, explored in this book by Roger B. Stein. Critics divide as to whether Williams is basically a realist or a poetic interpreter of sharply realistic actions and characters through a screen of illusion and memory. The most sensible position is perhaps that of Gerald Weales and Ruby Cohn, Cohn commenting that Williams creates "a symbolic resonance beyond the realistic surface," and Weales writing, in *Tennessee Williams* (1965), that he "has done his best to mask" the realistic through caricature, myths and rituals, lurid plots, symbols, distorted sets, and visual and auditory effects. Cohn shows Williams working within the realist convention to produce characters endowed with crisp colloquial speech but at the same time combining verbal and theatrical imagery symbolically in *Glass Menagerie, Streetcar,* and *Iguana,* and even allegorically in *Camino Real, Milk Train,* and *Slapstick Tragedy.*

Realistic or poetic, the big change in the style and tone of his plays after *Iguana* is discussed in an interview he had with Lewis Funke and John E. Booth *(Theatre Arts,* January, 1962) during the rehearsals of *Iguana.* Williams admitted dissatisfaction with with his old way of writing plays:

> I depended too much on language—on words. ... The whole attitude of this new wave of playwrights is not to preach...not to be dogmatic, to be provocatively allusive...human relations are terrifyingly ambiguous. ...I think my kind of literary or pseudo-literary style of writing for the theatre is on its way out. ...Poetry doesn't have to be words, you see. In the theatre it can be situations, it can be silences. ...My great *bête noir* as a writer has been a tendency to poeticize. ...*The Night of the Iguana* is a play whose theme...is how to live beyond despair and still live. ...I despair sometimes of love being lasting, and of people getting along together...as nations and as individuals.   (pp. 17-18,73)

The verbal excesses he is aware of occur most obviously in *Glass Menagerie, Streetcar, Summer and Smoke, Camino Real, Cat, Sweet Bird,* and *Iguana.* At least one central character in each falls into a long-winded, trite, or pretentious vein, even if, as Cohn shows in her chapter in this volume, it is in the nature of that character to do so.

One of the distinguishing features of the plays of the late fifties —*Orpheus Descending, Suddenly Last Summer, Sweet Bird*— was their violent plots. These plots were not meant to be realistic; they merely compressed certain gruesome realities of life and used violent events symbolically. By 1960, he was tired of them. In *Newsweek,* June 27, 1960, he said: "I'm through with what have been called my 'black' plays. ...Bestiality still exists, but I don't want to write about it any more. ... For years I was too pre-occupied with the destructive impulses. From now on I want to be concerned with the kinder aspects of life..." (p. 96).

What emerged was a new kind of desperate, self-mocking humor, as if to camouflage increasing anxiety about his health and doubt about his ability to write. After *Iguana* he did not have another commercial success until *Small Craft Warnings* in 1972. The emphasis in these later plays is upon a kind of survival, a resigned acceptance or grim endurance of life's ills. The increasingly grotesque humor of *Iguana, Milk Train, Slapstick Tragedy, Kingdom of Earth,* and *Small Craft Warnings* he has called his "wild black comedy." Harold Clurman in his review in this book finds that *The Mutilated* "requires its jokes to be horrible; its horror funny," and that *Gnädiges Fräulein* contains "an odd but effective mixture of gallows humor and Rabelaisian zest." Williams, Clurman asserts, is "avenging himself on the 'enemy' [critics? directors?] with satiric lunacy." Even a pessimistic play like *Out Cry* is permeated with what Williams calls "the jokes of the condemned," as Thomas P. Adler shows in his essay on the late plays. Humor or no, the sense of catastrophe is seldom absent; indeed, an aura of catastrophe hangs over all the major plays, and, as Stein shows, was heralded as early as *Glass Menagerie.*

These later black comedies, including *Period of Adjustment* (1960), *Slapstick Tragedy, Kingdom of Earth,* and *This Is,* have been characterized by a new terseness, a cynical and, at times, strained, farcical tone. Sometimes this new note is realistic, sometimes sur-realistic. In an interesting study, Leland Starnes finds it as early as *The Rose Tattoo* (1951).[11] The ominous cracking sound of the house settling an inch further into the cavern at the end of *Adjustment* and the funeral coach the honeymooners use for a car belie the successful adjustments they seem to have made, the "high point" they have reached. The vision of the Virgin seen by Celeste and Trinket at the end of *The Mutilated* is similarly cancelled in *Gnädiges Fräulein* by the gluttony of Indian Joe and the savagery of the coca-loonies whose cries, Weales reminds us, very much prevail. So, too, the dynamited levee sends the flood waters around the farm house at the end of *Kingdom of Earth,* as Chicken pulls Myrtle to safety; and in *This Is,* the rampaging Countess, a nymphomaniac who has

---

[11]Leland Starnes, "The Grotesque Children of *The Rose Tattoo,*" *Modern Drama,* 12 (February, 1970), 357-69. The quotation below is identified by page number.

cuckolded her husband, destroyed her lovers, and tried to conquer time, fears the dark (symbolizing death and disintegration).

In two of the plays written in this period of experiment, Williams has not yet successfully integrated his portrayal of the central character. The heroine of *Gnädiges Fräulein,* as Starnes notes, "vacillates confusingly between surrealism and naturalism and at last founders in ineffectuality for lack of definition; we have the frustrating impression, therefore, of a potentially exciting concept that might have worked but which was either carried too far or not "far enough." The explanation in this case...lies in Williams' present and hopefully transient uncertainty concerning point of view and subject matter in his work" (footnote to Starnes, p. 364).

In her review of the 1976 premiere of *This Is,* in San Francisco, Judith H. Clark suggests that this same vacillation between surrealism and realism blurs our perception of the protagonist. The Countess, in tentative revisions made by Williams during this production, is given a third layer of personality: a realistic, detached self (suggesting the future?) steps briefly out of the role of Countess and comments critically on her frenzied race with time (the present). The Countess is also seen in a relaxed mood at moments when she listens to her dead mother's voice (the past). Since these three aspects of the Countess have not yet been resolved in satisfactory dramatic terms, we cannot be sure what Williams is finally saying. The "transient uncertainty" about point of view and subject matter that Starnes finds in the Fräulein's portrayal is still present also in that of the Countess. Are these uncertainties transient or permanent? Judging from his habitual practice of revising and from his commitment to keep on writing, one hopes that Williams will remove them.

III

"Tennessee is the sort of writer who does not develop; he simply continues. By the time he was an adolescent he had his themes. Constantly he plays and replays the same small but brilliant set of cards" (17). Though Gore Vidal's compliment is double-edged, he is surely right in noting Williams' skillful and fresh variations on a formulized thematic pattern. This can be a weakness but also a strength. Are not many great writers limited in their use of themes? Writers who write "organically" (the term is Williams') write naturally about what they know at first hand—their own experience. To put it facetiously, if Ibsen's plays are acceptable despite the fact that they are thematically one play rewritten two dozen ways, why not Williams'? Let us examine more closely that "small but brilliant set of cards" that he keeps replaying.

In her chapter in this volume, Esther M. Jackson presents Williams as an existentialist rather than an absurdist. Through exposure and scrutiny of man's inner nature, he reveals man's anti-heroic qualities, his potential for moral and spiritual disintegration, his frequent lack of compassion, his own responsibility for his suffering, his sense of guilt, his quest for identity, and his possible redemption through compassion and love. One of Jackson's most interesting points is that Williams, with few exceptions, does not create heroes and villains, characters who are moral absolutes. The typical Williams anti-hero "is a schematic presentation of extended moral possibilities. In each of his characters Williams presents a composite image, a montage of the roles which together comprise the anti-heroic character." The playwright follows Pirandello's theory that character is "an agglomeration of roles," "a loosely unified grouping of identities," "a configuration of masks." This organization of character into multiple levels of identity, stratifications of the self, is the technique Williams has chosen to demonstrate his belief, already quoted, that "human relations are terrifyingly ambiguous." The Countess in *This Is* exemplifies, however imperfectly at an early stage of revision, his effort to create a Pirandellian central character—"to be provocatively allusive."

All Williams' ideas seem to follow from this basic concept of the anti-hero. Evil, for example, is not only to be found in society. Evil also exists within the self, and Blanche, Big Daddy, Jabe Torrance, Sebastian, Boss Finley, and Shannon are dramatic demonstrations of it. All have weaknesses of the flesh and are selfish—even brutal. Corruption, whether in others or one's self, is a cancer that gradually consumes and kills. And it causes its victims to hate, destroy, and kill, too.

But evil may be offset by good in Williams' interpretation of the anti-hero, both in society and the self. Good is spirit as opposed to flesh; dreams as opposed to mundane reality; ideals as opposed to brutality; above all it is love as opposed to selfish interests. The sensitive conveyors of spirit, dreams, ideals, and love are the misfits in a savage world who fight alone and are destroyed. In vain do the pursuers of good struggle to be free of this contaminating world. Gradually they too are polluted with the stain of evil. These are the "fugitive kind" that Donald P. Costello exhaustively depicts in his essay. The symbolism of sky, stars, birds (both predatory and heaven-seeking), and animals that Costello finds throughout the plays, from *This Property Is Condemned* to *This Is*, helps Williams to dramatize the difference between the instinctual, fleshly, and rapacious nature of the corrupting earth and the clean, white, serene sky which remains pure, inviolable. A virtue of Costello's essay is that it shows how poetically Williams has employed this symbolism of the tainted earth and the timeless, limitless kingdom of the fugitives. Almost all of his plays use this symbolism of nature to segregate the incorruptible, ideal world of man's dreams, where "the purity and the beauty of sensual life" can exist, from man's jungle world, the "kingdom of earth."

What happens when the fugitives fail to escape the corrupting earth? When they compromise with or yield to the forces of evil? When they are trapped in illusions? When they are guilt-ridden like Orestes or Hamlet but are not saved through love and compassion? Arthur Ganz argues forcefully that they reject life itself and for this most serious of all crimes they are punished. Not infrequently, Williams' victims of brutality and evil themselves become in some ambiguous sense the victimizers or rejectors, like Sebastian in *Suddenly Last Summer*. In a few plays, rejector and rejected (sometimes homosexual) are different characters (Blanche and Alan Gray; Hannah and Shannon).

A frightening version of this theme of the fugitive kind vainly trying to rise above a contaminating earth is described by Sy M. Kahn in his review of the Vienna premiere of *The Red Devil Battery Sign* (January, 1976). The play uses a cruder, less poetic symbolism than is customary in Williams to show that a genteel but puritanical and decadent cultural order (symbolized by the "Woman Downtown") will be replaced by a brutal and savagely instinctual one. It is a bleaker, more frightening vision than those perceived in *Streetcar* and *Kingdom of Earth*.[12] In the first, we

---

[12]Albert E. Kalson, in "Tennessee Williams' *Kingdom of Earth:* A Sterile Promontory," *Drama and Theatre*, 8 (Winter, 1969-70), 90-93 considers that play—an extended dramatic metaphor for the act of fellatio—to be Williams' "bleakest vision to date. ...[It] reinforces the dramatist's increasingly despairing vision of existence without hope."

see in a vivid metaphor that the apes will take over (Stanley says, "I am the king around here"); in the second, that "Chicken is king!" The indisputable fact of *Red Devil* is that Wolf is king.

In the plays just mentioned we encounter an ironic variation of another theme related to the anti-hero concept. If modern man is guilty of the human condition, he is redeemable, as Jackson says, through love and compassion. But in *Streetcar, Iguana, Kingdom of Earth,* and *Red Devil,* plays written in different periods of the author's career, "salvation" is grotesquely twisted into a kind of damnation and produces a note of horror. Blanche has always depended on the kindness of strangers and at the end is dependent on the doctor who leads her off to the mental institution; Myrtle is totally dependent on the mercenary Chicken for survival in a perilous flood; the "Woman Downtown," having lost everything in a world reduced to slag heaps, has but one chance of survival, to become a gang leader's moll; the defrocked priest Shannon's single hope of salvation through the restorative powers of the widow Faulk is at best a chance one. Many other examples could be added of this precarious and degrading dependence on others for salvation—in Williams the term means minimal survival. Yet, strangely, in the two latest plays produced in 1976, he seems to see violent revolt against the vested interests of the world as the only hope. Destruction of the conventional, the old, the decadent is preferable to apathetic endurance.

If salvation has lost its traditional religious meaning for the anti-hero, so has the universe. A metaphysical void can offer little comfort or solace to the troubled soul. Above all, there is the fear of time, of death. An early version of *Sweet Bird* was titled *The Enemy: Time,* and time dogs all Williams' characters. But love helps to conquer the fear of death. Thomas Adler interprets the search for God in the plays as a search for meaningful relationships between people, people meaning God to each other: "...Williams conceives of God as anthropomorphic, made in man's own image and likeness...the way we conceive of God is also the way we will see our neighbor and ourself." If we are, as Catharine Holly says in *Suddenly Last Summer,* "all of us children in a vast kindergarten trying to spell God's name with the wrong alphabet blocks!" then it makes a difference whether we spell it "God of Wrath" or "God of Love." Although, according to Adler, Williams himself prefers the latter spelling, several of his characters (Sebastian in *Suddenly,* Shannon in *Iguana,* Chicken in *Kingdom*) picture God as cruel, vengeful, or hard, and, except for Shannon, who sets the iguana free because "God won't do it," fall prey to their own visions of evil.

Gilbert Debusscher, taking an opposite position, tries to show that Williams' image of God resembles the deities of Sebastian, Shannon, and Christopher in *Milk Train*. In Debusscher's view, by naming each of these characters for a Christian saint, Williams creates grotesque parodies of the early martyrs who proved their faith in God and love of man through symbolic suffering and death. Williams does not wish to offer the nightmarish deific visions of these modern "saints" as simply subjective hallucinations imposed by the characters, but as reflections of his own spectral and frightened concept of a chaotic universe—"the savage grin on the face of God."

If we can find a thread of hope, a flicker of optimism, in the plays after *Milk Train*, it surely lies in the simple *caveat:* make the most of your short life; it's all you've got. All are characterized by a painful, desperate effort to cling to life at any price. The acceptance of life and death that Hannah and Christopher teach in *Iguana* and *Milk Train* (perhaps Williams' most optimistic works) is not to be found in more recent plays. A few weak rays of light may be discerned in an otherwise dismal scene: The mutilated Fräulein, getting herself together and going on (a parody of Hannah's endurance of pain?); the highly sexed Myrtle who will be gratified by Chicken; Bobby, the younger homosexual in *Small Craft Warnings,* who can say "My God!" instead of just "Oh, well"; the Countess in *This Is,* whose pregnancy by her revolutionary lover symbolizes the coming of a new order.

IV

Judging Williams a visceral not a cerebral writer, Tischler stresses in her essay in this volume the conflict in his work between instinct and intellect. In spite of his need to write "organically," spontaneously, he has frequently yielded to a persistent temptation to deal self-consciously with themes centered in Christ figures, Greek myths involving the rituals of death and rebirth, and other complex symbols. By universal agreement even among disparaging critics, his genius lies in his characterizations, his dialogue, his comic sense, and his symbols: the glass menagerie, the blue piano, the bandaged and bleeding Fräulein, the hot cat and the cool moon, the legless pure bird that never touches earth *(Orpheus Descending)*, the released iguana, the Mississippi flood

His visceral, romantic nature is most pronounced in his un-usual sensitivity to the multiple levels of the self: "We are pris-oners inside our own skins" *(Orpheus Descending)*. "I've always sensed the fact that life was too ambiguous to be presented in a cut and dried fashion" (Funke and Booth interview). "I always try to write obliquely...I am not a direct writer; I am always an oblique writer, if I can be; I want to be allusive..."(quoted in the De-busscher essay). "Truly, I have two sides to my nature" (*New York Times* interview). He has always tried to penetrate to facets of our innermost natures that are invisible when observed directly.

The two endings Williams wrote for *Cat* will succinctly illus-trate the two antithetical sides of his creative process, the visceral and the cerebral. The first ending he wrote "organically," from the heart. In Brick he unquestionably saw himself. In his explana-tion of the two versions of Act III that is inserted in most printed editions of *Cat*, the key sentence is: "I felt that the moral paralysis of Brick was a root thing in his tragedy, and to show a dramatic progression would obscure the meaning of that tragedy in him and...I don't believe that a conversation, however revelatory, ever effects so immediate a change in the heart or even conduct of a person in Brick's state of spiritual disrepair" (New Directions edition, p. 152). The parallel is to be found in the short story that preceded the play, "Three Players of a Summer Game." Brick will not make a sudden or miraculous adjustment to marriage; he will never be fully reconciled to Maggie. The text of the original version of Act III makes clear, as Cohn, Tischler, Robert B. Heil-man, Benjamin Nelson, and others have emphasized, that Wil-liams' sympathies lay with it; it is more tightly and convincingly written.

The second version of Act III, suggested by Elia Kazan, director of the Broadway production, is far more optimistic in its broadly hinted reconciliation. But we know from the looser texture of the writing and from Williams' later comments in interviews and the *Memoirs* that he rewrote the third act reluctantly—that is to say, insincerely, self-consciously. Eager for success, he yielded to Kazan, whom he wanted to direct the play. This Brick lacks the ambiguity, the obliqueness, and the depth of the first Brick. To be sure, Maggie is more charmingly presented, but at the expense of the real Brick and the integrity of the play. And Big Daddy's reappearance is disappointingly anticlimactic.

Williams has always sought to create anti-heroes whose behavior and direction are determined by inevitable circumstances. Except in a comedy like *The Rose Tattoo* or an expressionistic fantasy like *Camino Real,* their fates are pessimistically conceived. They seldom change their pattern of behavior, even in the face of disaster. Because of some inherent weakness or abnormality, they unconsciously will these disasters. This is certainly true of Brick, a latent homosexual who, as Williams has said, possesses unrealized abnormal tendencies. He will make a heterosexual adjustment with difficulty. In the rewritten third act, therefore, Williams has arbitrarily altered the inevitable course of a character whose nature plainly dictated that course. The first Act III of *Cat* is the one Williams meant to write. His heart was in it. It came spontaneously from his own nature and experience.

V

To sum up the achievement to date of Tennessee Williams is difficult. He has said that only "work," a four-letter word even lovelier than "love," sustains him. Just when many are ready to concede that his career as one of America's greatest and most influential playwrights is over, he has a way of coming back. At this writing, a Florida newspaper reports him as presenting a new ending to a stunned cast performing *Suddenly Last Summer* in Key West. "Come hell or high water," Gerald Weales in another connection has written, "Williams, like Chicken [in *Kingdom of Earth*], has no intention of abandoning familiar ground."

Since recovering from his breakdown in the late Sixties, he has resumed his prolific output. His recent publications include the collection of plays *Dragon Country,* and two others *(Small Craft Warnings* and *Out Cry),* a novel, a volume of short stories, and the *Memoirs.* He has had four plays produced: *Small Craft Warnings, Out Cry, Red Devil,* and *This Is,* all except the last more than once and in more than one version. After revisions, further productions of the last two of these can be expected. According to the *Memoirs, Gnädiges Fräulein* is now rewritten and will be staged as *The Latter Days of a Celebrated Soubrette.* If his health does not fail, he will publish and produce many more works.

But with this frantic compulsion to write, to keep on going, will he create, one surely wonders, another masterpiece like *Glass Menagerie, Streetcar,* or *Cat?* If he can follow the advice of critics like Nancy Tischler: that he "reveal his truth instead of pronouncing it," that he "lose himself in [his characters] and allow [them] to speak his thoughts in their own voices"; Ruby Cohn: that he create a vivid, supple dialogue embracing many emotional shadings; Arthur Ganz: that he control his warring impulses to punish and to extend sympathy without discrimination; and Gordon Rogoff: that he release his "stinging laughter never very far from even his darkest visions," Tennessee Williams may yet create another major work.

VI

A word about the arrangement of the essays in this volume. They have been divided—somewhat loosely—into three groups: (1) those that approach single plays or groups of plays from the perspective of dramatic technique—dialogue and poetic language, symbolism, black comedy, character complexity (Part II of this introduction considers most of these essays); (2) those that discuss plays in relation to a central theme (Part III outlines most of these); and (3) critical reviews of two plays produced in 1976 which are still in progress; they have not yet been seasoned and polished, for Williams refines his work only through many revisions and performances.

Tennessee Williams' Approach to Tragedy

by Robert Bechtold Heilman

Only about a half-dozen years elapsed between O'Neill's last complete play and, in the late 1940s, the first major successes of Tennessee Williams and of Arthur Miller. It is easy to think of the three together, for their thematic similarities are more marked than the patent differences among them. Their chief common ground is the portrayal of men and women who suffer disaster, who destroy themselves or move toward self-destruction, or are the victims of maladjustment, debility, or outright malady. For the most part, however, O'Neill and Williams are closer to each other than either is to Miller. Failures of personality are a special theme of O'Neill and Williams; but while Miller first achieved fame with a drama of a man who failed, he has moved on to deal with stronger characters. However, O'Neill and Miller do share a suspicion of would-be saviors, while Williams develops a considerable interest in savior-figures who succeed, either straightforwardly or ambiguously. Despite their common interest in characters who collapse or fail, O'Neill and Williams go about the subject differently. O'Neill's people, as we have seen, are self-conscious, striving, attuned to problems and ideas. Williams' people, to whom we now come, are more given to undefined feeling than to thought, and their troubles originate more often in faulty neurological mechanisms.

In Williams' work the sufferers who do not make the grade have an air of illness or something close to it. The early plays deal with hypersensitive characters who, from weakness or disability, either cannot face the world at all or have to opt out of it. Laura Wingfield in *The Glass Menagerie* (1945) cannot meet the ordinary problems of life; Blanche DuBois in *A Streetcar Named Desire* (1947) lacks stamina to bear up under the stresses that experience brings. Laura stays at home for good; Blanche ends up in a sanitarium. Williams' early predilection for the structure of melodrama appears in another way in his male protagonists, who face the world vigorously and in their own ways seem headed for triumph; Tom Wingfield escapes from financial constraint and family burdens to travel and write, and Stanley Kowalski, endowed with sexual virility and a keen sense of how the world goes, is ready to charge over all obstacles. So we have the familiar dualism of victors and victims.

But *Streetcar* has other convolutions that come out of a less simplistic imagination. There is the paradoxical attraction, for a moment at least, of opposites: Stanley, carrying the no-longer-resistant Blanche into the bedroom, tells her, "We've had this date with each other from the beginning!" (x).[1] The sexual common ground points up a world of imperfect choices: in Blanche, sexuality is allied with indiscriminateness, sentimentality, a decayed yet not wholly unattractive gentility, in a word, the end of a line, the collapse of a tradition; in Stanley, with a coarse new order, vigorous but rude and boorish. Stella, Stanley's wife and Blanche's sister, has to make a choice: she cries in bitter grief for the sister, but chooses Stanley, whose "maleness," as Williams' master D. H. Lawrence[2] might call it, is evidently meant to compensate for conspicuous narrowness, gaucherie, and arrogance

---

[1] *A Streetcar Named Desire* (New York: New Directions, 1947).

[2] In *The Glass Menagerie* (New York: New Directions, 1949) Amanda Wingfield is made to say "that hideous book by that insane Mr. D. H. Lawrence" (I.iii) and to become, in part, a Lawrence villain by opposing "instincts" and supporting "Superior things! Things of the mind and the spirit!" (I.v). Williams and Donald Windham coauthored *You Touched Me!*, a "romantic comedy" based on Lawrence's story of the same title, and produced in 1945; it is a rather gay theatrical version of the Lawrence melodrama of admirable body (lower-class boy and middle-class heroine) against villainous spirit (spinster and clergyman). *I Rise in Flame, Cried the Phoenix*, "A Play in One Act about D. H. Lawrence," was published in 1951 and again in 1970. Williams' preface, dated 1941, not only expresses admiration for "probably the greatest modern monument to the dark roots of creation" *(Dragon Country* [New York: New Directions, 1970], p. 56) but also shows critical detachment with respect to Lawrence's work. In Williams' Lawrentian works several shifts are worth notice. Lawrence's lower-class potent males have a sort of innate gentility, whereas Williams has not, for the sake of doctrine, purged Stanley Kowalski of his vulgarity. *Summer and Smoke* (1948), instead of simply deriving soul from body, attributes to the soul an independent restorative function. *The Rose Tattoo* (produced 1950), a comedy,

(though the arrogance is modified in turn by his dependence on Stella). What is notable here is Williams' complication of the basic Lawrence melodrama, which, as in *Lady Chatterley's Lover and St. Mawr*, tends to put sexuality and all the other virtues on one side, and nonsexuality and the vices on the other.

With Blanche, Williams goes a step further away from the univocal record of disaster. The crucial trauma in her life was the discovery that her young husband—"Blanche didn't just love him but worshipped the ground he walked on!" (vii)—was homosexual, and the shock of his consequent suicide. This might be simply something that happened to her. But Williams is feeling his way into personality rather than stopping at bad luck. He makes Blanche say, of her husband's suicide, "It was because, on the dance floor—unable to stop myself—I'd suddenly said—I saw! 'I know! You disgust me!'" (vi). Here is a flash of something new: Williams transcends the story of the victim and finds complicity, or tragic guilt, in the heroine. It is evident that Williams wants to give this episode major importance, for he has the "Varsouviana" —the music for the dance from which Blanche's husband broke away to shoot himself—played at key moments throughout the drama. And here several problems arise. If we grant that the music attaches to her sense of guilt rather than simply to the whole shocking experience, still the effect is lyric rather than dramatic: it creates an indefinite feeling rather than establishes a definite development of consciousness. Blanche speaks almost no additional words on this central experience; it remains a wound, the center of a morally static situation, in which it is not clear whether a sense of guilt persists as much as does a sense of shock and privation. At any rate, infinite regret, plus an infusion of self-pity, provides Blanche with no way of coming to terms with the disaster that borders on tragedy; when there is no reordering,

---

avoids the frequent Lawrence melodrama of the elect and the nonelect; here all are elect and their need is simply to divest themselves of mistaken ideals that temporarily obstruct salvation by the body. In writing the script for the film *Baby Doll* (1956), Williams made more conspicuous the Lawrence element in the Boccaccian one-act play of ten years earlier, *27 Wagons Full of Cotton:* in the film, as in *You Touched Me!*, sexual competence is accompanied by other virtues—somewhat at the risk, indeed, of making a Lawrentian Merriwell out of Silva Vicarro, the lover who is at once good businessman, imaginative playfellow, and philosophical commentator. But then in *Cat on a Hot Tin Roof* there is, in spite of the importance of sex in the lives of the central characters, something close to a reversal of Lawrence doctrine: sex does not produce, but is wholly dependent on, the integrated personality.

shock becomes illness, and illness eventually triumphs. By the end *Streetcar* has drifted back to the history of the victim, with its seductive appeal to the strange human capacity for sinking luxuriously into illness as an aesthetic experience. Yet its claims on the feelings are divided enough to prevent an unqualified *monopathic* structure. [*]

"SUMMER AND SMOKE"

In *Summer and Smoke* (first produced in 1948; subsequently revised) Williams appears to be making a more definite move toward a tragic complexity in his major characters, and then again to be drawn to a kind of theatrical effect that takes him away in a different direction. Almost from the beginning we are aware of divisions within two characters whose repeated confrontations provide, on the face of it, the principal dramatic tension—Alma Winemiller, a minister's nervous and genteel daughter, evidently in her mid-twenties, and her neighbor and friend from schooldays, Dr. John Buchanan, who in this Mississippi summer seems about to give up medicine, which he temperamentally shrinks from, for gambling, drink, and debauchery. Alma, believing in "culture," the finer things, ladies and gentlemen, noble actions, and above all in the primacy of the soul (that *alma* is Spanish for soul is carefully brought out in the dialogue), upbraids John for choosing the lower instead of the higher, for preferring worldliness, fleshliness, and deviltry to medical salvation for others, and for thus being false to himself. He, in turn, denies the soul, affirms the body, and taxes Alma with confused ideals, artificiality, hysteria, and self-delusion. In some ways quite like a medieval body-and-soul allegory (that is to say, a melodrama of concepts), *Summer and Smoke* is complicated, on the surface level, by the fact that there is attraction between Alma and John, indeed on her side a very strong one, and then, at the level of personality, by the conflicts within each of the two, and particularly in Alma. The play is more hers than John's, and we are given a fuller and

[* My emphasis. On pp. 57-58 of his book, Professor Heilman defines melodrama as "monopathic": the hero "has oneness of feeling" and is not torn or divided by conflicting drives; "all his strength or weakness faces in one direction." Tragedy is "polypathic": the audience experiences "the conflicting impulses of the divided man. ...The polypathic experience is complex, troubling, burdensome, as gaining knowledge must be." The monopathic produces a simpler emotional experience.—Ed.]

more immediate view of the clash of her ideas and ideals with her basic impulses, a clash that is making her into a textbook neurotic. Her split is first articulated when John tells her that she has "palpitations" because she has a *doppelgänger* who is "badly irritated" (i).[3] Alma herself is made to speak in terms that, from our point of view, are very significant: she tells John that she is "one of those weak and divided people" that contrast with "you solid strong ones," and she repeats that she is "a weak and divided person who stood in adoring awe of your singleness..."(xi). Though Alma is hardly right in thinking John "single" (she is more accurate in scene vi when she calls him "confused, just awfully, awfully confused, as confused as I am—but in a different way") and in identifying dividedness with weakness, nevertheless her key terms "singleness" and "divided" point to antithetical realities that are the issue in *Summer and Smoke*.

That Alma is "divided" and John "confused" is the groundwork of tragedy, and indeed here the potential is great. The situation is significantly like that in Samuel Richardson's *Clarissa,* where the intense struggle between Clarissa and Lovelace coexists with a strong attraction between them. What happens to Richardson's pair is that each of them resists his own doubleness and so fanatically preserves an inadequate singleness (she her ideal of chastity, he his will to conquer) that both are destroyed.[4] For a while it appears that Williams is sensing and tracing such a destructiveness, which is a familiar form of tragic hubris. But he decides not to follow through; the only violence is among minor characters (John's father is shot by the father of Rosa Gonzales, John's other-side-of-the-tracks girl); and the mode becomes essentially comic when therapeutic adjustments are made before any passion gets out of hand. The parallels are extraordinary as each instructs the other, and Alma sums up, "You've come around to my old way of thinking and I to yours..." (xi). John acknowledges the soul by becoming a medical hero, and does a turn for the body by marrying a floozie's gay and sprightly daughter, a morsel sent to Newcomb College and there made more colorful by new wiles rather than sicklied o'er by the pale cast of thought. In the improbable final scene Alma picks up a traveling salesman in the square, and they make off to a night club. She seems to have said a permanent farewell to her soul.

[3]*Summer and Smoke* (New York: New Directions, 1948).

[4]Compare the interpretation in Ian Watt, *The Rise of the Novel* (London: Chatto and Windus, 1957), pp. 228-38.

A situation that could lead into troublesome depths and irreversible plunges is smoothly planed off into a neat symmetry of reversals; a dramatist who is consciously experimental falls back into an old theatrical device used by both Ibsen and Wilde.[5] What Williams does here is not dissimilar to what he did a little earlier in *A Streetcar Named Desire*, that is, rely on an "effect" that turns him away from character. In *Streetcar* it was the repetition of a dance melody that substituted for a full verbal exploration of consciousness; in *Summer and Smoke* it is the surprise of an ordering of parts that precisely inverts a previous ordering. Not that a balance of elements is always an artifice; it could hardly seem so in a day when we have learned to see analogy as a frequent and admirable device of structure. But structural equations need to be somewhat elusive, to entice us to discover them behind a resistant surface; when a symmetry calls attention to itself, we suspect that it is imposed on the human actuality.[6]

Not until *Cat on a Hot Tin Roof* (produced 1955) did Williams again use the tragic perspective. In the meantime there were *The Rose Tattoo* (produced 1950), a comic variation on the recurrent D. H. Lawrence theme, and *Camino Real* (produced 1953), called a "pageant" (Block 16),[7] and, with the opening lines of Dante's *Inferno* ("In the middle of the journey [*cammin*] of our life") as epigraph, committed to an allegorical method, which, as often in more recent theater, subordinates individual lives to archetypal patterns of experience or traits of personality represented by large mythical figures.[8] Yet *Camino Real* has

---

[5]In *Rosmersholm* Rebecca West, who represents the will ruthlessly seeking its ends, comes to believe in Rosmer's ideal of nobility, while Rosmer loses faith in his mission to ennoble men. At the end of *Lady Windermere's Fan* Lord and Lady Windermere have essentially reversed their attitudes to Mrs. Erlynne. On the other hand, Williams uses a symmetrical structure very effectively in *Period of Adjustment* (1960), a "serious comedy" in which two married couples who are breaking up are in the end restored to at least a working harmony; the duplication emphasizes the spirit of compromise which is at the basis of the comic structure.

[6]In some analogous events Williams is much less obtrusive: in parallels between two generations, between different women inviting traveling salesmen, different men calling taxis for Alma. Symbols, which are in good supply, vary in subtlety: temperature, dress, statuary, fireworks, sleeping pills. This is true of most of his plays.

[7]*Camino Real* (New York: New Directions, 1953).

[8]Williams himself says that "its people are mostly archetypes of certain basic attitudes and qualities" (Foreword, p. viii). He adds, very soundly, that "symbols

some relevance for us in that it is essentially a drama of disaster: over it hangs the sense of death — of bodies and hopes and dreams — and of all the lesser simulacra of death that are in the human calendar; and the mood is one of the morning after, of wearing out, of *où sont les neiges d'antan* and of *post coitum triste*, and, in Dante's figure, of "a dark wood where the straight way was lost." There is an occasional touch of the paranoid that melodrama may entail: Esmeralda, the Gypsy's daughter, utters the symbolic cry, *"They've got you! They've got me!* Caught! Caught! We're caught!" (Block 6). But we are asked to feel not so much resentment and blame as sadness at the way things go, and Williams vigorously resists the tonal dangers of this structure when at the end he makes Don Quixote, who apparently has authority, say, *"Don't! Pity! Your! Self!"* (Block 16). The drift toward the nostalgic and pathetic is held in check by lively ironies of fact and word, by novel and ingenious detail, and by brisk epigram: "We're all of us guinea pigs in the laboratory of God. Humanity is just a work in progress" (Block 12). Nevertheless, despite the epic and panoramic frame, the picture is one of limited dimensions, as it must be when depth yields to spread.

II. *"Cat on a Hot Tin Roof"*

Cat on a Hot Tin Roof (1955) carries on, after eight years, from *Streetcar*, and in some ways also from the slightly later *Summer and Smoke*. In Brick Pollitt there is the inner split that is central in the earlier protagonists, but it is far more intense than those of Alma and John in *Summer and Smoke*. Brick is the product of the same kind of unrelenting imagination of inner discord that created Blanche DuBois. Indeed, his case history has some remarkable resemblances to hers: glamorous youth, the critical trauma that again involves homosexuality and the rejection of a homosexual, alcoholism, disintegration (with the possible loss of the great plantation as an accompanying symptom of decline), all this in a charismatic personality in which charm is the element that longest resists decay. This degree of likeness in key characters helps outline the differences in the plays taken as wholes.

---

are nothing but the natural speech of drama" and "when used respectfully, are the purest language of plays" (pp. x, xi). Perhaps "used respectfully" should mean giving them a dignified reticence instead of making them take the role of human beings in the dramatic arena.

Whereas in *Streetcar* hope lies in Stanley and Stella, with their hearty sexuality and insouciant energy, in *Cat* Williams all but demolishes the fertility myth: Gooper and Mae, with their six children, are made vulgar and grasping plotters, realistic versions of the quasi-human worldliness that is done expressionistically in Goldberg and McCann in Harold Pinter's *The Birthday Party* (1958). Such hope as there may be attaches to the title character, Margaret or Maggie, who, in her desperate struggle to save her husband Brick both for herself and for the plantation, and the plantation for them, might be merely a slick popular heroine. She is much more than that: she is, among other things, an embodiment of the Shavian life force, and that means that she is not so plain and simple as she manages to look. She had some complicity in her husband's downfall, since, in a calculated risk, she had broken up his ambiguous relationship with his best friend, Skipper; her devotion to Brick and the plantation is clearly interwoven with her passionate desire not to be poor again, her cool quest of advantage, and her detestation of Gooper and Mae; she can match them in laying strategic traps for the favors of Brick's parents, and in all the ruthless family in-fighting. So she is a person, not a cinematic madonna to the rescue. Still, insofar as the play is hers, it is concerned with a battle against outer forces by a character of what we have called pragmatic wholeness; win or lose, she herself is not looked at tragically, for, though she has some keen perceptions about herself—"[I've] become—*hard! Frantic!—cruel!!*"…"I'm not good," and "I destroyed [Skipper]" (I)[9]—her fight is not to discover herself or order herself but to escape from being a victim.

In terms of her vigor, of the frenzy of her struggle, and of the magnitude of her role, the play is Maggie's; after all, she is "the Cat." Yet Williams is pulled in two different directions, one toward the portrait of the strong competitive woman (the line that descends from Lady Macbeth through Ibsen's Rebecca West), the other toward inner conflict that has tragic potential. On the one hand there is all the tension that derives from Maggie's gladiatorial finesse and daring and her thrusts in various directions; on the other hand, there are the larger-looming problems of character that lie in Brick and in his powerful father, Big Daddy, whose presence alone marks a big jump ahead from *Streetcar*.

[9]*Cat on a Hot Tin Roof* (New York: New Directions, 1955).

The protracted confrontation of father and son takes up most of the long Act II, almost half the play in its original form. Bound by affection, they offer a sharp contrast: the mild, quasi-clear-headed pseudo serenity of the son, steadily drinking toward the inner "click" that signifies "peace"; and the violent boisterousness of the older man, ironically euphoric in the illusion of a reprieve from cancer (a faint reminiscence of Oedipus' certitude that he has defeated the malign oracle), triumphant, planning new triumphs, among them straightening out Brick.

Yet there is another bond: the old man's cancer, which will kill him, is paralleled by the thing in Brick's mind that Margaret literally calls "malignant" (I). (Symbols flow from Williams: trying drunkenly to repeat a youthful exploit, Brick gets a fractured foot that is analogous to the broken spirit partly due to the ending of football glories: he uses a literal crutch that also defines the role of alcohol for him.) A less tangible, but dramatically more important, bond is a concern for "truth," or, perhaps better, an incomplete invulnerability before it when the other uses it, therapeutically or punitively, as a flail. In the drama of self-knowledge, where tragedy has its roots, Williams appears to be again of different minds. Up to a point Brick does not muffle his sense of fact: he can say, "I'm alcoholic," he acknowledges, "I want to dodge away from [life]," and he defines, "A drinking man's someone who wants to forget he isn't still young an' believing" (II). Though these recognitions seem to go far, they do not "hurt," and that they do not is part of the dramatic evidence that there are still deeper levels of truth to be known.

The gradual revelation of these deeper levels, with an increase of pain that suggests a saving remnant of sentience in Brick, makes extremely effective drama. What is revealed cannot be defined simply; in a long interpolated note Williams inveighs against "'pat' conclusions, facile definitions" and rightly insists, "Some mystery should be left in the revelation of character..." (II). Brick is tensely and even explosively resentful of the view, partly held by Maggie and, it appears, by Gooper and Mae, that his relationship with Skipper was homosexual; he calls it "friendship," his experience of the "one great good true thing in [a man's] life" (I), and he passionately elaborates his notion to Big Daddy (II). He resents, too, Maggie's view that he and Skipper carried their college relationship on into professional football "because we were scared to grow up," were hanging on to adoles-

cent dreams of glory.[10] We can argue how much of the total truth
is represented by each of these views; what is clear is that, however we assess the mixture of ingredients, Brick was inhabiting
an idyllic Eden at whose breakup he began his determined push
into a surrogate realm of alcoholic peace. Maggie surely has
authority when she comments, "life has got to be allowed to continue even after the *dream* of life is—all—over" (I).

As the history is slowly set forth, Brick claims for himself the
virtue of honesty; yet his stance is on the whole the pretragic one
of defensiveness and blame—blame of a mendacious world and
particularly of Maggie: he punishes her by refusing to have sexual intercourse with her. She had destroyed the idyll by putting
it into Skipper's head that his feeling for Brick was homosexual
and thus destroying him. But at this moment Big Daddy, skeptical,
puts on the pressure and elicits the fact that, when Skipper had
phoned Brick to make a "drunken confession," Brick had hung
up. Big Daddy charges, "we have tracked down the lie with which
you're disgusted. . . . This disgust with mendacity is disgust with
yourself. *You!*—dug the grave of your friend and kicked him in it!
—before you'd face truth with him!" (II). It is at this point that we
sense the "two minds" in Williams. Big Daddy presses for the ultimate recognition of truth, and his great strength and passion apparently establish this value beyond question. Then Big Daddy
himself is challenged a little later when Brick retaliates by letting
it slip out to him that he has not escaped cancer, as he supposes;
on the contrary, he is really dying of it. But the truth that Big
Daddy has to face is that of physical fact, not moral act. Brick,
confronted with the latter, cries, "Who *can* face truth? Can *you?*"
(II). And insofar as Williams doubts the human ability to face
truth, he is of the same mind as O'Neill in the anti-tragic *Iceman,*
where an anesthetic Lethe of alcohol is all that makes existence
endurable. It is the reversal of George Eliot's requirement, "No
opium." Eliot may have had an illusion of strength, but she could
imagine the tragic situation rooted in power to endure. In Brick
what we find, on the contrary, is the disaster rooted in weakness.
He reflects that sense of human incapacity to endure that has
appeared in a good deal of modern "serious drama." Dr. Faustus
was the man who tried to be God; Miller's Quentin would casti-
gate himself for entertaining the illusion of divine power; but

---

[10]Football is also used to symbolize immaturity in Miller's *Death of a Salesman.*

Brick simply found himself accepted as a "godlike being" (I) and then went to pieces when one worshiper challenged another's purity.

Again, however, Williams has an impulse to go beyond the disaster of personality. He is not willing to let Brick be simply a victim, a good man destroyed by the actions of others. For what Big Daddy, acting as prosecutor, establishes is that Brick "dug the grave of [his] friend and kicked him in it" and that that is the source of his malaise. If this does not impute to Brick the hubris of the "overreacher," it at least makes him a man who does evil instead of one who simply suffers evil. We need now to see whether the play continues to regard him as a man of action or simply settles for his passivity and disintegration. It is here that Margaret's efforts to stir him into a resumption of sexual intercourse—including her final theatrical public claim that she is pregnant—take on great dramatic significance. For his rejection of sex is not only a symptom of illness, of one kind or another, but also, as we have seen, a punishment of her; and punishing her is his means of declaring that the guilt is hers, and of keeping his eyes off his own guilt. It is the old story from *Lear* to O'Neill's *Iceman*, of the man living in a melodrama of blame and resisting the tragic self-confrontation. To resume intercourse would be to declare Margaret innocent of his charges against her, or to forgive her, and thus to make possible his acknowledgment and understanding of his own role—in Skipper's death and in his and Margaret's subsequent misery. Williams has imagined an active tragic role for him. The problem is whether Brick can advance beyond the relative comfort of the melodrama he has created for himself, and beyond that, whether Williams is able to conceive of him as transcending the rather familiar role of the sad young man going under.

Again it appears that Williams is of two minds or at least that he was capable of being of two minds. For he wrote two versions of Act III, his own original draft and then, at the urging of his director Elia Kazan, a second one which was used in the first stage production.[11] While both versions end with at least a touch of the-lady-or-the-tiger ambiguity, the first gives little ground for supposing that Margaret can win her battle against Brick's punitive

---

[11]Printed editions usually contain both versions of Act III, and, after the first one, Williams' two-page "Note of Explanation" of the circumstances of his writing the second version.

and even self-righteous detachment. In the second version Brick
is a little less laconic, gives a touch of support to Margaret's game
of publicly claiming pregnancy, and views with admiration her
final tactic of throwing out every bottle of the whiskey that he
relies on. There is a little more reason to think that he may take
the critical step and break out of his own rigidity. Though even
here Margaret retains the line, "Oh, you weak, beautiful people
who give up...," still she is now permitted a stronger assertion
of her own will to rehabilitate him. However, Williams has more
of his heart in the first version: a subtly more urgent dialogue
conveys this, and besides, Williams is explicit in his prose comment. He cannot, he says, believe that "a conversation, however
revelatory," even a "virtual vivisection," can effect much change
in "a person in Brick's state of spiritual disrepair."

In rejecting the dramatic convention that a moment of revelation, even a brutally fierce one, can be the equivalent of a conversion, Williams is perhaps unconsciously seeking ground for
sticking to the disaster of personality—the history, not of the
person of hubris and of eventual insight, but of the person who
cannot cope and cannot face the record. Yet in speaking of Brick's
decline, Williams twice applies to it the word *tragedy*, another
evidence of his persistent attraction to the form.[12] In *Cat*, surely,
he reveals a further tendency to get away from, or at least to mod-
ify, the pathetic story of collapse. His central character is the man
who himself committed the originating deed and who is on the
edge of acknowledging his own guilt. Williams catches Brick at a
less irremediable stage of collapse than he does Blanche in *Streetcar*, he almost eliminates the element of the victim that is a bona
fide part of Blanche, he gives more authority to the protagonist's
crucial rejection of another (Blanche's injury to her husband we
see in her own memory only after she has become an undepend-
able witness). And in Big Daddy and Margaret there is a spon-
taneous emphasis on discovering the truth that is hardly present

---

[12]It appears to have been active in his imagination from the beginning. A
stage direction near the end of *The Glass Menagerie* refers to the mother's
"dignity and tragic beauty." Again near the end of *Streetcar* Williams uses a
stage direction to attribute to Blanche DuBois, now mentally ill and about to be
taken to a sanitarium, "a tragic radiance." He gives the subtitle, "A Tragedy in
One Act," to *Auto-Da-Fé*, which deals with another character whose inner stresses
have driven him out of his mind. He theorizes about the "tragic sense" in his
preface to *The Rose Tattoo*, a comedy, and in the foreword to *Sweet Bird of
Youth* he speaks of his satisfaction when "a work of tragic intention has seemed
to me to have achieved that intention, even if only approximately, nearly."

at all in *Streetcar.* Both of them are also potential tragic characters. ...

V. *Last Plays*

In the shorter plays to which Williams turned in the later 1960s, however, there are no major new developments; the collection entitled *Dragon Country* (1970)[13] works mainly from familiar Williams motifs. There are, of course, some emphases that belong to the later rather than the earlier work. One play has an explicitly, another an implicitly, Christian context. The scenes are not in the world of plantations and permanent homes, as in *Cat* and *Streetcar,* but in the world of hotels, bars, and boarding houses, as in *Night of the Iguana.* The dramatis personae may be transients or permanent residents, but even with the latter, their existence has much of the uprooted, the peripheral, the hanging on. Various people are on the edge of death, or hold out poorly against it, or are done in, or endure a sort of death-in-life. Against the nonsurvivors or the marginal survivors are ranged a few tougher types—crass or ruthless or simply gifted with more vitality. More than once there is a familiar melodramatic contrast of the weak and the strong, with overtones of the D. H. Lawrence dualism (the volume includes one very early play, *I Rise in Flame, Cried the Phoenix,* in which the characters are Lawrence, Frieda, and Brett) and of the allegorical shaping of experience toward which Williams' imagination occasionally turns (in addition to the life-versus-death[14] presence in various plays there is, in two of them, a generalized rendering of the fate of "the artist"). None of these materials looks naturally toward the tragic; the kind of words I have used implies rather an absence of the individuality and human stature essential to tragic quality. Yet Williams has used the word *tragedy* of two of the plays, and in two others he conceives of a character in terms that could lead to a tragic structure.

True, when he does use the word *tragedy* he is being suggestive rather than literal, and ironic rather than solemn. In 1966 two of

---

[13]*Dragon Country* (New York: New Directions, 1970) contains four very short plays that I do not deal with here and four others that might be thought of as long one-act plays or short two-act plays. Three of them have been produced: "The Mutilated" and "The Gnädiges Fräulein" in 1966, and "In the Bar of a Tokyo Hotel" in 1969. "Confessional" was copyrighted in 1970.

[14]One short play is entitled "The Frosted Glass Coffin."

the plays in *Dragon Country*—"The Mutilated" and "The Gnädiges Fräulein"—were produced in a double bill with the program
title of "Slapstick Tragedy." Here is an echo of the old concept
of the sorrowing clown and the jest that barely conceals grief. The
"slapstick" in these plays is the loud verbal conflict between the
characters—in both plays two women who belabor each other with
heavy irony, suspicion, abuse, threats, and even blows, but who
need, or can use, each other and hence grudgingly find an ac-
commodation.[15] "Slapstick" implies that the blows do not hurt,
but in these plays they do; survival has a price. "Tragedy" implies
the presence of something harsher than farcical shenanigans, but
the nonfarcical belongs less to tragedy than to disaster or potential disaster. In "The Mutilated" we are more aware of the needs
of the two women who abuse each other; in "The Gnädiges Fräulein" the personalities are cruder and more calculating. The
former is basically pathetic comedy; the latter relies strongly on
the grotesque, and the tone is dominantly satirical.

"The Mutilated" is about little people—a lonely woman, an
aging streetwalker, sailors, customers at a bar. The title character,
Trinket, is a woman who has had a breast removed; the sense of
being "mutilated" is a horror that hangs over her, makes her
forgo sex, and leaves her vulnerable to a blackmailing crony,
Celeste. The mutilation is symbolic as well as literal, however;
"we all have our mutilations," Celeste says (i); and death in one
form or another is just around the corner. The basis, then, is the
pathos of human insufficiency and vulnerability. But at Christmas the two women find a way of making up the quarrel which
is at the center of the action, and even manage to sense a visitation
by Our Lady. It is their experience of "the miracle" promised by
carolers whose carols, sung periodically throughout the play, are
charming in their union of freshly imaged faith and delicate irony.

Thus the pathos is modified by the slender comedy of spirit: the
momentary triumph of wholeness over mutilation. A gentle irony
hangs over the triumph and forecloses the sentimental. However,
what remains most vivid is the conflict that dominates most of
the play—the harsh idioms of hostility among various characters, but especially Trinket and Celeste, the "pair of old bitches"
as Celeste describes them (i). In all these plays Williams has a
good ear for the recriminative and vituperative style.

[15] Such a pair obviously has a strong hold on Williams' imagination. It appears
in two other plays in this collection, "Confessional" and "A Perfect Analysis
Given by a Parrot" (1958).

"The Gnädiges Fräulein" portrays an intrinsically tougher world of calculation and profit-seeking, with the two women who want to use each other combining the ludicrous and the sinister. Molly the boarding-house keeper wants a puff in the paper for which Polly writes; Polly wants a good news story from the boarding house and gets stud service from an Indian inmate there. The satirical keeps welling up through the surface farce. Besides, Molly and Polly have a common victim, the title character: an outcast from "show biz," she is treated like a workhouse inmate by Molly and is regarded as good copy by Polly. Thus the satire of crassness, as often, involves the melodrama of the victim.

But what dominates the play is the grotesque. This appears chiefly in the terrifying aggressiveness of the "cocaloony" bird, a "sort of giant pelican" who combatively invades Molly's rooming house, scares the people, and snatches a fish caught by one of them. At an offstage dock, we learn, the Fräulein has to compete with the cocaloony birds of the area for the unsalable fish tossed out by fishing boats; thus she pays her way in Molly's place. The struggle is desperate: the cocaloony birds have gradually stripped the Fräulein, plucked out one of her eyes and then the other, and half scalped her. Every time she appears on the stage she is bloodier and more nearly naked—a Williams horror story that inevitably reminds us of the end of Sebastian in *Suddenly Last Summer*.[16] While Sebastian was an eccentric courting disaster, however, the Fräulein is struggling for survival. Since the word *competition* is used, the tale is really a fierce parable on economic rivalry and its threats to plain subsistence (there is a casual reference to the Mafia and "the Syndicate"). But still deeper than this is another theme that recurs in Williams: the fate of the original artist both in the commercialized theater and in the outside competitive world. The Fräulein, we learn, got black-balled in show biz when her innovations in a performance infuriated a "trained seal," and he beat her. Ever since, she has battled desperately for a marginal subsistence, her life as fish-catcher analogous to her role on stage. It is as if an original playwright was driven out of the theater because of his originality, had to write commercials for a living, and was then hated by the pros in this grosser field.

---

[16]Williams seems mildly haunted by an image of people-and-birds, people as victims of birds, or people victimized as birds. In "The Mutilated" there is a "Bird-Girl" in a freak show, and Celeste reports that she once had this role. Speaking of the present Bird-Girl, "poor Rosie," Celeste voices one of the best ironic remarks in the volume: "If she was a bird, the humane society would be interested in her situation but since she's a human being, they couldn't care less" (i).

Viewed reductively, this is the old romantic melodrama of the innovator victimized both by his fellow professionals and by society generally; yet it is translated into fantastic terms that create a satiric melodrama of originality and force. The expressionistic voice gives freshness and toughness to a theme that could spawn the trite and the sentimental.[17]

HUBRIS AND DIVIDEDNESS

Three years later, in "In the Bar of a Tokyo Hotel" (produced, 1969), Williams returns to the subject of the artist and his fate, this time the overt theme. The expressionistic appears in some of the details, but the general procedure is realistic. The artist is still in part a victim, but there is a new element in that he is in some sense also a victim of himself. Here, then, Williams moves into the realm of tragedy.

Mark, the painter, is a febrile and almost hysterical version of Ibsen's master-builder Solness—endeavoring to control a new style, sensing a dangerous breakthrough of old limits and all limits, terrified, exhausted by the intensity of a struggle that is imaged as a sensual conflict, as if canvases were women to be sexually subdued by force. Like Solness, Mark dies at the end, not in a sudden theatrical accident, but in a climactic dissolution prophesied from the beginning by a fantastic physical and spiritual debility. Mark's own view is that he is worn out by wrestlings with problems of creation; as he says, "An artist has to lay his life on the line" (i). In Mark's striving to go beyond limits there is a tincture of the Faustian. After his death his wife Miriam argues that he has erred by not staying within "the circle of light," which is "our existence and our protection." She rejects the "romantic" view that "the circle of light is the approving look of God" (ii), but she has managed to get it expressed and thus to set loose in our imaginations the idea of the artist as actuated by a demonic drive. What we sense here is a version of the tragic passion to exceed human limits.

Disappointingly, this possibility is not realized. For one thing, we have only Mark's word for the intensity of his aspiration, and the play does not make him a reliable witness. We do not see enough of Mark's consciousness to be sure that his striving is hubristic, an assault on limits that, like Faust, he cannot ultimate-

[17]Cf. a different expressionistic treatment of the same theme (the artist and society) in Pinter's *The Birthday Party* (produced 1958).

ly deny. For another, it is by no means clear that he is not deceived about his breakthrough or is not just sick. Though we are told that he has been a successful and productive painter, he is, during the action of the play, so emaciated and feeble as to be almost a caricature. In this lack of robustness he seems a distant echo of Brick Pollitt, of Shannon in *The Night of the Iguana,* and, in his off-center nervous organization, of Sebastian in *Suddenly Last Summer.* Here is a recurrent Williams problem of a lack of tragic stature in a character who is potentially tragic.

But Miriam is not going to play Maggie the Cat or Hannah Jelkes to what she calls Mark's "tyrannical dependence" (i). Indeed, her intention to withdraw support from him is implicitly a murderous act, if she is truly the bitch that he calls her, then we have a melodrama of evil woman and her victim. The play is rather, I believe, a more complex melodrama with dividedness of appeal: neither is wholly justified against the other. The life of the play is the intensity of the conflict between them. At the same time there is an ironic balance between them: Mark lusts after art, Miriam lusts after other men.

Insofar as Mark is "the artist" and the subject is "the creative life," there is a touch of the allegorical which has occasionally cropped up in Williams since *Camino Real.* It appears again in "Confessional" (copyright 1970), where there is much talk of "birth" and "death," in one speech called "holy miracles" and "holy mysteries" (i). Death is introduced most ingeniously in the fact that Leona, the strong woman in the play, is on a quarrelsome drunk in ritual mourning for her brother on his "deathday." We are meant to feel these abstract themes in the heart of the action. The play is in part a documentary on kinds of vitality and nonvitality (an echo of the old Lawrence strain in Williams), and at the same time on kinds of sexuality. The result is a panorama of types of psychological subsistence in which the habitual is varied by cathartic binges.

The allegorical had a strong hold on O'Neill too, and "Confessional" reminds us of O'Neill in more ways than one. The scene is a bar which is reminiscent of Harry Hope's place in *The Iceman Cometh;* though in no way so far gone as O'Neill's, the characters lead a limited, in-turning life—an unfrocked M.D., a whimpering, disintegrating whore, a middle-aged short-order cook who barely makes a living, a weary homosexual, a self-centered male hustler (a more limited Chance Wayne); the stage directions are lengthy and novelistic; periodically one character or another, spotlighted, addresses the audience in a "confessional," a rather mechanical revelatory device such as O'Neill used more than once. It is more a theatrical self-exposé than an essential coming to knowledge in a tragic manner. But this is the right style for these characters, who, as often in O'Neill and Williams, have a limitedness or weakness that is not the raw material of tragic life.

The possible exception is Leona, the vigorous, combative, promiscuous hairdresser who tells people off, levels with herself, combines a tough mother-earth good sense with a passion for sentimental music, and is always ready to defy loneliness and hit the road in her trailer when the joys of the current stand run out. Not only does Leona have the strength for a tragic role; she is specifically defined in terms that we have seen more than one dramatist apply to tragically conceived characters: "She's got two natures in her" (i). But the "two natures" are less divergent passions than they are moods which alternate. Leona may be easy to get on with, or very quarrelsome, but in either phase she is completely unified, not disturbed by a conflicting impulse. Rather than divided, she is remarkably well held together, despite shifts in emotional state. Indeed what might in a truly complex character be dividedness of appeal is here rather an easily agreeable mingling of dissimilar elements—itself a kind of cliché. But at its best the treatment of her manages a subdued pathos laced with irony.

THE WILLIAMS MODE

Williams has not again come as close to the tragic structuring of character and experience as he did in *Streetcar, Cat on a Hot Tin Roof,* and *Summer and Smoke.* The vigorous characters in these plays do continue to appear, in many variations, in the dramas up to 1970; likewise the weak and disintegrating characters, victims sometimes of others, sometimes of their own fragility. But the life of the play is rarely in the inner discords of strong characters who in hubris or error make choices that lead to catastrophe. What especially attracts Williams is the built-in liability to disaster, and he often infuses a remarkable vitality into the portrayal of characters with limited powers of survival. Death and a deathlike state frequently hang over the heads of people troubled either by their own inadequacies or perversities, or by the malice that comes out of the needs or perversities of others. The death theme is treated most complexly in *Milk Train,* with an ambiguity that lies less in richness of character than in the meaning that attaches to action; the complexity is more in symbol than in passion. In that play, Chris Flanders is from one perspective the artist, the figure who appears in two of the recent short plays: we regularly see the artist in a tense conflict with others, more often than not victimized, yet keeping to his last as best he may. Williams is consistently good in representing the spirit and style of hostile confrontation, the drama of counter-forces and counterpurposes. When he internalizes his drama, he is on the road to tragedy.

The Glass Menagerie Revisited:
Catastrophe without Violence

by Roger B. Stein

The Glass Menagerie (1945) was Tennessee Williams' first major theatrical success. Over the years he has written much, some of high quality indeed, but nothing better than this play which established him as an important post-war playwright. "The dramatist of frustration," John Gassner dubbed him in 1948 after *Streetcar,* but unlike most of his later plays, *The Glass Menagerie* projects not a series of violent confrontations leading to catastrophe but a vision of lonely human beings who fail to make contact, who are isolated from each other and from society, and who seem ultimately abandoned in the universe.

What holds the play together are Tom's remembrances of things past, not plot or characterization. Tom, the poet-narrator and author's surrogate, called "Shakespeare" in the warehouse, organizes the drama symbolically through language and image. This is the "new plastic theatre" of which Williams spoke in his production notes, a revelation not through dramatic struggle but through the allusive power of the word, the accretion of symbolic clusters which bear the meaning, reinforced dramaturgically through lighting, music, the distancing devices of a narrator and, as originally planned, of screen images.

The glass menagerie is itself the most obvious organizing symbol. It embodies the fragility of Laura's world, her search for beauty; it registers sensitively changes in lighting and stands in vivid contrast to the harshness of the outer world which can (and does) shatter it so easily. The unicorn can become the gift to Jim the Gentleman Caller, whose anticipation and appearance form the plot of the play, only when it has lost its mythical unique-ness, the horn, when dream becomes momentarily possibility be-fore it is obliterated at the end. The magic of Prince Charming's kiss can not work ("Stumblejohn," he brands himself in the pub-lished version of the play, taking on for the moment Laura's crippled condition). The "little silver slipper of a moon" on which Amanda has asked Laura to wish becomes an ironic image of Laura's isolated condition, but Amanda, wrapped up in her own illusions and selling magazine subscriptions and brassieres (like the "Gay Deceivers" with which she tries to stuff Laura before Jim appears) prefers to believe not in Tom's favorite D. H. Lawrence, but in Cinderella and courtly love and *Gone With the Wind,* the novel to which she compares Bessie May Harper's latest effort in *The Homemaker's Companion.* The ironies of the allusive imagery proliferate: Amanda's heroic efforts as homemaker are unsuc-cessful (the father appears only as a happy doughboy photo-graphic image), and Margaret Mitchell's depression romance about the desirable Scarlett O'Hara in a lost Eden, a South fan-tasized in the national imagination during the Depression, only makes Laura look more forlorn. Finally one may note that the title image itself of *Gone With the Wind* underlines the evanes-cent quality of this dream and all of the Wingfields' illusions. As such, it points directly to the last line of the play and Tom's in-junction to "Blow out your candles, Laura."

On the level of plot, this widening circle of reference enhances the credibility of the dramatic situation. Given Amanda's sham version of idealized love and a fantasy past, how could the Gentle-man Caller's visit be other than a failure? Despite Amanda's dress which is "historical almost," despite the attempt to live in the nineteenth century when the electric power goes off, Jim is not Rhett Butler but an "emissary from a world of reality," as Tom calls him, an engaged twentieth-century man on vacation. The flickering candlelight of Jim's scene with Laura is not enough to sustain the illusion; at the end of their scene this illusion col-lapses and we are left in darkness.

But *The Glass Menagerie* is built upon more than the poignant plot of illusion and frustration in the lives of little people. Wil-liams has deepened the losses of individuals by pointing to social and even spiritual catastrophe. The time of the play is 1939, as the narrative frame makes explicit both at the beginning and the end. The life of illusion is not confined to the Wingfields alone. As Tom says, "the huge middle class of America was matricu-

lating in a school for the blind." What he calls the "social background" of the play has an important role. The international
backdrop is Guernica and the song America sings is "The World
is Waiting for the Sunrise," for the sober truth is that America is
still in the depression and on the brink of war. The note of social
disaster runs throughout the drama, fixing the lives of individuals
against the larger canvas.

Amanda's anxieties are in large part economic and there is
money behind many of her illusions: her mythical suitors were all
wealthy men, as are her magazine heroes; she computes the money
Tom would save by giving up smoking. When Tom complains of
the grimness of life in the shoe factory, she replies, "Try and you
will SUCCEED!" If this is another of Amanda's illusions, it is one
shared by her fellow Americans, for "try and you will succeed"
is the traditional motto of the American dream of success, the
theme of confident self-reliance canonized in the romances of
Horatio Alger.

It is not Amanda, however, but Jim, the emissary from reality,
who is the chief spokesman for the American dream. To Jim the
warehouse is not a prison but a rung on the ladder toward success.
He believes in self-improvement through education, and the
lecture on self-confidence which he reads to Laura is part of the
equipment of the future executive. He is awed by the fortune
made in chewing gum and rhapsodizes on the theme of the future
material progress of America: "All that remains is for the industry to get itself under way! Full steam—*Knowledge—Zzzzzp!
Money—Zzzzzp! Power!* That's the cycle democracy is built on!"

Yet when the theme of success is superimposed upon the lives
of the characters, the social irony emerges. Father was not the
successful businessman, but a telephone man who "fell in love
with long distances." Tom, the substitute father, refuses to pay
the light bill, plunges his family into darkness, and then runs out,
and Amanda sells subscriptions and brassieres only at the loss of
her dignity. Jim's own dream of success seems to have reached its
peak in high school. (Williams later explored this theme more
fully in *Cat on a Hot Tin Roof.*) The trek upward through the depression years is disappointing, but the indomitable optimist is
not discouraged.

The experience of the 1930s did not turn Williams into a pro-
letarian writer or social realist, but it did open up for him a
darker vision of American life which he suggests to his audience
but which is denied to his characters, still "matriculating in a

school for the blind": a belief that the American dream is itself a sham and a failure. In his essay "The Catastrophe of Success," Williams said that "the Cinderella story is our favorite national myth, the cornerstone of the film industry if not of the Democracy itself." The social catastrophe inherent in *The Glass Menagerie* lies precisely in the fact that Laura is *not* Cinderella: the silver slipper does not finally fit, and Jim is not Prince Charming but one of the innumerable Americans who would soon be moving overseas in troop ships. As Tom says at the end, "for nowadays the world is lit by lightning! Blow out your candles, Laura—and so goodbye...."The world which had been waiting for the sunrise burst with bombardments instead, and the lives of the Wingfields at the end are absorbed in the larger social tragedy.

Williams goes even further than this, however. The end of the play involves more than just the snuffing out of Laura's hope; it is even more than social tragedy. It is a *Götterdämmerung*. For the candles and the lightning which close the play have appeared together before. We are told by Amanda that the candelabrum "used to be on the altar at the church of the Heavenly Rest. It was melted a little out of shape when the church burnt down. Lightning struck it one spring." Amanda's comment opens up another dimension of the drama, and reminds us that Williams, inheritor of a Southern religious tradition which includes writers like Faulkner and Robert Penn Warren, has persistently drawn upon the language of Christian symbolism to define his characters' human situations. Amanda's quiet comment is a far cry from the hysterical ravings of the defrocked Reverend T. Lawrence Shannon in *Night of the Iguana* about wanting "to go back to the church and preach the gospel of God as Lightning and Thunder." The pervasive religious overtones of *The Glass Menagerie* never obscure the literal line of the story or seem self-conscious, as they frequently do in the later plays. Ultimately they try to locate the catastrophe at the end beyond human pathos and social tragedy.

Williams' stage directions clearly indicate his intention. The lighting for Laura should resemble that "used in early religious portraits of female saints or madonnas." The scene where Tom tells his mother that a Gentleman Caller will appear Williams entitles "Annunciation." The dressing of Laura for the Caller's appearance should be "devout and ritualistic." During her scene with Jim she is lit "inwardly with altar candles," and when Jim withdraws after kissing her Williams informs us that the "holy candles in the altar of Laura's face have been snuffed out. There is a look of almost infinite desolation."

Those overtones extend beyond Williams' hints to the director and become part of the fabric of dramatic action. The first scene in both the acting version and the library edition of the play opens on this note. In the former, Amanda narrates her "funny experience" of being denied a seat in the Episcopal church because she has not rented a pew. The idea of the Wingfields' exclusion from Christian ceremony is established thus at the outset, and it is underlined by the ensuing talk of digesting food, mastication, and salivary glands. In the Wingfield apartment, eating is an animal process only; it lacks ritual significance. The library edition opens with Amanda's call to Tom, "We can't say grace until you come to the table," and then moves on to the question of digestion. The lines are different, but their import is the same. When the Gentleman Caller comes, the scene is repeated, only this time it is Laura whose absence holds up "grace."

Amanda, who condemns instinct and urges Tom to think in terms of the mind and spirit, as "Christian adults" do, is often characterized in Christian terms. Her music, in the library edition, is "Ave Maria." As a girl she could only cook angel food cake. She urges Laura, "Possess your soul in patience," and then speaks of her dress for the dinner scene as "resurrected" from a trunk. Her constant refrain to Tom is "Rise an' Shine," and she sells subscriptions to her friends by waking them early in the morning and then sympathizing with them as "Christian martyrs." Laura is afraid to tell her mother she has left the business school because "when you're disappointed, you get that awful suffering look on your face, like the picture of Jesus' mother in the museum!"

The next picture Laura mentions is the one of Jim in the yearbook. Though the context seems secular enough at this point— Jim is a high school hero—his religious function emerges later on. In the "Annunciation" scene, when Amanda learns that the Gentleman Caller's name is O'Connor, she says, "that, of course, means fish—tomorrow is Friday!" The remark functions not only literally, since Jim is Irish Catholic, but also figuratively, for the fish is the traditional symbol of Christ. In a very real sense both Amanda and Laura are searching for a Savior who will come to help them, to save them, to give their drab lives meaning.

Tom is unable to play this role himself. Though he appears as the angel of the Annunciation, he denies the world of belief and in a bitter speech to his mother calls himself "El Diablo." With him Christian terms appear only as imprecations: "what in Christ's name" or "that God damn Rise and Shine." When Tom returns home drunk one night, he tells Laura of a stage show he has seen which is shot through with Christian symbolism, none of which he perceives. Here the magician, Malvolio, whose name suggests bad will, dislike, or even hate, plays the role of the modern Christ. He performs the miracle of turning water into wine and then goes on to blasphemy by turning the wine into beer and then whiskey. He also produces his proper symbol, the fish, but it is gold-fish, as if stained by modern materialism. Most important, he escapes from a nailed coffin. But Tom reads the symbolism of this trick in personal terms only. When Laura tries to keep him from awakening Amanda, Tom retorts:

> Goody, goody! Pay 'er back for all those "Rise an' Shines." You know it don't take much intelligence to get yourself into a nailed-up coffin, Laura. But who in hell ever got himself out of one without removing one nail?   (Scene 4)

The illumination of the father's photograph at this point suggests one answer to this question, but the pattern of Christian imagery in the drama, especially when reinforced here by the "Rise an' Shine" refrain, should suggest to us another answer—the resurrection itself—which Tom's rejection of Christian belief prevents him from seeing.

It remains therefore for Jim to come as the Savior to this Friday night supper. The air of expectancy is great, with the ritualistic dressing of Laura, the tension, and the oppressive heat. Jim's arrival is marked by the coming of rain, but the hopes of fertility and renewal which this might suggest are soon dashed. Laura's attempt to come to the dinner table is a failure, signaled by a clap of thunder, and Tom's muttered grace, "For these and all thy mercies, God's Holy Name be praised," is bitterly ironic, mocked by what follows. The only paradise within reach is Paradise Dance Hall, with its "Waste Land" mood of slow and sensuous rhythms and couples kissing behind ashpits and telephone poles, "the compensation for lives that passed...without any change or adventure," as Tom remarks. The failure of electric power after dinner—previsioning the blackout of the world—leads to Amanda's joking question, "Where was Moses when the lights went off?" This suggests another savior who would lead his people from the desert into the promised land, but the answer to her question is "In the dark."

Jim's attempt to play the modern savior is an abysmal failure. In the after-dinner scene, he offers Laura the sacrament—wine and "life-savers," in this case—and a Dale Carnegie version of the Sermon on the Mount—self-help rather than divine help—but to no avail. At the end of the play Laura and Amanda are, as the joke bitterly reminds us, "in the dark," and Tom's last lines announce the final failure, the infinite desolation: "For nowadays the world is lit by lightning. Blow out your candles, Laura—and so goodbye. ..."

Here as elsewhere in his plays Williams draws upon his frightened characters' preference for soft candlelight to harsh daylight or electric bulbs, not only because it serves him dramaturgically to establish his conception of a new plastic theater where evanescent characters and images flicker across the stage momentarily, but also because his characters so often want to withdraw from the blinding light of reality into the softer world of illusion. At the end of *The Glass Menagerie*, however, the blackout is even more catastrophic, for it not only envelops the Laura of Tom's memory and serves as another reminder of the blackout of war which shrouds the world: it is also the denial of any final "Rise an' Shine" for these frail creatures. The church has been struck by lightning, and all hope of resurrection has been lost in this damned universe where belief turns into metaphor, where humankind seems abandoned by its God, and where the echoes of prayer are heard only in blasphemy or irony. The bleakness of Williams' vision in *The Glass Menagerie* is complete. If Tom is released finally, it is in the words of Job, "And I only am escaped alone to tell thee." It is as the author's surrogate, as writer and chronicler of catastrophe, that he emerges at the end.

Postscript 1976

Published criticism of *The Glass Menagerie* since this essay was originally written in 1964 has confirmed in other particulars my sense of the importance of the religious language of the drama, and my interpretation, in turn, has been used to attack Marxist readings of the play as a dramatization of the disintegration of a lower middle class family under a ruthless capitalist system during the Depression.* It is a tribute to the play's richness that it has

*Gilbert Debusscher, in "Tennessee Williams' Unicorn Broken Again," *Revue belge de Philologie et d'Histoire*, 49 (1971), 875-85, builds upon my analysis and stimulated both kinds of criticism. What I would emphasize now in rethinking these issues is that a Marxist analysis of the play, though incomplete, is both ideologically accurate and descriptively useful. Williams did serve his aesthetic apprenticeship during the 1930s, and in the first part of his opening description of the apartment building he does point us towards a class analysis of "this largest and fundamentally enslaved section of American society." But this intention loses force in the last few words of the paragraph.

Williams' understanding of and compassion for the illusions of the Wingfields are based upon an implicit recognition that work in America is alienating drudgery: Rubicam's Business College for Laura, selling illusions for Amanda, Continental Shoes for Tom ("the warehouse is where I work, not where I know people," he tells Amanda, with, as it turns out, devastating consequences for Laura). They are indeed victims of a larger social failure, for humane democratic values have been redefined and inverted by Jim, the economic system's apologist, as a use of knowledge to gain power and money. In this Depression world, as Tom tells us, it takes a war to make adventure available to the masses, to release them from the social trap. Which is of course precisely what happened.

In the light of these social clarifications, it seems to me now that Williams' religious language in the play becomes—however unconsciously—a strategic mode for evading the implications of his social analysis, about which, like Amanda ("We live in such a mysterious universe, don't we?"), he is finally muddled. If his sense of cosmic catastrophe and of the metaphysical abandonment of his characters in the universe is, as I have shown, in some ways a great dramatic and linguistic strength of the play, it is from another point of view a typical weakness of Williams and American writers in general. Failing in their art to explore humankind

---

weakens the argument of Grigor Pavlov's Marxist "Comparative Study of Tennessee Williams' *The Glass Menagerie* and *Portrait of a Girl in Glass*," *Annuaire de l'Université de Sofia,* Faculté des Lettres, 62 (1968), 111-31.

[For another Marxist reading of Williams, see Maya M. Koreneva, *Contemporary American Drama:* 1945-70, published doctoral dissertation (Moscow: Gorky Institute of World Literature, Academy of Sciences, U.S.S.R., 1975). She thinks that Williams' significance lies in his exposure (in the early plays) of decadent social conditions in America at the time of World War II. When he switched from social to sexual studies, however, he ceased to be a playwright of the first rank.—Ed.]

adequately in society, they shift responsibility for the human condition to the divine and write metaphysical romances rather than trenchant social drama, in a series of dramatic gestures which fluctuate between Byronic defiance and ultimate despair. This weakness is especially apparent in Williams' later plays, which frequently exploit what I would call the romance of violence. The greatness of *The Glass Menagerie*, as art and as human statement, still lies in Williams' ability at that point in his career to sustain a sense of the individual, the social, and the religious dimensions of our experience poised in delicate poetic balance.

The Garrulous Grotesques
of Tennessee Williams

by Ruby Cohn

The last plays of Eugene O'Neill were produced after World War II; the first plays of Arthur Miller and Tennessee Williams were produced after World War II. Though Miller and Williams strain, like O'Neill, toward tragedy, each of them early settled into his own idiom, little tempted by O'Neill's restless experimentation. Since Miller and Williams dominated a decade of American theater, their names have often been coupled, if only for contrast. Kenneth Tynan, the British critic, has written: "Miller's plays are hard, 'patrist,' athletic, concerned mostly with men. Williams' are soft, 'matrist,' sickly, concerned mostly with women. What links them is their love for the bruised individual soul and its life of 'quiet desperation.'"[1] What also links them is the way the dramatists convey the bruises; not at all quiet in their desperation, each of these victim-souls evokes our pity through the author's distinctive idiom. The most effective dialogue of Miller often relies on his Jewish background, whereas that of Williams leans on his Southern background. In this milieu, Williams often reuses the same materials—phrase, theme, scene, or character. Williams himself acknowledged: "My longer plays emerge out of earlier one-acters or short stories I may have written years before. I work over them again and again."[2] Consistently, Williams reworks by expansion, and comparison of the short works with the longer plays illuminates his focus on dialogue of pathos. ...

[1]Kenneth Tynan, *Tynan on Theatre*. (Baltimore: Penguin Books, 1961), 141.

[2]"Talk with the Playwright," *Newsweek* (March 23, 1959), 75.

Three years separate *The Glass Menagerie* from Williams' next extended drama, *A Streetcar Named Desire* (1947). Two one-act plays written during that interval point toward the latter. *Streetcar,* like *The Glass Menagerie,* is a poignant portrait of a Southern gentlewoman who is "extinct in the modern world." Similarly, the pathetic protagonists of two 1945 one-acters take refuge from reality in a world of fantasy. Thirteen-year-old Willie in *This Property is Condemned* invents her own romanticized life in imitation of her prostitute sister, Alva, who is dead. Miss Lucretia Collins, a demented old maid in *Portrait of a Madonna,* imagines herself pregnant by a youthful lover; like Blanche DuBois in *Streetcar,* she is taken to an institution by a doctor and nurse.[3] Both Willie and Miss Lucretia are as garrulous as Amanda Wingfield. Lacking her energy, however, they exist only through their brave, bright words, which are contradicted by the sexless pathos of their visual stage reality—child and old maid. But Blanche Du Bois is Williams' masterpiece of contradiction.

The very name Blanche DuBois suggests her duality. In the play, she herself translates it for Mitch as "white woods. Like an orchard in spring." But even her translation is a fantasy. Blanche is past her spring, and the purity of Blanche-white is undermined by the thicket of DuBois-woods. Anglicized, Blanche's name is DuBoys, and under her chaste surface, Blanche lusts for boys. Comparably, her clothes reflect her divided nature—mothlike white for day and red satin robe for intimacy. More pointedly, the two streetcars—Desire and Cemeteries—suggest the opposing forces that claim Blanche. Her deeds—impulsive and reckless—give the lie to her words—consciously poetic and proper. Blanche never understands the deep division within her, as Williams understands that division in himself: "Roughly there was a combination of Puritan and Cavalier strains in my blood which may be accountable for the conflicting impulses I often represent in the people I write about."[4] The DuBois sisters seem to have only the one Puritan (French Huguenot) strain in *their* blood, but Blanche is nevertheless prey to "conflicting impulses." Preserving the veneer of an aristocratic belle of the Old South, criticizing her sister for an animal marriage, Blanche herself slips into vul-

---

[3]Jessica Tandy was chosen to play the role of Blanche in the New York production of *Streetcar* because she had played Miss Lucretia in the Los Angeles Actors' Laboratory production of *Portrait of a Madonna.*

[4]Program for the Los Angeles Mark Taper Forum Theater production of *El Camino Real,* n.p.

garisms. Though she claims to be "compiling a notebook of quaint little words and phrases" of the New Orleans milieu, she has, as Stanley charges, heard them all before.

Early in the play, Blanche sprays Stanley with her atomizer, so that he responds: "If I didn't know that you was my wife's sister I'd get ideas about you!" Later, Blanche tells Stella that the only way to live with Stanley "is to—go to bed with him." While waiting for Mitch, Blanche toys amorously with a newspaper boy who has just had a cherry soda. "Cherry!" Blanche teases, confessing, "You make my mouth water." Much later that night, Blanche mocks Mitch: *"Voulex-vous coucher avec moi ce soir?"* The question has wider currency than the French language, and Blanche takes a risk for her poor little joke—the risk of destroying her pure Southern Belle image in Mitch's eyes. A few minutes later, *"she rolls her eyes"* when she mentions her "old-fashioned ideals" to Mitch. But that is the last time she shows any awareness of playing a role.

During most of the eleven scenes of the play, Blanche appears to believe in her role of proper Southern lady, and that way her madness lies. In Scene 1, Blanche plays the *grande dame* for her own sister, until her impassioned outburst about death at Belle Reve. In Scene 2, she plays a sex kitten for Stanley (which is compatible with the cliché portrait of a vivacious Southern lady); as she protects her love letters and delivers the Belle Reve papers to him, she explains that all the male DuBois "exchanged the land for their epic fornications." Only obliquely does she admit that the plantation is finally foreclosed to pay for her own fornications. The very name Belle Reve feminizes dreams since *rêve* is a masculine noun and *belle* a feminine adjective.

In Scene 3, Blanche plays the refined lady—her sustained pose with Mitch: "I can't stand a naked light bulb, any more than I can a rude remark or a vulgar action." In Scene 4, Blanche plays the outraged aristocrat, complaining of animal Stanley, and culminating in her plea to Stella: *"Don't—don't hang back with the brutes!"* In Scene 5, Blanche acts superior to Stanley even when he hints at her past. In Scene 6, Blanche continues to play the refined lady for Mitch, but the memory of her marriage tears through that role. She is only momentarily present in Scene 7, but her aristocratic role is shattered in Scene 8, when Stanley gives her a bus ticket back to Laurel, an ironic name for the town of her humiliation. When Mitch arrives in Scene 9, Blanche attempts briefly to resume her refined lady role, then abruptly confesses

and explains her promiscuities: "Death...The opposite is desire."
Rather than suffer the desire of Mitch, however, Blanche cries out
wildly: "Fire! Fire! Fire!" In the climactic tenth scene, both
Blanche and Stanley have been drinking. We are not quite sure
whether her story of Shep Huntleigh is an illusion or a brave
front against Stanley, who scoffs at her pose of purity. Forcing
Blanche to drop the broken bottle-top of self-defense. Stanley
calls her "Tiger." Earlier, she had called Stanley an animal, but
now the animal accusation is turned against her. In the final
scene, Blanche is the victim of her own Southern-belle fantasy;
the role has become her reality as she seems not to recognize the
poker-playing men. Expecting Shep Huntleigh, Blanche responds
to the Institution doctor, who is both her Hunter and her Shep-
herd. Her exit line, addressed to the doctor, intensifies her
pathos: "Whoever you are—I have always depended on the kindness of strangers." But we know that Blanche has found no kindness among strangers, and we may recall an earlier use of the
word "strangers," in her confession to Mitch: "After the death of
Allan—intimacies with strangers was all I seemed able to fill my
empty heart with."

To play her role in the two-room Kowalski apartment, Blanche
has brought a trunk full of clothes; her stage business involves
drinking, dimming lights, emerging from hot baths, and seeking
compliments about her appearance. But it is mainly through her
dialogue that Blanche underlines her manor-born superiority.
She introduces cultural references into the French Quarter dwell-
ing, which evokes an Edgar Allen Poe horror story for her. She
recognizes that the lines on Mitch's cigarette case belong to a
sonnet by Mrs. Browning; she has evidently taught American
literature, since she mentions Poe, Hawthorne, and Whitman.
She calls the newspaper boy a young Prince out of the Arabian
nights, and Mitch her Rosenkavalier, Armand, and Samson. In
the last scene, Blanche is blind to the reality of her situation, but
she specifies that her jacket is Della Robbia blue: "the blue of the
robe in the old Madonna pictures."

Blanche's speech is distinguished not only by her cultural
references. She alone uses correct grammar and varied syntax.
Her vocabulary contains such Latinisms as "heterogeneous,"
"absconding," "judicial," "transitory," and "recriminations."
But when Blanche uses images, they are stale or incongruous.
Defeated, she tells Mitch that she had viewed him as "a cleft in
the rock of the world that I could hide in." A little later, she

compares her past to "an old tin can [on] the tail of the kite." Of her soldier boy-friends, Blanche remarks: "The paddy-wagon would gather them up like daisies." Even her most moving speech —the story of her husband's suicide—closes with pretentious imagery: "And then the searchlight which had been turned on the world was turned off again and never for one moment since has there been any light that's stronger than this—kitchen— candle." Seemingly related but not functionally linked is her hope that Stella's baby will have eyes "like two blue candles lighted in a white cake."

When Blanche tries to be uplifting, her images are most inadequate. Seeking to inspire Stella, she becomes trite and abstract: poetry and music, new light, tender feelings, our flag. When Blanche insists upon her superiority to Stanley, she can summon only the cliché phrases of popular magazines: "But beauty of the mind and richness of the spirit and tenderness of the heart —and I have all of those things—aren't taken away, but grow!" Whatever Williams may have intended, Blanche DuBois is trapped by the poverty of her imagery which reflects the poverty of her dreams, like Miller's Willie Loman. But whereas Miller supplies Willy with weak foils, Blanche is challenged and destroyed by a strong antagonist, Stanley Kowalski, whom she correctly views as her executioner.

The hard consonants of Stanley Kowalski contrast with the open vowels of Blanche DuBois. As opposed to her mothlike whiteness, Stanley moves in a world of vivid color; Williams compares him to *"a richly feathered male bird."* Stanley wears a green bowling shirt or bright silk pajamas. He and Stella make love under colored lights. His poker party resembles Van Gogh's *Night Cafe,* with its *"raw colors of childhood's spectrum."*

Visually and verbally, Williams opposes Stanley to Blanche. Each character is summarized by his opening lines:

> *Stanley.* Hey, there! Stella, Baby!....Catch!...Meat!
> *Blanche.* They told me to take a streetcar named Desire, and then transfer to one called Cemeteries and ride six blocks and get off at—Elysian Fields!

Stanley has trained his wife to catch his meat, in every sense. Blanche has come to the end of the line named Desire, and Williams' drama traces her ride to Cemeteries. Forcing her toward that destination is the implacable solidity of Stanley's speech: "Be comfortable is my motto." "You going to shack up here?" "To hold front position in this rat-race you've got to believe you are lucky." "You left nothing here but spilt talcum and old empty perfume bottles—unless it's the paper lantern you want to take with you."

On stage, Stanley's physicality contrasts with Blanche's ready verbalizations. His cruellest gesture in the play is to tear the paper lantern off the light bulb. His other rough acts are understandable—tossing the meat package to Stella, ruffling Blanche's rich clothes, throwing the radio out of the window, breaking plates when he is insulted, and handing Blanche a one-way ticket to Laurel. We do not see Stanley hit Stella, and we do not see him rape Blanche; the first deed is mitigated by his contrition, and the second by Blanche's provocation. In the last scene of the play, however, when Blanche is helpless and defeated, Stanley acts with the kind of cruelty that Blanche has called "unforgiveable," and of which she herself was guilty when she told her young husband: "You disgust me."

Blanche and Stanley are protagonist and antagonist in *Streetcar*, and yet, whatever Williams has said in commentary, his play is not a simple picture of victim and villain. Blanche is cruel to her husband, rude to Eunice, patronizing to Stella, and arrogant to Stanley. Though Stanley is finally cruel to Blanche, he is a faithful friend to Mitch and a satisfying husband to Stella. Especially as played by Marlon Brando, Stanley hides vulnerability beneath taunts and boasts; his cruelty defends his world.

Between Blanche and Stanley are Stella and Mitch, each part-victim and part-brute. Naturally kind, admittedly sensual, Stella is ironically named for a star. She remembers Belle Reve without nostalgia, and she lives contentedly in the Elysian Fields, acquiescing to Stanley's dominance as quietly as she evidently did to Blanche in their childhood. "Thrilled" by Stanley, she accepts all facets of his violence—except the truth of his rape of her sister.

Like Stella, Mitch is pulled between Stanley and Blanche. Responsive to women, Mitch willingly accedes to Blanche's instructions in gentility, and he suffers visibly at Stanley's revelations about her past. An Army buddy, fellow-worker, and poker pal of Stanley, Mitch shares Stanley's ethics—"Poker should not be played in a house with women." But he also shares Blanche's awareness of death. Mitch has a dead girl-friend as Blanche has a dead husband. As Blanche watched the members of her family die, Mitch is watching his mother die. Mitch's feeling for his dying mother elicits Blanche's confession of her husband's suicide. Death makes them realize their need of one another. But after Mitch learns about Blanche's past, a Mexican woman chants: "Flores. Flores. Flores para los muertos." It is not clear whether Blanche understands the Spanish, but she reminisces on the same theme: "Death—I used to sit here and she used to sit over there and death was as close as you are." Death of the mind is as close to Blanche as Mitch is. By the next scene, even before the rape, Blanche panics into derangement.

The play's last scene so victimizes Blanche—sister, brother-in-law, poker players, nurse—that it borders on sentimentality, which is aggravated, in reading, by such pretentious stage directions as *"tragic radiance"* for Blanche, on whose face *"all human experience shows."* But Williams saves the scene by the very triviality of the dialogue—Blanche's preoccupation with her adornments, the men's preoccupation with their poker game. Both preoccupations have been repeated during the course of the play, so that they take on cumulative significance in this last scene. Other repeated motifs culminate in this scene—the Shep Huntleigh of Blanche's fantasy, her hot bath and search for compliments, her references to death, the distortion of the "Varsouviana" into jungle noises, Stanley's revelation of the naked light bulb. At the last, Blanche follows the doctor as blindly as she followed Stella during the first poker game. Once Blanche is gone, civilized discourse vanishes, Stanley and Stella relax into an almost wordless animal abandon as we hear the blue piano music and the final words of the play: "This game is seven-card stud," which summarizes life in the French Quarter.

Williams had intended at first to call his play *The Poker Game,* and the actual title may indicate his shift of focus from Stanley to Blanche. Elia Kazan's much-publicized Director's Notes center every scene on Blanche, whose role has been called an "actor-killer."[5] Though the psycho-pathology of Blanche has absorbed three decades of critics, directors like Kazan build from climax to climax of the play on the firm ground of Stanley's brute vigor. While Blanche's desire goes the way of Belle Reve, Stanley and his entourage raucously ride the streetcar named Desire. Like D. H. Lawrence, Williams presents desire as synonymous with life, and its opposite is Cemeteries. Before the play began, Blanche

---

[5]Published in Toby Cole and Helen Chinoy, eds, *Directors on Directing* (New York, 1963). See, too, Harold Clurman, *Lies Like Truth* (New York, 1958), 72-80, for a view that Brando was acting "against" Kowalski as written.

used desire to escape from death, but in the Elysian Fields, the
world of seven-card stud, her past desires turn to present death,
and Williams summons our pity with light, music, repetition,
and her paste-images that she displays like diamonds. ...

...Some time between 1952, when Williams published "Three
Players of a Summer Game" and 1955, when *Cat on a Hot Tin
Roof* was first produced, Williams came to associate Margaret
Pollitt with that metaphor of monosyllables—cat on a hot tin
roof.

Of the "three players of a summer game," none is Margaret
Pollitt. In the story she is never compared to a cat, and she is
never called Maggie. But Brick Pollitt, her husband, is trans-
planted almost intact from story to play. In both story and play,
Brick takes to drink for sexual reasons, but in the story it is Margaret's parasitic masculinity that is responsible. "Margaret Pollitt
lost her pale, feminine prettiness and assumed in its place something more impressive—a firm and rough-textured sort of hand-
someness." Margaret thrives on Brick's weakness, but a widow
and her daughter play croquet with Brick, seeking to restore his
self-respect. When the summer is over, widow and daughter leave
town, and Brick returns to liquor and wife, who drives him in
their Pierce-Arrow "as Caesar or Alexander the Great or Hannibal
might have led in chains through a capital city the prince of a
state newly conquered."

In *Cat on a Hot Tin Roof*, Williams reverses Brick's passion for
his wife to hers for him, and he changes Margaret's masculinity
to Brick's fear of his own homosexuality. The story's widow and
daughter disappear, to be replaced by Big Daddy, Big Mama, and
Gooper Pollitt's brood. But the most important change is reflected in the new title: "Three Players of a Summer Game" suggests the ephemeral nature of their activity, whereas *Cat on a Hot
Tin Roof* couples animal and metal, two durables in uncomfortable contact.

The prevalence of animal imagery in *Cat* has been noted by
Bernard Dukore:[6] the Negro servants pronounce the family name
as "Polly;" Big Daddy eats like a horse; Big Mama charges like
a rhino; Mae and Gooper jaw, jabber, and watch like hawks; their
children are compared to county fair animals, monkeys, pigs, and
no-neck monsters; the celebrants of Big Daddy's birthday sound
"like a great aviary of chattering birds," and they are all deep

[6]Bernard Dukore, "The Cat Has Nine Lives," *Tulane Drama Review* (Fall,
1963), 95-100.

in "catty talk." For no specified reason, Margaret has been nick-named Maggie the Cat, and she makes three references to her-self as a cat on a hot tin roof (in the original version). In reviewing her affair with Skipper, Maggie calls herself a mouse and says she "shot cock-robin" Skipper. Brick alone is free of animal reso-nance, and Maggie even calls him "godlike." Only in his con-fession to Big Daddy does Brick liken his marriage to "two cats on a fence humping." But he refers to the past, before he sought refuge in alcohol.

Like the roses in *The Rose Tattoo* and desire in *Streetcar*, animality in *Cat* is synonymous with life. Grasping, screeching, devouring, the Pollitts are greedily alive, and the shadow of cancer on Big Daddy has made them all the more aggressive in their vigor. The Reverend Tooker announces sententiously that "the Stork and the Reaper are running neck and neck." In *Cat on a Hot Tin Roof,* Mae Pollitt is pregnant while Big Daddy is dying of cancer. By the end of the play Maggie Pollitt lies that she is pregnant while Brick Pollitt may die of alcoholism. Fear of dying and zest for living distinguish the dialogue of *Cat,* and they dramatize Brick rather than Big Daddy as the moribund stranger in this vital family.

Like O'Neill's drinkers, Brick holds his liquor well. So courte-ous is he that it is difficult to believe that Big Mama and Big Daddy are his parents; so aloof, it is difficult to view acquisitive Gooper as his brother; so cool, it is difficult to imagine him with desire for either woman or man. The darling of father, mother, and wife, Brick repeats the word "disgust" almost as a leitmotif. When Maggie admires Big Daddy because he "drops his eyes to my boobs an' licks his old chops," Brick comments: "That kind of talk is disgusting." In the crucial scene between Brick and his father, Big Daddy asks: "Why do you drink? Why are you throw-ing your life away, boy, like somethin' disgusting you picked up on the street?" As if taking the word for a cue, Brick answers the question in one word: "DISGUST!" When Brick realizes that Big Daddy is not horrified that he and Skipper might have been lovers, he exclaims: "Don't you know how people *feel* about things like that? How, how *disgusted* they are by things like that?" The word "disgust" is repeated six times before Brick shifts to mendacity as his reason for drinking. Rejecting this excuse, Big Daddy concludes a long speech to Brick: "*I've* lived with men-dacity!—Why can't *you* live with it? Hell, you *got* to live with it, there's nothing *else* to *live* with except mendacity, is there?"

Though the words appear abstract out of context, they are a coda to the specific lies of Big Daddy's life, and the italicized words give rhythm and meaning to the coda, which declares that lies are life.

Cat on a Hot Tin Roof thrives on the life of its lies and animality, to all of which Brick reacts with the tall drinks of his disgust Ironically, his liveliest reaction emerges from his disgust, and it serves death. When Big Daddy accuses Brick of drinking to kill his disgust with his own lie, Brick bares the truth of mortality to his father: *"How about these birthday congratulations, these many, many happy returns of the day, when ev'rybody but you knows there won't be any!"* At the end of the second act, Brick and Daddy enunciate the theme of the play, each in his own idiom:

> *Brick.* Mendacity is a system that we live in.
> *Big Daddy.* Yes, all liars, all liars, all lying dying liars!...Lying! Dying! Liars!

The original version of the play stresses the contrast between Big Daddy's acceptance and Brick's rejection of the lies that are life. Big Daddy proclaims a sexual aversion to Big Mama, as Brick does to Maggie. As Brick voices his disgust, Big Daddy voices *his* disgust. But Brick will not touch his wife, and Big Daddy *"laid* [his]!—regular as a piston" and fathered his two sons. In the Act II birthday celebration, Big Mama tells Big Daddy: "I even loved your hate and your hardness, Big Daddy!" He muses: *"Wouldn't it be funny if that was true..."* In the original ending of the play, after Maggie has lied that she is pregnant, after she has locked Brick's liquor away, she turns out the lights and declares her love for Brick, who responds: "Wouldn't it be funny if that was true?" to close the play.

Williams supplied an alternate ending for *Cat,* at the suggestion of Broadway director Elia Kazan, who wanted 1) Big Daddy to reappear, 2) Brick to change, and 3) Maggie to be more sympathetic. The five new pages introduce slack into the already slack third act. Brick's declaration of life to Gooper, and of admiration to Maggie, is no more convincing than mere declaration ever is. And Maggie becomes more garrulous rather than more sympathetic. In the original version, the last scene highlights the ambiguous relationship of truth and lies; living is lying, but if one continues to live, any lie can become truth. In that context, Brick's curtain line is a meaningful echo of Big Daddy: "Wouldn't it be funny if that was true?" In the Kazan-inspired ending, however,

Williams confusingly introduces the titular metaphor. Maggie tritely links her love with Brick's life, then closes the play with the line: "I'm determined to do it—and nothing's more determined than a cat on a tin roof—is there? Is there, Baby?" The comparison is preposterous, for the whole play has equated the metaphor with nervousness and discomfort, not determination. On the other hand, if Williams *intends* the metaphor to be preposterous in order to win sympathy for Maggie's determination in the face of impossible odds, then Brick cannot acquiesce tacitly, undergoing the change that Kazan requested. In either case, repetition of the metaphor emphasizes the more flaccid writing of the alternate version.[7]

In both *Streetcar* and *Cat,* the life of the dialogue lies in animal vigor. But *Streetcar* is more dramatic because of the tension between a genteel dream and that vigor, whereas catty energy easily overwhelms aloofness in *Cat.* Kazan's directorial instinct did not err in clinging to Big Daddy, who, without pretentiousness, looms like a god of life from his first word "Crap" to his final furious cry. His speech embraces all the living kingdoms: "The human machine is not so different from the animal machine or the fish machine or the bird machine or the reptile machine or the insect machine!" For all the repetitions of the word "machine," they are organic to him. He is tolerant of all forms of sexuality except what is sold. Big Daddy is the richest planter in the Delta —the man whose life and livelihood are organically interrelated. And this man reacts to the news of his death with rage. It is for Big Daddy that Williams precedes his play by the Dylan Thomas line: "Rage, rage against the dying of the light."

Like many colorful characters, Big Daddy manhandles his creator, growing too big for his play. Thus, his reminiscences about Europe, his generalizations about mendacity, and his elephantine joke diffuse the dramatic drive. Unlike Maggie, he never becomes maudlin. In spite of Big Daddy's digressions and Maggie's unfeline sentimentality, however, *Cat* contains concrete and cohesive dramatic dialogue. All Williams' subsequent plays, like, many of his previous ones, are marred by pretentious symbols that seek to inflate psychopathology into poetic myth....

Though Williams is often called a poetic playwright, he usually accepts the realist convention of psychologically and sociologically coherent characters, grotesque though they may be.

[7]Cf. William Sacksteder, "The Three Cats," *Drama Survey* (Winter, 1966-67), 252-266, for a different viewpoint.

These grotesque characters are exceptionally verbal, given to a degree of imagery that is unusual in American realistic drama. In a few of his plays, Williams combines verbal with theatrical imagery to insist upon a symbolic resonance beyond the realistic surface — *Glass Menagerie, Streetcar Named Desire, The Rose Tattoo, The Night of the Iguana*. There is also a more candidly symbolic strain in his playwriting, bordering on allegory. His first excursion into this domain was the short *Ten Blocks on the Camino Real*, revised and expanded in 1953. With modification, Williams continued the non-realistic form in *The Milktrain Doesn't Stop Here Any More* and his two "Slapstick Tragedies." In contrast to their experimental, often expressionistic form, these plays use crisp, colloquial dialogue.

Though five years separate *Ten Blocks on the Camino Real* from the first Broadway production of *Camino Real*, no substantive change occurs. The earlier play is subtitled "A fantasy," and the fantastic elements are increased in the full-length play. The hero in each play is Kilroy, whose name derives from the ubiquitous American solider of World War II; in Williams' plays, however, he is not a soldier, but an ex-Golden Gloves winner. He speaks in American slang of the 1940's, which contrasts with the more literary locutions of such characters as Marguerite Gautier, Jacques Casanova, Baron de Charlus, a gypsy daughter Esmeralda, Don Quixote, and a sinister Mr. Gutman. In the shorter play, Kilroy appears on seven of the ten blocks; in the longer one, he is present on eleven of the sixteen blocks, his importance steadily increasing as the play progresses. Moreover, a prologue suggests that the entire play is a dream of Don Quixote, and Williams' Expressionistic technique is thus indebted to Strindberg's *Dream Play*, often considered the first Expressionist drama.

A quest play like *The Dream Play, Camino Real* mirrors Kilroy's quest by the separate quests of Jacques Casanova, Proust's Baron de Charlus, Lord Byron, and the arch-dreamer Don Quixote. Trapped in sixteen blocks of no man's land, all these dreamers are rejected from the Royal Way, so that they are compelled to stray on the Real Road — as Williams puns on the Spanish and English meanings of "real." There are three possible exits from this country of fantasy: escape in an airplane appropriately named Fugitivo; bold egress into the desert of the Terra Incognita; death and degradation at the hands of the sinister Streetcleaners who deliver corpses to a medical laboratory. In the diffusion of scenes, action centers on the Camino *Real;* none of the major characters reaches the Fugitivo, Lord Byron sets out for Terra Incognita, Baron de Charlus falls to the Streetcleaners, and, in his fidelity to Marguerite Gautier, Jacques Casanova will spend eternity shuttling back and forth from Royal Way to Real Road. But Kilroy, ex-champ and ex-Patsy, pure-hearted lover of an ever-renewed Virgin, becomes garbage for the Streetcleaners, guinea pig for the medical students, to be resurrected as the companion to Don Quixote in his venture into Terra Incognita.

Williams summarized the play's theme: *"Camino Real* doesn't say anything that hasn't been said before, but is merely a picture of the state of the romantic non-conformist in modern society. It stresses honor and man's sense of inner dignity which the Bohemian must re-achieve after each period of degradation he is bound to run into. The romantic should have the spirit of anarchy and not let the world drag him down to its level."[8] In the play itself, Esmeralda, the gypsy's daughter, who is a prostitute and always a virgin, utters much the same sentiment in more determinedly colorful idiom: "God bless all con men and hustlers and pitch-men who hawk their hearts on the street, all two-time losers who're likely to lose once more, the courtesan who made the mistake of love, the greatest of lovers crowned with the longest horns, the poet who wandered far from his heart's green country and possibly will and possibly won't be able to find his way back, look down with a smile tonight on the last cavaliers, the ones with the rusty armor and soiled white plumes, and visit with understanding and something that's almost tender those fading legends that come and go in this plaza like songs not clearly remembered, oh, sometime and somewhere, let there be something to mean the word *honor* again!" Not only does the prayer embrace the literary characters of the play, but it uses the clichés of romantic literature —heart, love, green country, armor, plumes, legends, songs, honor. Camille accuses Casanova: "Your vocabulary is almost as out-of-date as your cape and your cane." And the charge can be made against much of Williams' dialogue in this play.

What distinguishes Kilroy, however, is his colloquial innocence in this literary company. Announced as "the Eternal Punchinella," Kilroy arrives with his concrete idiom: "I just got off a boat. Lousiest frigging tub I ever shipped on, one continual hell it was, all the way up from Rio. And me sick, too. I picked

[8]Program for the Los Angeles Mark Taper Forum Theater production of *El Camino Real,* n.p.

up one of those tropical fevers. No sick-bay on that tub, no doctor, no medicine or nothing, not even one quinine pill, and I was burning up with Christ knows how much fever. I couldn't make them understand I was sick. I got a bad heart, too. I had to retire from the prize ring because of my heart. I was the light heavyweight champion of the West Coast, won these gloves!—before my ticker went bad." Decades after the original version of the play, when its staging no longer seems inventive, the play's spine lies in Kilroy's idiom. His slang has dated with his legend, so that Williams' wandering American is a pathetic anachronism, who talks too much, but who endears himself to us because all that talk is a whistling in the dark at the human condition.

Other than Kilroy, only the Gypsy speaks vigorously in the cynical language of commercial enterprise, which has dated less than Kilroy's slang. Before the farcical scene in which the Chosen Hero Kilroy courts the Prostitute Virgin Esmeralda, the Gypsy summarizes the action: "There's nobody left to uphold the old traditions! You raise a girl. She watches television. Plays be-bop. Reads *Screen Secrets.* Comes the Big Fiesta. The moonrise makes her a virgin—which is the neatest trick of the week! And what does she do? Chooses a Fugitive Patsy for the Chosen Hero! Well, show him in! Admit the joker and get the virgin ready!"

As the concreteness of Stanley overwhelms Blanche's esthetic abstrations and clichés, the commercial vigor of the Gypsy and the visual menace of the Streetcleaners overwhelm the ethical abstractions and clichés, the commercial vigor of the Gypsy and Real. But with determined optimism, Williams gives the final inspiring words to Don Quixote, in whose shadow walks Kilroy. Earlier, on Block X, faithful Jacques Casanova had attempted to convince faithless Marguerite Gautier: "The violets in the mountains can break the rocks if you believe in them and allow them to grow!" Though there is no evidence of belief on Marguerite's part, we last see her rising from the bed of her young lover to invite Jacques from Skid Row to her sumptuous hotel. As they embrace, Don Quixote raises his lance to proclaim: *"The violets in the mountains have broken the rocks!"* The old idealist *"goes through the arch with Kilroy."* Clearly, Williams intends triumph for the grotesque Bohemians, in spite of stale slang and stale literary phrases.

As in his more realistic dramas, Williams plays upon a theatrical symbol—the heart. Kilroy's heart is as large as a baby's head, and Kilroy himself calls it a "ticker" in this land where time is running out. Lord Byron describes how Trelawney "snatched the heart of Shelley out of the blistering corpse!" Byron disapproves of Trelawney's action, asking: "What can one man do with another man's heart?" Jacques Casanova responds with passion; speaking for himself and all lovers, he takes a loaf of bread and accompanies his words with actions—twisting, tearing, crushing, and kicking the heart-loaf. By Block XV, Esmeralda has done all this to Kilroy's heart, and he lies dead on a dissecting table. When his heart is removed, it is seen to be the size of a baby's head, and it is made of solid gold. Kilroy rises from the operating table, grabs his heart, and escapes from the laboratory to the loan shark, where he pawns his heart for gifts for Esmeralda—romantic to the last. When she rejects him and the gypsy ejects him, Kilroy joins Don Quixote on Skid Row, with words that summarize the action more truly than the violets in the mountains: "Had for a button! Stewed, screwed and tattooed on the Camino Real! Baptized, finally, with the contents of a slop-jar!—Did anybody say the deal was rugged?!" ...

In spite of his prolific output, Tennessee Williams is narrow in range. Most of his plays are set in Southern United States, focused on protagonist-victims who manage to combine humor and weakness. Unlike the monosyllabic characters of many American realistic plays, Williams' grotesques are loquacious, rambling on in free imagery and incantatory repetitions. In addition to image and rhythm, Williams uses set, music, and light to extract symbolic meaning from his realistic surfaces; the more blatant the symbolism, the more frail the play. Like Tom in *Glass Menagerie*, Williams has "a poet's weakness for symbols." Thus, insistence on symbols *weakens* the dramatic drive of several Williams plays—*Summer and Smoke, The Rose Tattoo, Suddenly Last Summer, Cat on a Hot Tin Roof* (Kazan version), *The Milktrain Doesn't Stop Here Any More, Slapstick Tragedy,* and *Kingdom of Earth.* Williams' symbolic imagery is most effective when its very weakness is woven into the fabric of the drama— the stale nostalgia of Amanda in *Glass Menagerie,* the cultural yearning of Blanche in *Streetcar,* the dated slang of Kilroy in *Camino Real.* In these plays the inadequacies of Williams' lyricism function thematically and theatrically, to evoke our sympathy for his garrulous grotesques.

Pithy or more leisurely, Williams' dialogue has endowed the American theater with new rhythms and a larger vocabulary. Though Williams' prose lacks the taut coherence of Southern poetry of a Tate or Ransom, and though Williams' plots lack the complex density of Southern novels of a Faulkner, Welty, or O'Connor, he has given Southern grotesques dignity on the Broadway stage. Even the farcical *Rose Tattoo* is peopled with giants, by comparison with *Tobacco Road.* Though shocking sexuality rather than human warmth may account for his Broadway success, Williams has managed to combine shocking sexuality with human warmth, sometimes in the same play. His major instrument in this combination is a dialogue that can embrace nostalgia, frustration, sadness, merriment, cruelty, and compassion. Like O'Neill and Miller, Williams has written few flawless plays. He does not often hammer like O'Neill, he does not often preach like Miller, but he tends to indulge in gratuitous violence or obstreperous symbol. At his best, however—*Menagerie, Streetcar,* first version of *Cat, Iguana,* and even *Camino Real*—Williams expands American stage dialogue in vocabulary, image, rhythm, and range.

Tennessee Williams' Achievement
in the Sixties

by Gerald Weales

...The 1960's is the decade in which Tennessee Williams saw his winning streak as a popular dramatist come to an end, and Arthur Miller, wearing a new philosophical look, returned to the theater. From the successful production of *The Glass Menagerie* in 1945 until well into the 1960's, Tennessee Williams averaged rather better than a play every two years, most of which had respectable New York runs—100 performances or more. Working for the most part in Southern settings and presenting somewhat lurid surface events, Williams told again and again the story of an outsider, one of the fugitive kind, who by virtue of his (or her) differentness—his artistic inclinations, his sexual proclivities, his physical defects—becomes a victim of an uncongenial society. As the number of plays grew, it became clear that, for Williams, all men are outsiders and the enemy is the character himself or time eating at him or a godless universe, from which there is no escape, and the best he can do is to take what comfort he can from the temporary palliative, sex.[1] Although a persistent strain of social comment remained in his work, by the end of the 1950's he had become a kind of existential melodramatist. From the beginning, Williams has been essentially a nonrealistic dramatist, using everything from mechanical tricks (the television screen in *Sweet Bird of Youth*) to artificial soliloquies (the set pieces in the same play), from significant names (Val Xavier) to

"Tennessee Williams' Achievement in the Sixties" (editor's title). Excerpted from Gerald Weales, *The Jumping-Off Place: American Drama in the 1960's* (New York: Macmillan, 1969), pp. 3-14. Copyright © 1969 by Gerald Weales. Reprinted by permission of the author and publisher. The pages reprinted here form part of a longer chapter.

[1]For a detailed examination of Williams' thematic and theatrical practices see my *Tennessee Williams* (1965), one of the University of Minnesota Pamphlets on American Writers.

symbolic stage sets (the body-soul balance in *Summer and Smoke*) to break out of the realistic tradition of American drama, a tradition, incidentally, in which he works extremely well (consider the breakfast scene in *The Glass Menagerie*).

Williams' work in the 1960's begins with the highly deceptive *Period of Adjustment* (1960), which many critics dismissed as the Broadway marital comedy it pretended to be. On the surface it looks like—and it is, to some extent—a conventional attack on suburbia, making its satirical points while it tells the story of two marriages, one brand-new and unconsummated, the other five years old and teetering, both going through periods of adjustment. The resolution brings both couples together in a curtain scene that would be the familiar Broadway side-step if it were not that the whole house shakes at this point, settling a little deeper into the cavern over which the suburban development is built. The subtitle, "High Point over a Cavern" (High Point is the name of the development), with its sexual *double-entendre,* suggests that the familiar off-to-bed ending is not all that happy. The play is still another instance, lightly disguised, of the Williams world in which men live tentatively, in an unending period of adjustment, over an abyss that is more than simply social. It is sprinkled with Williams lines that help make the point ("The whole world's a big hospital, a big neurological ward, and I am a student nurse in it") and, as though the sinking house were not enough, he throws in an even more apt image: the honeymoon car in which George and Isabel arrive is a funeral coach.

Period of Adjustment is obviously an experiment for Williams, an attempt to use a popular dramatic form for his own purposes; it succeeded too well, for—in the original production, at least—it came across as a heavy-handed light comedy, this despite the fact that, in Isabel, Williams has created one of the best of his nervous Southern women. "And I had the impression *Period of Adjustment* was a happy play," Williams told Lewis Funke and John E. Booth in an interview, "but when I saw it this summer in the stock production with Dane Clark, I realized that it was about as black as *Orpheus Descending.* "[2] Black it is, certainly, but Williams' remark is an overstatement in the other direction. If we take the play seriously, it is possible to see the "happy" ending not simply as a joke but as a kind of assent to chaos rather than an attempt to escape it. In that case, the play is a first step toward what

[2]*Theatre Arts,* January, 1962. Williams also said that his "style of writing for the theatre is on its way out."

is genuinely new in Williams' work in the 1960's, a retreat from the inescapable violence of *Orpheus Descending* and *Suddenly Last Summer* to an acceptance of life and death, a resignation that is almost positive in its refusal to be sentimental or to indulge the self-pitiers. *The Night of the Iguana* (1961) and *The Milk Train Doesn't Stop Here Anymore* (1963) exemplify that change in Williams.

In *Iguana*, which gets its title and the name of its heroine and very little else from an early Williams story (*One Arm and Other Stories*), the action takes place in a run-down hotel in Mexico. T. Lawrence Shannon, defrocked clergyman and alcoholic, comes running for shelter—dragging behind him a gaggle of outraged Texas teachers whom he is supposed to be taking on tour, including a sixteen-year-old he has seduced and her lesbian chaperone—only to find the hotelkeeper dead and his widow, Maxine, too eager to let him fill Fred's shoes. Hannah Jelkes pushes the wheelchair of her ninety-seven-year-old grandfather uphill through a rain forest to reach the Costa Verde, the last refuge for Nonno in a world through which he and Hannah have wandered, she making sketches, he reciting his poems to pick up the pennies that have kept them alive. So they arrive, priest, poet and painter, buffeted and suffering creatures, as the lines keep insisting, directly identified with the iguana tied under the porch, scratching in a vain attempt to escape before it is eaten. "At the end of its rope?" cries Shannon. "Trying to go on past the end of its goddam rope? Like *you!* Like *me!* Like Grampa with his last poem!"

Yet, this is not the usual Williams struggle in which the victims are destroyed by the ugly forces they face; this is a contest between Hannah and Shannon—oddly enough, a kind of conversion play. Shannon's view of the world is contained in his description of one of the sights he tried to force his "ladies" to see—a great pile of human refuse across which tattered beggars crawled, stopping to eat bits of still undigested food. His God, at once cruel ("stray dogs vivisected") and impersonal ("His oblivious majesty"), is embodied in the storm that strikes at the end of the second act ("Here is your God, Mr. Shannon"); the description in the stage direction, borrowed from the story ("like a giant white bird attacking the hilltop"), recalls Sebastian's God from *Suddenly Last Summer*, the birds diving on the young turtles. Shannon's reaction to the random cruelty of the universe and the ugliness of the world's inequities is to become cruel in his own right;

like a child, he strikes out at everyone—Maxine, Hannah, the teachers for whom he has such contempt—wounding with words. He swims in self-pity. In the dark-night-of-the-soul scene in the third act, in which he is tied in a hammock, presumably to save him from suicide, Hannah taunts him: "Who wouldn't like to suffer and atone for the sins of himself and the world if it could be done in a hammock with ropes instead of nails. ...Isn't that a comparatively comfortable, almost voluptuous kind of crucifixion to suffer for the guilt of the world, Mr. Shannon?" She suggests an alternative, an idea of God that she learned in the House for the Dying in Shanghai, the "little comforts beside the death-pallets" that the "children and grandchildren and the custodians" left there. Instead of forcing his God of "Lightning and Thunder" on others, even if He exists, she tells him to look into the longing faces and "Lead them beside still waters because you know how badly they need the still waters." If there is no comfort to be gained in heaven, there are "Broken gates between people so they can reach each other, even if it's just for one night only." This suggests the way characters in the earlier plays used sex—Blanche in *A Streetcar Named Desire,* Marguerite in *Camino Real,* Carol Cutrere in *Orpheus Descending*—and Hannah's description of the masturbating traveling salesman in Hong Kong intensifies that suggestion, as does Shannon's decision to stay with Maxine.

In the end, Williams goes beyond this limited sense of human contact. Hannah, who has thrown herself on Maxine's mercy in Act I, says, in effect, that if one cannot have God, then he must act like God. Shannon goes down and cuts the iguana loose, "because God won't do it." At this point, Nonno, just before he dies, finally finishes his poem about the orange branch in which growth is only half the story, decay the other, and the tree faces it "Without a cry, without a prayer,/ With no betrayal of despair." Shannon's "spooks" and Hannah's "blue devils" are defeated, or at least held at bay, by an endurance that is strengthened by help given and help received. Since Shannon spends so much of the play fighting off Maxine, his staying (and there is no alternative) might be seen as his final destruction; if that were the case, Hannah's gentle God, like Dr. Sugar's in *Suddenly Last Summer,* would be as frightening as that of Shannon and Sebastian. This, however, is not the effect *The Night of the Iguana* finally conveys. Although there is something almost touchingly corny in the last exchange between Maxine and Shannon, in which she promises to help him get back up the hill and he "chuckles happily" (this being Maxine and Williams, it is also a sex joke), it is intended to convey that Shannon has found Hannah's "still waters," not undergone Dr. Sugar's lobotomy. Even Hannah's last scene, with the dead Nonno, is one of release, not defeat.

If, as Williams told Funke and Booth, *Iguana* is about "how to live beyond despair and still live," *Milk Train* is about how to go beyond despair and learn to die. It is an attempt to still that terrible cry Big Daddy makes at the end of the second act of *Cat on a Hot Tin Roof* when Brick forces him to face the fact of his death. *Milk Train* is based on the story "Man Bring This Up Road" (*Mademoiselle,* July, 1959; reprinted in *The Knightly Quest*), but the earlier fictional version, unlike the play, is not an exercise in *Iguana*-like theology. The much-married, fabulously rich heroine of the play, Flora Goforth, a Georgia swamp girl come up in the world, recalls Big Daddy in her vitality, her vulgarity, her sense of her own power; but also in her fear of death and her refusal to recognize the cancer that is killing her. She sits on an almost impregnable mountaintop in Italy, guarded by *lupos,* animal and human, and dictates her memoirs, from which she hopes to learn something about her life. "Sometimes I think, I suspect, that everything that we do is a way of—*not* thinking about it. Meaning of life, and meaning of death, too." Christopher Flanders, poet and mobile-maker, who is jokingly known as the Angel of Death because he has a habit of visiting old ladies just before they die, manages to invade the estate. Flora tries to make him sleep with her, but his job is to give the ladies "something closer to what they need than what they think they still want." He convinces Flora that she is not that self-sufficient, that "sooner or later, you need somebody or something to mean God to you," and, having taken him on his terms, not hers, she is ready to Goforth peacefully. She accepts the death that she could not escape in any case, recognizes it as simply the last of a great many moments that make up life, and, in doing so, alters her view of life itself. At the end, she asks Chris to help her into her bedroom ("I can't make it alone") and, thus, like Shannon in *Iguana*, comes around to Hannah's God.

Milk Train is an interesting play, particularly to anyone who has watched the subtle alterations and acceptances that have come to Williams over the last twenty years, but it is not a very good one. Even *The Night of the Iguana*, Williams' last popular success, suffers from a surfeit of argument. Williams has always been at his dramatic best when, as in *Streetcar* and *Cat*, character predominates over idea; when a too neat formulation *(Summer and Smoke)* or a too heavy mythic superstructure *(Orpheus Descending)* takes over, the characters have to fight for life. Although a sensitive actress can make something moving out of Hannah, as Margaret Leighton did in the original New York production, she is essentially nondramatic, a walking world view, and her third-act scene with Shannon is a little like a debate, artificially enlivened by his attempts at violence. Compare that vitally important scene with the business in the second act in which Maxine tempts Shannon with a rum-coco; the latter is much more dramatic, a confrontation of characters rather than ideas. Still, there is a genuine clash of ideas in *Iguana* and, for all that Hannah is a bit pale, they are given flesh enough to hold our attention, even to elicit our sympathy. This is not true of *Milk Train.* Flora is potentially a vibrant comic character, but except in some of her exchanges with her neighbor, the Witch of Capri, she operates in a vacuum. Chris is so bland a symbolic character that there is no conflict, no real abrasion, simply a reversal on Flora's part that is not presented dramatically or defined in any terms but philosophic generalization. The play is further hampered by the bogus Kabuki framework in which stage assistants set the scene and offer explanations where none are needed. *Milk Train* suggests *Camino Real* in its imaginative ponderousness, its determination to make its point, but, for all its obviousness, there is more fun in the early work.

The play I have been describing is the third—the published—version of *Milk Train.* It was first done at the Festival of Two Worlds in Spoleto, Italy, in the summer of 1962. It came to New York in January of the next year and ran for two months; in 1964, revised, it tried again and lasted for only five performances. Williams has always been a relentless reviser, turning stories into plays, short plays into long plays, old plays into new plays, but this was the first time that he brought the same material back so quickly, as though he were determined to say what is in this play. Its rejection, by critics and audience alike, marked a change in Williams' relationship to the American theater. He is still indisputably one of the leading American playwrights, but, as Broadway figures such things, he is no longer a safe property; the milk train doesn't stop here anymore.

In 1964, *The Eccentricities of a Nightingale* was tried out in summer stock but never came to New York, and it was published in a double volume with *Summer and Smoke,* of which it is a revision. Neater in action, simpler in theme, *Eccentricities* differ from the earlier play most importantly in that it allows Alma the temporary fulfillment of one night with John. Its best invention is Aunt Albertine, whose story Alma tells in Act II. Albertine lost her respectability and found happiness when she eloped with Otto Schwárzkopf, who ran the Musée Mécanique. On the night the Musée burned, Otto, who was drunk, would not leave the mechanical bird-girl, and Albertine, trying to save him, reached and got only a button. The moral, as Alma explains, is in her aunt's dying words, an echo from an early Williams story, "The Yellow Bird" (in *One Arm and Other Stories)*: "'Some people,' she said, 'don't even die empty-handed!'" In a note to the published play, Williams says that he wrote the revision to be performed in England but got to London too late, after the original *Summer and Smoke* was in rehearsal; that was presumably 1951. *Eccentricities,* then, does not really belong to Williams' work in the 1960's, except for the fact that he chose to release it almost fifteen years after it was written. It is, of course, a play about the "Broken gates between people" that Hannah speaks of in *Iguana*—a gentle, almost genteel example of one of Shannon's "One night stands."

During 1965, a bill of Tennessee Williams one-acters was repeatedly announced for production, but it was not until 1966 that *Slapstick Tragedy* finally got to Broadway. Even though the two plays—*The Mutilated and The Gnädiges Fräulein*—are minor Williams, "diversions," as he called them in his Preface when they were published in *Esquire* (August, 1965), it was surprising that the production lasted for only seven performances. In *The Mutilated,* the weakest of the two plays, two old friends, or friendly enemies, spend Christmas Eve trying and failing to find peace on earth for themselves. One of them is Trinket, who has had a breast removed because of cancer; the other is Celeste, a shoplifting, streetwalking wino who knows and threatens to divulge the secret of Trinket's mutilation. Much of the play deals with the quarrel between them, but it ends with their reconciliation on Christmas Day, when, in a haze of Tokay and sugar wafers, they have a vision of Our Lady, which, as Trinket says, takes away the pain. With the ironic religious experience, the omnipresent carolers chanting their miracle message *a cappella* ("I think the strange, the crazed, the queer/ Will have their holiday this year") and some standard Williams comic lines, the whole thing should probably not be taken too seriously. It certainly should not be played for pathos, as it was in the original New York production.

The Gnädiges Fräulein is a grotesque comedy in which the heroine, down on her luck, is forced to compete with the coca-loony birds (the costumer's delight) for the fishing-boat rejects that provide her room and board. A decayed artist, recalling Alexandra in *Sweet Bird of Youth*, she is no match for organized parasites like the cocaloonies; the play is the account of how she fights the good fight for survival even though it sends her back to the docks, blind and bleeding. Her action forms the spine of the play, the flesh being the running commentary provided by Polly and Molly, the Greek chorus reduced to a comedy team. Williams has used this device before, as in *Orpheus Descending*, where the two comic sisters comment on the disastrous affair of Val and Lady, but now the comic duologue has stepped to the front of the stage and the suffering figure is reduced to an almost mute scare-crow, shivering on the periphery of the scene. Even so, in the last moment of the play, the comedy is upstaged; the final rush of the heroine, while Molly, Polly, and Indian Joe sit down to dinner in the background, should be frightening. Although the two plays have been published in separate acting editions, it is easy to see why Williams suggested, in his *Esquire* note, that they be per-formed together. The first is a sad and occasionally brutal work that ends on a note of ironic exaltation; the second is wild slap-stick that finishes on a note of horror. "In production," Williams wrote, "they may seem to be a pair of fantastic allegories on the tragicomic subject of human existence on this risky planet." Since the heroine of *The Gnädiges Fräulein* provides a ludicrous ex-ample of the endurance Hannah embodies in *Iguana* and since the vision at the end of *The Mutilated* is a wine-soaked variation on the peace that Flora Goforth finds in *Milk Train*, the relation of *Slapstick Tragedy* to the more serious plays of the 1960's is a highly ambiguous one, particularly when one remembers that, as a double bill, the world ends not with Our Lady but with the cry of the cocaloony—*awk, awk, awk*.

Since the appearance of *Slapstick Tragedy*, Williams has pub-lished two short plays in *Esquire: I Can't Imagine Tomorrow* (March, 1966) and *Kingdom of Earth* (February, 1967). The second of these is still another grotesque comedy, suggesting *Baby Doll* rather than *The Gnädiges Fräulein*, in which an unlikely triangle is acted out in the face of an impending flood. The tuber-cular Lot comes back from Memphis with a new wife, Myrtle, and threatens the position of Chicken, his bastard half-brother who has been promised the farm when Lot dies. While Lot calls, then crawls for help, finally dying on the stairs, Chicken explains to Myrtle that only he can save her when the flood comes ("If you get on the roof tomorrow, it'll be Chicken, not Jesus, that gets you up there") and makes it clear that he wants her as much as she wants to stay with him. "There's nothing in the world, nothing in this whole kingdom of earth, that can compare with one thing, and that one thing is what's able to happen between a man and a woman, just that thing, nothing more, is perfect." At the end, he looks out at his land ("Chicken is king!") and then goes up to Myrtle, past the dead Lot, while outside we hear the "distant dynamite blast" which indicates that Mr. Sikes ("like God, he's got more to think about than people below him") has blown up one of his levees and the water is on its way. What the play has to say, beyond its anecdote, is that the only thing anyone can depend on is other people and, given "the scoop," as Myrtle has learned it ("The hardness of people"), this is at best a chancy dependence. The short story treatment of the same material, "The Kingdom of Earth" (in *The Knightly Quest*), is somewhat softer, partly because Chicken as narrator can carry us beyond Lot's death to their fructifying life together (Myrtle is expecting a child whom they will name either Lot or Lottie) and partly because there is no flood in the story and, therefore, no dynamite ending.

The Iguana-like choice of life over death is still implicit in the full-length version of the play—*The Seven Descents of Myrtle* (1968)—but it is no longer a neat if grotesque little parable. There are still the triangle, the shift in partners, and the flood, but the longer play has altered the characters. Chicken becomes a variation on the conventional Williams priapic figure, an uncomfortable compromise between a calendar-caressing recluse and the speaker of the salvational sex lines carried over from the one-act play. Lot is no longer simply tubercular. He is an impotent aristocrat of sorts (he cleans the crystal chandelier while Chicken works the land), ridden by the memory of his dead mother, whom he becomes in a rather trying transvestite death scene. There is no contest, then, for Myrtle. Inevitably she chooses potency over impotency, even if it means, as Stella's choice of Stanley meant twenty years earlier, the choice of vulgarity over gentility. Since Chicken is part Negro and he and Lot are half-brothers, Williams may intend some allegorical statement about racial changes abroad in the land, but such significance is finally irrelevant. What *Seven Descents* becomes is Myrtle and not much else. Most of Williams' invention in stretching his short play has gone into the creation of a Myrtle who is not so much a character of substance as a vehicle for a talented actress. If there is life at all in *The Seven Descents of Myrtle,* it does not come from character or theme or plot, but from an accumulation of funny bits.

Still another Williams play, *The Two-Character Play,* opened in London in December, 1967. According to the reviews, it is about two performers, Felice and his sister Clare, who have been deserted by the other actors, who consider them insane; it takes place in the theater where, at Felice's insistence, they act out what is apparently their own story. David Wade, reviewing the play in the London *Times* (December 13, 1967) under the headline "Tennessee Williams' New Voice," compared Williams to Samuel Beckett. As long ago as the interview with Funke and Booth, Williams expressed his admiration for Harold Pinter. In the production of *Slapstick Tragedy,* directed by Alan Schneider, who made his reputation directing Beckett, Pinter, and Albee, *The Mutilated* nodded in the direction of Pinter, at least to the extent of being unspecific about Trinket's mutilation, which is clearly identified in the printed play; the acting edition offers variants for some of the speeches, showing how the definition was befogged. A hint of undefined terror, however, will not turn a Williams play into a Pinter play, particularly when the Williams play contains themes and devices that we have known as his for years; nor did Williams intend it to, for he said in the *Esquire* note, "They are not 'Theatre of the Absurd.'" If Wade is right, Williams may finally have moved tentatively in the Beckett-Pinter direction in *The Two-Character Play.* If so, that would be somewhat ironic, like Hellman echoing Williams just at the moment when his voice was being drowned out by the absurdists. In any case, *The Seven Descents of Myrtle* is evidence that, come hell or high water, Williams, like Chicken, has no intention of abandoning familiar ground.

The New Note in Tennessee Williams

by Harold Clurman

Tennessee Williams did himself an injustice by having his two
one-act plays, collectively entitled *Slapstick Tragedy,* produced
on Broadway. They might have gained considerable esteem had
they been given in a more modest manner. Their closing was announced after six performances.

A second injustice, almost as great, is the plays' critical reception. *Slapstick Tragedy* is not the author's "top-drawer" work,
but he has struck a new note in at least the second of the two plays
and both have a peculiarly personal stamp that merits attention.

The plays are melancholy but masked avowals. The first, called
The Mutilated, might be described as a freakish Christmas Carol.
Two whores—the first has had one of her breasts removed, the
other has just been released from a short-term jail sentence for
shoplifting—become reconciled in wretched companionship one
Christmas Eve, because although they have reviled each other
through corrupt professional rivalry, they realize that they have
only their mutual deprivation, and the understanding of it, to
give them solace in their common exile from respectable society.

As in certain of his former plays, Williams in *The Mutilated*
reveals his compassion—more, his sense of identification—with
the insulted and the injured, the misfits and the maimed. But
while the earlier plays were soft in sentiment, *The Mutilated* is
savage.

Its "slapstick" consists of deliberate bitchiness. Even the final
moments in which the two whores induce a vision in themselves
of the Blessed Virgin who will forgive and heal them are bitterly
ironic. (This is Williams' squint-eyed flirtation with mysticism.)
The intention is to make us see that the two women, one stupidly
infantile, the other horribly stricken with shame at her affliction,

"The New Note in Tennessee Williams" (editor's title) by Harold Clurman.
From *The Nation*, 202 (March 14, 1966), 309. Copyright © 1966 by *The Nation*.
Reprinted by permission of *The Nation*.

are as absurd as they are pitiable. Williams refuses to gush over them; they are meant to be both grotesque and ridiculous, and these qualities themselves are to lend the women all the commiseration they need to make them kin to us. The play requires its jokes to be horrible; its horror funny.

To make clear how *The Mutilated* differs from other Williams plays the production should not dodge the play's cruelty. Perhaps the director (Alan Schneider) and the author felt that an emphasis on its savagery would alienate an "uptown" audience.

Margaret Leighton, whose voice touches the heart and who is blessed with the very appealing look of a Pre-Raphaelite beauty in anguish, never for a moment suggests anything but noble sorrow. She doesn't seem to have a bitchy bone in her body. Kate Reid, a gusty and essentially good-natured actress, is amusing but hardly conveys anything soiled or mean. The result is that the play strikes us as a minor repetition of an old Williams theme, when it is really an acid variation.

The second slapstick tragedy, *The Gnädiges Fräulein*, is more interesting in several ways than the first. It is a stylized essay in farcical fantasy altogether new for Williams. It is filled with sardonic mirth at the plight of the artist applauded and glamorized in his triumphs and then repudiated and derided when he fails. The "artiste" in the play is a once celebrated middle-European *chanteuse*, but the inner motivation for the personage is Williams' projection of his present situation. He attempts to ward off self-pity through self-mockery, avenging himself on the "enemy" with satiric lunacy.

The Fräulein earns her keep in a God-forsaken boarding house at the seaboard of the southernmost point of our States by fighting to catch fish in the waters whipped by the hurricanes which harass the place. The difficulty of bringing in the fish (prestige, status, success) is compounded by the jealousy and competition of a bird of prey, the Cocaloony, who not only snatches the fish from the Fräulein's grip but pecks out her eyes in the process.

The play abounds in symbols. The Cocaloony may represent the Critics. The public becomes a Permanent Transient at the boarding house. Certain aspects of the Press appear in the person of Polly, a madcap society reporter who combines impregnable complacency with malice. The clownish lady who runs the boarding house may stand for managerial powers, producers, editors, publishers and the like. There is also a blond Indian who steals and makes a banquet of the fish which the Fräulein has struggled and lost her eyes to catch. Is this meant to stand for one of Williams' directors?

However we interpret this nightmare it is written in an odd but effective mixture of gallows humor and Rabelaisian zest. On opening night the audience laughed uproariously at the broad-stroked slapdash language, but though I was able to appreciate the style I could not bring myself to smile. I was too conscious that its author was in pain.

The outstanding performance in *The Gnädiges Fräulein* was that of Zoe Caldwell as Polly, a truly remarkable creation, all venom and sugar, risible and appalling. Both plays are sure to be seen and acclaimed in future productions at universities, community theatres and on foreign stages.

The Dialogue of Incompletion:
Language in Tennessee Williams'
Later Plays

by Thomas P. Adler

In her recent study entitled *Dialogue in American Drama,* Ruby Cohn concludes her assessment of Tennessee Williams' plays up through *Slapstick Tragedy* (1966) by stating that so long as Williams refrains from "indulg[ing] in gratuitous violence and irrelevant symbol" he "expands American stage dialogue in vocabulary, image, rhythm, and range."[1] Yet to discuss Williams' use of language in the three plays written after *Slapstick Tragedy,* it is necessary to focus on verbal aspects other than just those explored by Ms. Cohn's treatment of the earlier plays. Specifically one must focus on the soliloquy and, most especially, on those experiments with syntactical patterns which suggest a new direction in Williams' theatrical technique. Of the three dramas, only *Small Craft Warnings*—the most traditional of the three in its verbal elements—was a critical and popular success, running for 200 performances off-Broadway in 1972. The other two, which are more radical departures in their use of language from Williams' earlier plays, failed with both critics and audiences alike: *In the Bar of a Tokyo Hotel* lasted only 25 performances off-Broadway in 1969, while *Out Cry* stayed on Broadway for just 12 performances in 1973.[2] Even so, these plays are still note-

From Thomas P. Adler, "The Dialogue of Incompletion: Language in Tennessee Williams' Later Plays," *The Quarterly Journal of Speech,* 61 (February, 1975), 48-58. Copyright © 1975 by *The Quarterly Journal of Speech.* Reprinted by permission of the author and publisher.

[1]Ruby Cohn, *Dialogue in American Drama* (Bloomington: Indiana University Press, 1971), p. 129.

[2]There were two earlier productions of *Out Cry:* a London version in 1967 under the title *The Two-Character Play,* and a Chicago version in 1971 under the

worthy for their experimentation with theatre language, at times successful, at other times not, as well as for being the most recent dramatic works of America's—some would say the world's—best living playwright.

At first glance, Williams' innovations in theatre language, particularly in the two failed plays, might remind one of similar techniques employed by Beckett, Ionesco, and Pinter. Seeing Williams' practice against the background of these dramatists, however, makes it clear that the verbal techniques new to Williams are used to express a metaphysics very different from that of the Absurdist playrights. Among Beckett, Ionesco, and Pinter, Beckett is the most skeptical of the continued potency of the word to deal with what Karen Stein terms "the universal, metaphysical silence, the inexplicable abyss."[3] Martin Esslin quotes Beckett as saying: "There is nothing to express, nothing with which to express, nothing from which to express, no power to express, no desire to express, together with the obligation to express."[4] For Ionesco, on the other hand, there *is* something to communicate, but it is very nearly incommunicable: "There are no words for the deepest experience. The more I try to explain myself, the less I understand myself. Of course, not everything is unsayable in words, only the living truth."[5] So for Ionesco, the experience or the something to express does exist, and he emphatically denies that he considers man as totally bereft of the ability to reach others through the word: "I simply hold that it is difficult to make

---

title finally used on Broadway. [However, an August, 1975 New York production and the most recent printed edition retain the original title. See footnote (1) to Judith Hersh Clark's "The Countess..." and *Chronology of Important Dates* in this volume.—Ed.]

[3]Karen F. Stein, "Metaphysical Silence in Absurd Drama," *Modern Drama*, 8 (1971), 424.

[4]Samuel Beckett, quoted by Martin Esslin, "Introduction," *Samuel Beckett: A Collection of Critical Essays* (Englewood Cliffs: Prentice-Hall, Inc., 1965), p. 17. Beckett has, of course, written "Acts Without Words".

[5]Eugene Ionesco, quoted by George Steiner, "Silence and the Poet," in *Language and Silence: Essays on Language, Literature, and the Inhuman* (New York: Atheneum, 1967), p. 52. Steiner makes further comments in the same essay that are relevant to the Theatre of the Absurd: "But the poet's choice of silence, the writer's relinquishing his articulate enactment of identity in mid-course, is something new. ... This revaluation of silence—in the epistemology of Wittgenstein, in the aesthetics of Webern and Cage, in the poetics of Beckett—is one of the most original, characteristic acts of the modern spirit" (pp. 47-8).

oneself understood, not absolutely impossible."[6] What the Absurdist dramatists force us to consider, then, is a world where, in the words of John Killinger, "every individual is condemned to his own private hell and discovers that language is only a tossed yoyo, either coming back upon the speaker or dribbling out flatly and uselessly between him and the world he is trying to reach."[7]

But whereas much of the anguish for the characters in Absurdist drama is imposed from the indifferent world without, for Pinter's people the anguish more often than not derives from within. Although the initial comic exchange between Meg and Petey in *The Birthday Party* (so famous by now that it is oftentimes parodied) cannot help but remind theatregoers of Ionesco's *Bald Soprano* in its repetitiveness and banality and irrelevancy, Pinter goes beyond such language games to suggest a more disturbing type of verbal trickery. Man, Pinter believes, really does not desire to reveal himself to others, employing any available "stratagem to cover [his] nakedness"[8]: "people fall back on anything they can lay their hands on verbally to keep away from the danger of knowing, and of being known."[9] So—and this distinction between Pinter and the Absurdists has too often been glossed over—"instead of any inability to communicate there is a deliberate evasion of communication. Communication itself between people is so frightening that rather than do that there is a continual crosstalk, a continual talking about other things rather than what is at the root of their relationship."[10]

Williams, though, writes about people who, rather than go to extremes to evade communication, crave it·obsessively as a means of breaking out of the self and making contact with the other, of

[6]Eugene Ionesco, *Notes and Counter Notes*, trans. Donald Watson (New York: Grove Press, 1964), p. 90.

[7]John Killinger, *World in Collapse: The Vision of Absurd Drama* (New York: Dell Publishing Co., Inc., 1971), p. 113. Significantly, Williams himself has said: "Hell is yourself. When you ignore other people completely, that is hell" ("The Angel of the Odd," *Time*, 9 March 1962, 53).

[8]Harold Pinter, quoted by John Russell Brown, *Theatre Language: A Study of Arden, Osborne, Pinter and Wesker* (London: The Penguin Press, 1972), p. 18.

[9]Harold Pinter, "Interview" in *Theatre at Work: Playwrights and Productions in Modern British Theatre*, ed. Charles Marowitz and Simon Trussler (New York: Hill & Wang, 1967), p. 103.

[10]Harold Pinter, quoted by John Russell Taylor, *Anger and After: A Guide to the New British Drama*, 2nd. ed. rev. (London: Methuen & Co. Ltd. 1971), p. 334.

overcoming the aloneness that is the human condition and entering into a saving communion of shared humanity. Perhaps Williams' most explicit treatment of the theme of noncommunication—a theme he shares in common with the Absurdist dramatists—is found in his short play "I Can't Imagine Tomorrow" (1966), in which a man, named simply Two, is emotionally unable even to complete a sentence without the constant, helpful prodding of his "only friend," a woman named One. Two, who lives in what One calls a "hotel mortuary" and is terribly afraid of the "changes" time brings ("time," according to the woman, "lives in the world with us and has a big broom and is sweeping us out of the way, whether we face it or not") says he has always found it "difficult...to put what I think and feel into speech" and "to look in the eyes of another person."[11] One understands that each person must eventually leave his "last friend behind...and...go on alone" into Dragon Country, in which place "of endured but unendurable pain each one is so absorbed, deafened, blinded by his own journey across it, he sees, he looks for, no one else crawling across it with him" (IT, pp. 148, 138), but for the time being she will help Two be not separate from but united with her through language. In order for this verbal union to occur, after each few words that Two speaks One must goad him on by interjecting "What?" before he can speak the next few words and bring his utterance closer to completion. If man's ability to use language is what gives him the power to know and define himself, then Williams seems to be suggesting that without her Two's identity as an individual is incomplete.

In the [two*] dramas under discussion in this essay, there are strong indications that an interconnection achieved through words is one antidote for the characters' sense of incompleteness. In *Small Craft Warnings,* we learn that Violet, when alone and deprived of the sensation of touching another (physical gesture is a kind of stage language), is "Something more like a possibility than a completed creature."[12] In *In the Bar of a Tokyo Hotel,* Miriam asks Mark, despite his insistence that she not pursue the

---

[11]Tennessee Williams, "I Can't Imagine Tomorrow," in *Dragon Country: A Book of Plays* (New York: New Directions, 1970), pp. 140-1. Further references will be cited in the text by IT and page number.

[*In this volume, Professor Adler's section on *In the Bar of a Tokyo Hotel* is omitted.—Ed.]

[12]Tennessee Williams, *Small Craft Warnings* (New York: New Directions, 1972), p. 12. Further references will be cited in the text by SCW and page number.

question, "—Are we two people, Mark, or are we—...Two sides
of!...One!"[13] And, finally, in *Out Cry,* Felice and Clare recognize that to face the threat from the world outside "Each of us
would have to confirm the statements of the—....Other."[14] In
every instance, the completion of dialogue and/ or self-identity
depends on the presence of and interaction with the other, and it
is this interdependence which is sometimes being conveyed
dramatically through Williams' experiments with syntax.

The theoretician of language who comes closest to explaining
the relationship between character and dialogue that underlies
Williams' syntactical experiments in his latest plays is George
Steiner, in his essay "The Retreat from the Word":

> The crisis of poetic means, as we now know it, began in the later
> nineteenth century. It arose from awareness of the gap between the
> new sense of psychological reality and the old modes of rhetorical
> and poetic statement. In order to articulate the wealth of con-
> sciousness opened to the modern sensibility, a number of poets
> sought to break out of traditional confines of syntax and definition.
> ...They realized that traditional syntax organizes our perceptions
> into linear and monistic patterns. Such patterns distort or stifle
> the play of subconscious energies, the multitudinous life of the
> interior of the mind....[15]

Although Steiner is referring here specifically to the poet's use
of language, what he says applies equally well to any given
character's language patterns in a dramatic work.

1

In *Small Craft Warnings,* Williams does not break with "linear
and monistic patterns" in the speeches of his characters; instead,
he employs eleven fairly extended soliloquies or interior monologues to convey "the multitudinous life of the interior of the
mind." At least once during the play each of the characters "dis-
engages himself from the group to speak as if to himself," at which

[13]Tennessee Williams, *In the Bar of Tokyo Hotel,* in *Dragon Country* (New
York: New Directions, 1970), p. 30. Further references will be cited by BTH and
page number.

[14]Tennessee Williams, *Out Cry* (New York: New Directions, 1973), p. 44.
Further references will be cited in the text by OC and page number.

[15]Steiner, p. 27.

times "the light in the bar should dim, and a special spot should illuminate each actor as he speaks" (SCW, p. 11). Variations on the soliloquy form are not new to Williams's dramaturgy: we have Tom's narrative passages in *Glass Menagerie* as he remembers the past in order to gain release from his guilt, or the addresses to the audience by Trinket in *The Mutilated* and by Polly in *The Gnädiges Fräulein,* the two plays produced together as *Slapstick Tragedy.* The technique as it appears in *Warnings* is most reminiscent of O'Neill's use of the interior monologue in *Strange Interlude,* though in Williams' play it occurs with less regularity and consistency and is not made to carry so much weight. O'Neill considered the "'Interlude' aside technique [as] special expression for special type of modern neurotic, disintegrated soul,"[16] a technique that Winifred Dusenbury likens in function to the Shakespearean soliloquy: "As Hamlet's soliloquies define his aloneness, O'Neill's device of spoken thoughts, although overworked, signifies loneliness in every character."[17] Williams' people, too, are lonely: they are isolates, many of them down-and-out, for whom Monk's bar, somewhat like Harry Hope's in *The Iceman Cometh,* is "a place of refuge" (SCW, p. 15), a home-away-from-home. Monk regards himself as something of a combination priest/ analyst: "I'm fond of, I've got an affection for, a sincere interest in my regular customers here. ...And all their personal problems, I want to know that, too" (SCW, p. 51). The relationship between Monk and his "patients," however, is reciprocal, since hearing "the stories, the jokes, the confidences and confessions...makes [him] feel not alone" (SCW, pp. 51-2). For he, like the rest of them, is a "vulnerable human vessel" for whom the "small craft warnings" are out (SCW, p. 15).

The patrons in Monk's bar are vulnerable for reasons other than just loneliness. Some, especially Violet, suffer from a lack of respect for themselves which is aggravated still more by a lack of affection for others. Some, mainly Doc, are horrified by the absurdity of life and a seemingly malevolent God. Yet an equally terrifying and more pervasive malady is to have lost the sense of wonder in life, "to've never had anything beautiful in your life

---

[16]Eugene O'Neill, "Working Notes and Extracts from a Fragmentary Work Diary," in *American Playwrights on Drama,* ed. Horst Frenz (New York: Hill & Wang, 1965), p. 10.

[17]Winifred Dusenbury, *The Theme of Loneliness in Modern American Drama* (Gainesville: University of Florida Press, 1960), p. 110.

and not even know you've missed it" (SCW, p. 32). In drama, of
course, a symbolic stage property speaks to the audience as clearly as does dialogue, and so stage symbols become an element of
theatre language. Here, the central visual prop is the sailfish that
hangs suspended from the ceiling as an ironic reminder to the
characters of their limited lives; it is "hooked and shellacked and
strung up like a flag over...over...lesser, much lesser...creatures
that never, ever sailed an inch in their...lives" (SCW, p. 25).

In the soliloquy that is the thematic center of the play, the
homosexual Quentin talks about no longer being "startled by the
sense of being alive" or "lightning-struck with astonishment...
by the existence of everything that exists," whereas Bobby, an
adolescent in the throes of indecision over his own sexual identity

> still has the capacity for being surprised by what he sees, hears and
> feels in this kingdom of earth. All the way up the canyon to my
> place, he kept saying, *I can't believe it, I'm here, I've come to the*
> *Pacific, the world's greatest ocean!*...as if nobody, Magellan or
> Balboa or even the Indians had ever seen it before him; yes, like
> he'd discovered this ocean, the largest on earth, and so now, be-
> cause he'd found it himself, it existed, now, for the first time, never
> before...And this excitement of his reminded me of my having lost
> the ability to say: "My God!" instead of just: "Oh, well."
>
>   (SCW, pp. 46-7)

As Leona, the pivotal character in the play, says, so long as she
can find somebody to quench her loneliness "then, all at once,
something wonderful happens....Life! Life! I never just said,
'Oh, well,' I've always said 'Life!' to life, like a song to God, too,
because I've lived in my lifetime and not been afraid of...
changes" (SCW, p. 55). And, as is usually true in Williams'
dramas, it is the artist or artist figure whose vocation it is to create
the beauty in our life that allows us to say "My God!" and not just
"Oh, well": the artist's vision is essential, for "Without one
beautiful thing in the course of a lifetime, it's all a deathtime"
(SCW, p. 34).

Technically—and this is the basic difference between Williams' technique in this drama and O'Neill's in *Interlude*—
there is nothing in the interior monologues in *Warnings* that
could not have been presented through straightforward dialogue
between characters, for these soliloquies do not uncover the dark,
underside of his nature that man ordinarily feels compelled to
keep hidden from others. If in O'Neill's drama the normal
dialogue showed only the surface, outer man while the mono-

logues revealed the inner man usually masked from others,[18] the shifts from dialogue to soliloquy in *Warnings* do not express any such fragmentation between inner and outer. While a few of these monologues could be looked upon as "confessions," most of them do not divulge any "confidences" one would usually keep secret. All of them do, in a sense, characterize the speaker; several provide exposition about other characters; and a few are thematic in intent. What they contribute to the drama, however, is an ambience, a mood of loneliness and wistfulness that it might otherwise not possess. And so, even though the soliloquies in *Warnings* fall into no very definite structural pattern, they enhance rather than disrupt the theatrical experience. We do not demand strict consistency in the use of this technique here because the painful lives of this cross section of humanity are pictured so compellingly and with such compassion. ...

In *Out Cry*, another of Williams' highly personal plays about fear and the courage needed to face it, the only two characters are artists—this time a brother and sister acting team—who are torn between, on the one hand, the necessity of venturing out of the self and into the unknown and, on the other, the concomitant tendency to shy away from going out for fear of possible rejection by others. Williams classifies the play as "a parable," and "hope[s] that it is...of enough meaning to compensate for the apparent slightness of its dramatic content."[19] So on one level, it is a parable about the artist whose very existence and self-identity depend upon being heard by others, and yet because of fear of continued rejection by those who do hear is afraid to expose his work—and therefore himself—to an audience. As such, it is first and foremost the intensely private story of Williams himself (he likes to refer to the play as his *"cri de coeur"*) as a dramatist whose works from *Milk Train* on never achieved—and, with the possible exception

---

[18]In "Memoranda on Masks" (1932), O'Neill commented: *Dogma for the new masked drama. One's outer life passes in a solitude haunted by the masks of others; one's inner life in a solitude hounded by the masks of oneself."* (Reprinted in *O'Neill and His Plays: Four Decades of Criticism,* ed. Oscar Cargill, N. Bryllion Fagin, and William J. Fisher [New York: New York University Press, 1961], p. 117.)

[19]Tennessee Williams, unpublished "Author's Notes" to *Out Cry,* March, 1970, unpaged, but the quotation is from page 2 of 3 pages. These Notes were written after the London production but before the Chicago version, and Mr. Williams shared these Notes with me on the occasion of his visit to Purdue University in 1972 when a reading with script of *The Two-Character Play,* combining sections from both the London and Chicago versions, were presented.

of *Small Craft Warnings,* do not merit—the stature of his plays
from *Menagerie* through *Night of the Iguana.* But no matter how
searing a cry from the heart, here the personal, again as in *Bar,*
has not been adequately transmuted into so universal "an essence
that a wide audience can somehow manage to feel in themselves: 'This is true,'"[20] A comment of Clare's to Felice about *The
Two-Character Play* that they act out perhaps belies Williams'
own recognition of the central drawback of *Out Cry* as drama:
"I wonder sometimes if it isn't a little too personal, too special, for
most audiences" (OC, p. 62).

One of the verbal techniques which concretizes the fear of Clare
and Felice is a variety of witty dialogue, funny, but with an edge
of terror just beneath the surface, that Williams refers to as "the
jokes of the condemned": "the two performers...must relieve the
dark content of the plays [sic], interior and total, with a carefully
measured lightness—the jokes of the condemned?..."[21] In a line
of Mark's in *Bar,* there is one example of this kind of humor
which will become so much more pervasive in *Out Cry:* "I'll
tell you something about what's called—the breath of life in us.
No, I don't have the breath to tell you" (BTH, p. 47). *Out Cry* is
rife with this kind of dark verbal wit, oftentimes based on pun-
ning: sometimes it works purposively and elicits the intended
audience response, while at other times it falls flat, as puns so
often do, because it is too unsubtle, too cute, or too precious. In
the successful category one might include such lines as Felice's
reference to an actress who "had a passion for incineration. Burned
to death in a hotel fire and then had herself cremated," or such
exchanges between Felice and Clare as, "I yelled my head off."
"Oh—Decapitated?", or—referring to their absent theatrical
manager named Fox—, "Well, we'll track him down." "I don't
feel like fox hunting" (OC, pp. 63, 9, 61). On the debit side of the
ledger might appear such lines as Clara's question about the
theatre they are trapped in, "Is this the subterranean—pleasure-
dome of—Kabla—Kubla—Koon?", or such an artificial exchange
as Clare's comment that "cloth and wood are two inflammable
things. Your eyes make three!", to which Felice responds, "No
four! I'm not a one-eyed Cyclops!" (OC, pp. 11, 40).

[20]On page 3 of the "Author's Notes," Williams admits "that in my later plays
there is a bit of emotional obscurity, perhaps because the world becomes darker
to me as I pass through it. ...."

[21]Williams, "Author's Notes," page 3.

Along with these "jokes of the condemned," there is an even more extensive use than in *Bar* of the unfinished sentence that is only completed by the other speaker, but when this device occurs in *Out Cry* it generally has a deeper resonance than in the earlier play. Indeed, here it is sometimes a provocative technique which attains a certain beauty not unlike the rhythmic quality of some of the later dramas of Pinter, especially *Landscape*, "Night," and *Old Times*. One long example from early in the play will suggest the quality of this technique:

> *Felice.* The telephone company would send us a notice before
>   they turned off the phone.
> *Clare.* [vaguely and sadly] : Sometimes notices aren't—noticed.
> *Felice.* The house is—
> *Clare.* Still occupied but they might have the idea it wasn't,
>   since it's not lighted at night and no one still comes and goes.
> *Felice.* We would have received a notice if one was sent.
> *Clare.* We can't count on that.
> *Felice.* We musn't start counting things that can't be counted on,
>   Clare.
> *Clare.* We must trust in things—
> *Felice.* Continuing as they've—
> *Clare.* Continued?
> *Felice.* Yes, as they've continued, for such a long time that they
>   seem—
> *Clare.* Dependable to us.   (OC, pp. 24-5)

In this very Pirandelloesque drama, Felice and Clare find themselves as actors on the stage of a "state theater of a state unknown" (OC, p. 9), and the play-within-the-play, entitled *The Two-Character Play,* which they are to perform is set in a house in a Southern town and is actually the drama of their own lives and of their parents, of their father who killed their mother and then himself. But *"The Two-Character Play* never had an ending" before, Felice tells us (OC, p. 15), and so during this performance of it, art and life will merge and become one as Clare and Felice, in the process of acting it out, bring not only the play to completion but their own lives as well. Felice and Clare—both as actors in the play, and as characters in the play-within-the-play who are, in turn, identical with their real selves—are desperately in need of courage. As actors, they require the courage to go on with the performance: "if we're not artists, we're nothing. And play...the best we've ever played it no matter what our condition of panic may be" (OC, p. 22). Both in real life and as char-

acters in *The Two-Character Play,* they exist in "one endless—
continuum of—endurance," so "terrified of [their] shadows" that
it demands "unusual courage" (OC, pp. 12, 22) just to live from
day-to-day.

One of the sources of their fear, dramatized largely through
visual symbols as well as through certain physical gestures such
as Felice turning a ring on Clare's finger in "a sort of love-
making" or their "compulsive embrace—like two lovers meeting
after a long separation" (OC, pp. 27, 56), is evidently an incestuous relationship between them.[22] Dominating the scenic decor is
"a huge, dark statue upstage, a work of great power and darkly
subjective meaning. Something about it, its monolithic presence
and its suggestion of things anguished and perverse (in his [i.e.,
Felice's] own nature?) rivets his attention, which is shocked and
fearful" (OC, p. 7). Also, both mentioned in the dialogue and later
seen through the means of "images...projected on the stage backdrop" are the phallic, two-headed sunflowers "grown tall as the
house," which are "shouting sensational things about [them]":

> *Clare.* Call it [the sunflower] the poem of two and dark as—
> *Felice.* Our blood?
> *Clare.* Yes, why don't you say it? Abnormality!—Say it! And
>   point at me!
> *Felice.* At myself, first.   (OC, pp. 29-30)

And Williams very deftly and intriguingly employs the syntactical device of chiasmus to reinforce through the dialogue the
suggestion of an incestuous union of the brother and sister, as
in: "just in case a desperate situation—" "Increases in desperation—", or in "Stared without recognition!" "With nothing to
recognize!" (OC, pp. 32, 46).

When Clare somewhat hopelessly but defiantly suggests that
she will find a way out of the locked theatre, Felice more realistically counsels, "Give it up. ..." and then he says, in words that
Williams might have intended at the time as his own Prospero-
like farewell to his art: "There are punctuation marks in life and
it's time to admit that they include periods—one of which is final
..." (OC, p. 68). But just as Felice failed to end his sentence with a

----

[22]At the beginning of the "Author's Notes," apparently intended as guide-
lines for the actors and director, Williams states: "There may be no apparent
sexuality in *The Two-Character Play,* and yet it is actually the *Liebestod* of
the two characters from whom the title derives. This fact should be recognized
by the director and players, but then it should appear to be forgotten."

definite period, Williams, despite disavowals that he would ever again write for Broadway production, reportedly has completed a new play, entitled *The Red Devil Battery Sign,* which "abandons the static musings of Williams' recent works and returns to the dynamic style of such earlier (and more successful) efforts as *A Streetcar Named Desire.*"[23] So his generally unsuccessful experiments with new syntactical patterns in such plays as *In the Bar of a Tokyo Hotel* and *Out Cry* are evidently the product of Williams' own "strange interlude" now ending. Nevertheless, these innovations in theatre language do impart to the [two] dramas discussed in this essay much of their distinctive tone and quality, while evidencing a playwright who was not satisfied with repeating the tried-and-true, and so sought to expand the range of his dramatic technique at a relatively late point in his career. But the measure of his language in these plays must also include an awareness of the visual symbols that are essential to the engagement between play and audience. In their use, Williams remains without peer among contemporary American dramatists.

[23]"Tennessee Williams Recharges." *Newsweek,* 1 October, 1973, 23.

PART TWO

Themes

The Anti-Hero in the Plays
of Tennessee Williams

by Esther Merle Jackson

One of the most controversial aspects of the drama of Tennessee Williams is his use of an anti-heroic protagonist as an image of man. Williams appears to reject the Aristotelian concept of the protagonist and to substitute for it an anti-hero, the personification of a humanity neither good, knowledgeable, nor courageous. In Blanche, Alma, Brick, Kilroy, Val, Chance, and Shannon, we see this anti-heroic image of man. Even those figures who command some sympathy, characters such as Tom in *The Glass Menagerie* and Catharine—the victim of *Suddenly Last Summer*—may be described...as "non-beings."...Williams claims that such is the image of modern man—poised as he is between the contrary imperatives of his world. As he examines humanity through the patched glass of his synthetic myth, the playwright perceives a creature transfixed in a moment of stasis, halted at the point of transition in the process of becoming.[1]...

Although contemporary dramatists accept certain aspects of the ethics of Aristotle, they do not feel that his definition of the hero is in every sense an accurate description of a virtuous man in the twentieth century. Arthur Miller, for example, points out that many aspects of Aristotle's system of ethics are today obsolete. The image of man in the twentieth century, writes Miller, must be rooted in an open system of values appropriate to a

"The Anti-Hero in the Plays of Tennessee Williams" (editor's title). Excerpted from Esther Merle Jackson, *The Broken World of Tennessee Williams* (Madison, Wisconsin: University of Wisconsin Press, 1965). Copyright © 1965 by Esther Merle Jackson. Reprinted by permission of the author and publisher. The pages reprinted here form part of a longer chapter.

[1]Williams, like Eliot and others among twentieth-century artists, accepts a dynamic theory of reality. Like post-Hegelians such as Bergson, Williams regards art as the image of process, and form as a "still" picture drawn out of the moving spectacle. See Henri Bergson, *An Introduction to Metaphysics*, trans. T. E. Hulme (New York: The Liberal Arts Press, 1949), pp. 25-27.

democratic society.[2] Tennessee Williams writes that the most pressing moral problem of man in the twentieth century is to avoid extinction: "to beat the game of being against non-being."[3] The crux of the argument which has led to the modification of the Aristotelian hero lies in changes in the perception of experience, in the accumulation of new knowledges about and new hopes for the human species.

One of the most dramatic of the changes which have affected the idea of the hero is that embodied in the science of psychology, for classic ideals of "goodness," "nobility," and "courage" have, under psychological scrutiny, assumed a significantly different aspect. Equally affecting, perhaps, has been the political history of modern Europe: a record of suffering, wars, and conflicts which have exacted a tremendous physical, spiritual, and psychological toll. Because of a new sense of historical crisis, the hero, a man of action, has grown less appealing as an image of present moral and ethical aspirations than the anti-hero, a man of reflection and contemplation. But perhaps an even more profound change in perspective is represented in the growing influence of the Judaeo-Christian ethic on the moral aspirations of the common man. Despite the apparent record of history, the principles of Christianity have become, in the past century, a more meaningful part of a common standard for human action. The substitution of the "inner-oriented" ethic of the Christian protagonist for the "outer-directed" heroism of the Greek hero is one of the significant contemporary adjustments in Western drama. It is this change which has materially altered the idea of tragic action and which has produced a new concept of dramatic character.[4]

In a discussion of contemporary form, René-Marill Albérès describes the contemporary anti-hero as a "theological protagonist." He is an image of man seeking to know the universe, to define its purpose, and to discover his ultimate meaning in its pattern. Albérès describes the contemporary motive in these words: "The contemporary theatre, like the novel, becomes a research and a quest. It makes itself idealistic, its characters

[2]Arthur Miller, Introduction to the *Collected Plays* (New York, 1957), pp. 8-12.

[3]Introduction to *The Rose Tattoo,* p. ix.

[4]Such a change in perspective appears in late Greek drama, especially in plays such as *Oedipus at Colonus,* a work which shows many correspondences to "Christian drama." In the main, however, the movement toward an "inner direction" must be attributed to the passage of Christian perspectives into the medieval drama.

force themselves toward that which they can never find."⁵ For Albérès the anti-heroic quest is a journey toward moral commitment. Williams seems to confirm this judgment in his play *The Night of the Iguana;* he gives in this work the account of a heretic, the story of the world-weary priest Shannon who searches the earth for the face of God. Shannon follows the moral progression described by St. John of the Cross as the "dark night of the soul." He proceeds in contrary motion, in flight from the presence of God; but, like St. John, he finds that the "way down" leads up. Shannon declares that his search has brought him finally to that presence which he has sought:

> Yes, I see him, I hear him, I know him. And if he doesn't know that I know him, let him strike me dead with a bolt of his lightning.
> (Act II, p. 78)

Williams' construction of his anti-heroic protagonist, his "negative saint," is based on a radical perception of new dangers for mankind, as well as on the recognition of new modes of courage. What are these dangers? In *A Streetcar Named Desire* the playwright cautions the spectator against societal regression, against the capitulation of humanity to the laws of the jungle. In later plays—*Cat on a Hot Tin Roof, Camino Real, Suddenly Last Summer, Sweet Bird of Youth,* and *The Night of the Iguana* —he warns against the moral and spiritual disintegration of mankind. To interpret present dimensions of the human dilemma, Williams creates a protagonist who is conceived in anti-traditional terms. Brick, Kilroy, Catharine, Chance, and Shannon are not "mankind" in the sense of classic, neoclassic, romantic, or realistic definitions. They are images of a humanity diminished by time and history. They are each characterized by an inner division, by a fragmentation so complete that it has reduced them to partialities. They are "un-beings," caught in the destructive life-process. They are fragments of debris, thrown up by "time the destroyer."⁶ In the short story *One Arm,* Williams describes this anti-heroic man: "He never said to himself, I'm lost. But the speechless self knew

⁵René-Marill Albérès, *La Révolte des écrivains d'aujourd'hui* (Paris, 1949), p. 141. (The translation is my own.)

⁶This is Eliot's phrase. It appears in "The Dry Salvages," the third of *Four Quartets* (New York: Harcourt Brace Jovanovich, Inc, 1943; London: Faber and Faber, Ltd., 1944): "Time the destroyer is time the preserver", copyright © 1943, by T. S. Eliot; copyright © 1971, by Esme Valerie Eliot. Reprinted by permission of the publishers.

it and in submission to its unthinking control the youth had begun as soon as he left the hospital to look about for destruction."[7]

The portrait of the anti-hero is not confined to the work of this playwright. Its fusion of pessimism and mysticism was the trademark of both the poetic realists and the early expressionists. The image of an anti-heroic man may be seen in the plays of Strindberg, Tolstoy, Ibsen, and Chekhov, as well as in the writings of expressionist artists such as Oskar Kokoschka. Moreover, this same contour is apparent in the work of existential dramatists such as Jean-Paul Sartre and Albert Camus. Some of the most telling portraits of the anti-hero have appeared in the work of the orthodox Christian dramatists Paul Claudel and T. S. Eliot. Claudel's *Partage de Midi*, like Eliot's *Murder in the Cathedral*, interprets an anti-heroic image with eloquence....

Clearly, this view of character is not entirely the creation of the twentieth century. Rather, it represents the intensification of perspectives which have been present throughout the history of Western letters. Albert Camus observes that much of existentialist dogma parallels the fundamental teachings of Jesus Christ. Certainly there are clear correspondences between existential teleologies and New Testament pronouncements on man's guilt, his search for truth, and his need for faith. Expressionism, existential theory, and "radical" Christian theology are agreed that man may find salvation only in love—in sympathy for his fellow man. Williams finds, then, considerable support for his vision of humanity from Christian theology and existential philosophy, as well as from the modern arts. His anti-hero is the symbol of a widely recognized condition: a "sickness unto death." Like the classic protagonist, the anti-hero searches for a mode of healing. But unlike the earlier protagonist he does not expect to find it. That which forbids his immediate salvation is himself. For the anti-hero is possessed of a profound fault, not merely of a single flaw, but of a comprehensive condition of evil, an inner impurity far greater than the Greek *hamartia*. Albérès describes this inner condition as "original sin."

The playwright gives shape to his anti-hero through the manipulation of a mythic glass; that is, Williams reveals his flawed image of man by showing his relationship to archetypal patterns. Throughout his work, Williams superimposes parallel visions— shadow images—of modern man. His anti-hero is a man of many

[7]In the collection *One Arm and Other Stories*, pp. 9-10.

identities; his Tom a "Hamlet," his Catharine a "Cassandra," his
Brick an "Orestes," his Big Daddy an "Agamemnon." In *Orpheus
Descending* his use of this technique of multiple vision is vivid.
The Orphic figure Val descends into the underworld of Williams' mythical Mississippi town and there is brought to destruction by reveling maenads— Vee, Carol, and Lady—who envy his
strange and magical music. Perhaps less obvious is Williams' use
of a simultaneous treatment of character in *A Streetcar Named
Desire*. Blanche—the poetic figure—descends into the underworld described as "The Elysian Fields." The symbology is set
forth in the protagonist's opening speech (Scene I, p. 11): "They
told me to take a streetcar named Desire, and then transfer to
one called Cemeteries and ride six blocks and get off at—Elysian
Fields!" In the critical scene preceding Blanche's destruction,
Williams gives Orphic voice to the night:

> [... The night is filled with inhuman voices like cries in a jungle.
> [The shadows and lurid reflections move sinuously as flames
> along the wall spaces.
> [Through the back wall of the rooms, which have become trans-
> parent, can be seen the sidewalk. ...   (Scene X, p. 148)

There is in this work a second source of character interpretation which, like the Orphic myth, has its major presentation
in Greek mythology. Williams has found one of the antecedents
for his anti-hero in the figure of the Euripidean Orestes. The
Oresteian protagonist, like the contemporary image, is an anti-
hero. He is a symbol of man in flight from the consequences of
his own transgression, in search of his identity in the universe.
Modern European dramatists, for reasons associated with their
own intellectual history, have been more inclined to develop
studies of the Aeschylean pre-tragic protagonist Prometheus.
Throughout the work of Sartre, Anouilh, and Camus we see the
outline of Prometheus in revolt against cosmic law. ... The
Americans, on the contrary, have been attracted to the late tragic
apprehension of Euripides, especially by his images of Orpheus,
Electra, Medea, and Orestes. While O'Neill reflects a certain
interest in "Promethean man" in plays such as *Mourning Becomes Electra* and *Lazarus Laughed,* Williams, Miller, Inge, and,
more recently, Albee conceive a protagonist closely akin to the
anti-heroic image of Euripides.

The differences between these two apprehensions are significant. Promethean anti-heroism is revolutionary in nature. The

pre-tragic protagonist of Aeschylus is, like Milton's Satan, a rebel: he is a creature in revolt against a powerful and inscrutable divinity.... The Oresteian hero, treated in Aeschylus' trilogy, comes into sharper focus in the work of Euripides. For Euripides' Orestes—undoubtedly a fragment of a longer study—is the product of a particularly modern sensibility. Orestes is not a tragic hero in the Sophoclean tradition. He is, rather, an image of man concerned with his own power, responsibility, and complicity in the evil of the universe. Unlike the Sophoclean hero, the Euripidean anti-hero is himself the microcosm of universal evil as well as the image of universal good.

In an eloquent essay on Greek tragedy, Edith Hamilton attributes the continuing appeal of the Euripidean anti-hero for writers to the timeless nature of this playwright's perception. She describes Euripides as the "first modern mind." ...

The Oresteian anti-hero is not, then, the virtuous man of Aristotelian description: he is, on the contrary, the symbol of a guilty humanity, the distillation of a fatal weakness in man. He cries out:

> O! human nature, what a grievous curse thou art in this world! and what salvation, too, to those who have a goodly heritage therein![8]

Moreover, Orestes is a transgressor whose sins are supported, rather than diminished, by intelligence. For his fault is his lack of human compassion. While the gods have indeed preordained the punishment of Clytemnestra for the murder of Agamemnon, Orestes makes a free choice to act as her executioner. The brutal manner of his crime—a murder devoid of pity, calculated in vengeance, and executed without a trace of compassion—strikes horror even in the heartless gods. Orestes thus demonstrates a capacity for evil which is anti-human in its very aspect. Jean-Paul Sartre, in his modernization of the Euripidean legend, describes Orestes as a man who defies the gods in order to assume full responsibility in the universe. ...

It is, then, primarily in consequence of his own choice that Orestes suffers. How does he suffer? The sophisticated dramatist Euripides, living at the beginning of the decline of the Greek Empire, saw in the sense of guilt a more ruinous form of pain

[8]Euripides, *Orestes*, translated by E. P. Coleridge, in *The Complete Greek Drama*, edited by Whitney J. Oates and Eugene O'Neill, Jr. (London: G. Bell & Sons, Ltd., 1938), II, 114. Reprinted by permission of the publisher.

than any devised by the gods or by man's enemies. In the opening scene of his *Orestes,* he portrays a man whose body is wracked by this corrosive inner disease: guilt. Orestes demonstrates all the symptoms of spiritual disintegration that afflict the modern antihero: the malaise, the fevered hallucinations, and the attacks of rage.[9] For his consciousness of transgression, Orestes pays the penalty of fragmentation, disorientation, and despair....

The Euripidean myth, like the drama of Williams, is concerned not merely with defining the nature of sin; it seeks to find a human answer to suffering. Aeschylus, consistent with his theological orientation, summons man before the gods, where accused humanity is given a suspended sentence, a conditional acquittal. Euripides, on the other hand, places the responsibility for evil fully on man and challenges him to find a solution for the ills of his world.

The image of the anti-heroic Orestes seems always to have been present in the transgression-conscious American literature.[10] It is a clear motif in works such as *The Scarlet Letter, Billy Budd,* and *Moby Dick* as well as in William Faulkner's Euripidean studies of the mythical South. The Oresteian myth is a more subtly defined element of interpretation in the work of other Americans: in that of Walt Whitman, Robert Frost, T. S. Eliot, Emily Dickinson, and Edna St. Vincent Millay. In the works of all of these writers there appears the contour of the guilty protagonist, *man in exile,* in flight from his own transgression. D. H. Lawrence has commented that the study of guilt—the residue of the Puritan heritage—is one of the most persistent themes in American literature.[11] But the theme of metaphysical guilt is also an important element of modern European literature. The anti-hero of Tennessee Williams belongs to the lineage of Shakespeare, Goethe, Dostoevski, Gide, Kafka, and Thomas Mann, as well as to that of Hawthorne, Melville, and Faulkner. Like these writers, Williams explores one of the most persistent themes in modern letters: the significance of human transgression.

In order to examine this metaphysical problem, Williams sets in motion an anti-heroic cycle of human experience. Like Dante's poet, his anti-hero traverses the downward way in his "dark night

[9]The indebtedness of Freud to Euripides is clearly illustrated in this work.

[10]See Doris Falk, *Eugene O'Neill and The Tragic Tension* (New Brunswick, New Jersey, 1958).

[11]See D. H. Lawrence, *Studies in Classic American Literature* (New York, 1923).

of the soul."[12] Blanche, in *A Streetcar Named Desire,* describes her descent in the spiritual cycle:

> There are thousands of papers, stretching back over hundreds of years, affecting Belle Reve as, piece by piece, our improvident grandfathers and father and uncles and brothers exchanged the land for their epic fornications—to put it plainly!...The four-letter word deprived us of our plantation, till finally all that was left—and Stella can verify that!—was the house itself and about twenty acres of ground, including a graveyard, to which now all but Stella and I have retreated.   (Scene II, p. 45)

Blanche, in her downward progress toward salvation, comes to the realization of her own responsibility for suffering. She becomes aware that she suffers more for her own transgressions than for the actions of her guilty ancestors. Like Orestes, she has made a guilty choice: a choice which has involved her in the suffering of others. She suggests that she is the effective cause of her husband's death. In her moment of partial "enlightenment" she describes the critical moment when she withdrew "sympathy" from a morally helpless being:

> He'd stuck the revolver into his mouth, and fired—so that the back of his head had been—blown away!
> It was because—on the dance-floor—unable to stop myself—I'd suddenly said—"I saw! I know! You disgust me..." And then the searchlight which had been turned on the world was turned off again and never for one moment since has there been any light that's stronger than this—kitchen—candle.
>
>   (Scene VI, pp. 109-10)

Blanche records her descent into the hell of suffering. She describes her agony:

> I, I, *I* took the blows in my face and my body! All of those deaths! The long parade to the graveyard!...And funerals are pretty compared to deaths. ... You didn't dream, but I saw! *Saw, Saw!* And now you sit there telling me with your eyes that I let the place go! How in hell do you think all that sickness and dying was paid for? Death is expensive, Miss Stella!...   (Scene I, pp. 25-26)

---

[12]In a seminar on *Camino Real* convened at Bochum, Germany, in 1953, one of the first of its kind given Williams, the critics thought Dante to be among Williams' strongest influences, especially in *Camino Real.* [In her book, Prof. Jackson cites several critical opinions expressed at the seminar. See pp. 54, 121, 127-28, 129-30, 149—Ed.]

The play begins at a point late in the development of the anti-heroic cycle. In his record of this movement, Williams exposes Blanche's progressive fragmentation, her progress toward the last circle of hell. In *A Streetcar Named Desire*, Williams concludes his development at the ultimate point of descent; that is to say, this play closes without a clear resolution.

If his earlier works trace the protagonist's descent into the private hell of consciousness, it is only in later plays that Williams begins the description of the long and torturous ascent of the anti-hero to a limited enlightenment. We see some hint of resolution in *Summer and Smoke* in the redemption of Dr. John by the young and lovely Nellie. Similarly, in *Cat on a Hot Tin Roof*—a vivid transposition of the Oresteian myth—there is some suggestion of hope in the renewed bonds of sympathy between the dying father and son, as well as in the possibility of a new life which may cancel out old sins. A second movement—the ascent to light—is more clearly marked in *Camino Real,* a play in which Williams offers, as savior of mankind, the American soldier of fortune Kilroy, a protagonist who redeems the world with a simple display of sympathy. A more complete cycle of understanding is suggested in *The Night of the Iguana,* where the world-weary Shannon finds God through the friendship of Hannah, a woman who offers him sympathy.

A review of the whole body of Williams' work would seem to indicate that the playwright has not as yet completely resolved the problem of reconciliation in his cycle of anti-heroic development. He has succeeded in stating the case against man, in describing his anti-heroic condition. Moreover, he has formulated the general outlines of a kind of virtue appropriate to this condition. His greatest achievement, perhaps, is his definition of present conditions of heroism. For in his drama the anti-hero engages himself to suffer the agony of conscience, to confront hidden truth, and to accept the heavy burden of metaphysical guilt. ...

If the willingness to engage inner conflict is the nature of heroism in the theatre of Williams, his organization of character is designed to reveal such action by exploring, in relation to the protagonist, the full range of possibilities affecting his moral choice. The anti-hero, in this sense, is not a man; he is a schematic presentation of extended moral possibilities. In each of his characters Williams presents a composite image, a montage of the

roles which together comprise the anti-heroic character. Alma, in
Summer and Smoke, speaks of this view of character:

> I've thought many times of something you told me last summer,
> that I have a *doppelganger*. I looked that up and I found that it
> means another person inside of me, another self, and I don't know
> whether to thank you or not for making me conscious of it!—I
> haven't been well.... For a while I thought I was dying, that that
> was the change that was coming.   (Scene XI, p. 115)

In his presentation of character, Williams follows the method of
exposition which in modern theatre is associated with the theories
of Luigi Pirandello....

Pirandello attempted to provide for modern drama a concept
of character consistent with the relative perspective of twentieth-
century thought: to create an image of man in all of his complexity,
in the full reality of his inner disharmony. It is important to observe that Pirandello's theory corresponds not only to the relative vision of artists such as Picasso, but also to that of the great
creative thinkers such as Jung.[13] Like Jungian psychology,
Pirandello's theory defines character as a loosely unified grouping of identities. Pirandellian Man, like Jungian Man, is a configuration of masks. He is an image of man in search of a
reconciling symbol, in need of a self above selves.

This pattern of organization, despite its intellectual validity,
presents serious theatrical problems. How can such a concept
of character be realized in the sensible form of the drama?
European playwrights such as Brecht have solved this problem
by introducing into the drama large quantities of discursive
material. They explain the conflicted nature of the protagonist's
character through the use of monologues, films, notes, and other
"teaching devices." Americans such as O'Neill and Miller have
also on occasion used such techniques. Although Williams makes
some use of the interior monologue, he has been inclined to
figure inner conflict in more theatrical terms. He follows the
example of Shakespeare in revealing character through schematic arrangement. Like Hamlet, Blanche DuBois reveals her
inner nature by playing out her conflicted roles: schoolteacher,
Southern belle, poet, sister, savior, and prostitute. Similarly,
Alma, Brick, Quixote, Chance, Val, Shannon, and others play out

[13]This Jungian language also seems to be employed by Pirandello. The relationship between Jung and Pirandello has not, to my knowledge, been fully
explored.

a range of characters, as they don first one mask and then another.

Although it was interpreted by Pirandello, this idea of character development should be credited to Shakespeare. Indeed, it may be described as the "Hamlet organization": for the anti-heroic Hamlet is perhaps the most effective theatrical example of this multiple concept of human personality. Hamlet is organized from simultaneous visions in much the manner of the modern anti-hero. Shakespeare rationalized his use of montage by attributing to his protagonist the consciousness of an actor. ... [He] revealed the nature of Hamlet's character by exposing the possibilities of *action* and *being* contingent upon a moment of choice. In the course of his time upon the stage, Hamlet plays many roles; he is alternately prince and jester, lover and knave, courtier and politician, poet and ribald jester.

A study of the work of Williams would seem to show that he takes this "existential" Hamlet as his point of departure in his organization of anti-heroic character. For he seeks to affirm in character the present; his protagonists have little real past and no hope for a future. They are locked within a moment of choice. The form of Williams is thus a record of a critical instant in individual destiny. The stage for action is consciousness: it is a consciousness filled with spectres who are in effect extensions of the self. This principle is perhaps most clearly demonstrated in *The Night of the Iguana,* one of his latest plays. Here, as in other works, Williams creates a mythical way station in his progression of understanding. To this "point" he brings a number of characters, each personifying a particular virtue or vice in the consciousness of the protagonist. The aged poet is at one extreme of the continuum. A man who has lost the will to live, he is countered by a young and eager girl. The energetic German family is posed against the casual Mexicans; the corrupt agent Latta against the anti-heroic Shannon; the saintly Hannah against the "insatiable widow" Maxine. *The Night of the Iguana* is a kind of modern *Everyman,* a moment when the protagonist watches his own vices and virtues parade across the great stage of his consciousness.

A more subtle use of the Hamlet device may be seen in an earlier work, *The Glass Menagerie.* For Williams creates in this drama a conscious self: the observing and reflecting "Tom" who projects the flow of experience from his own recall. Within his stream of consciousness there exists another "Tom," the acting self. As the play progresses, it becomes evident that each of the other members of Tom's family represents a position in his pattern of understanding. *The Glass Menagerie,* like O'Neill's *The Great God Brown,* is an exploration of life possibilities, a review of the roles conceived by an anti-heroic man. In *The Glass Menagerie* Williams conceives three of these masks: that of Amanda, the self of natural life; of Laura, the self of poetry and illusion; and of the father, the self of action. Tom explains his choice of a life role in these words,

> I didn't go to the moon, I went much further—for time is the longest distance between two places—....
> I left Saint Louis. I descended the steps of this fire-escape for a last time and followed, from then on, in my father's footsteps. ...
>
> (Scene VIII, p. 123)

In *The Glass Menagerie,* as in the other major works of Tennessee Williams, the protagonist pursues his "odyssey," his journey toward selfhood. Within the "lyric instant," the moment of escape from the corrosive life process, the protagonist conducts his search for a principle through which he may bring meaning to experience. He does this by exploring the alternatives mirrored within this image of his own consciousness. Williams thus examines a comprehensive theme of twentieth-century arts, the search for identity: the journey toward meaning. It is because of his perception of a moral crisis that Williams has abandoned more flattering images of man. Apparently shocked and frightened by the growing threat of human annihilation, he suggests that the theatre cannot afford to exalt man, to praise and to commend his nature. He insists that the proper function of the modern drama is to expose man's hidden nature, to search out his motives, to discover his limits, and, ultimately, to help him to find a mode of salvation. There is little doubt that in his anti-hero Williams states the case against modern man effectively. However, he has been able to evolve only a limited resolution for his cycle of suffering. He concludes that the only hope for man is compassion. It is love that redeems the damned city of Camino Real and sets the "water to flowing again in the mountains."

The anti-heroic protagonist of Williams is designed to reveal the nature of suffering as it appears in the life of the twentieth century. He is intended as the object of pity and terror in the modern world. A question is often asked about this aspect of Williams' work: Of what meaning is the fate of his emotional, spiritual, and moral cripples? The answer given by Williams reflects the gradual usurpation of the pagan idea of tragedy by the Christian concept of human worth. For the Christian ethic holds every man a sinner, redeemable only through love. Similarly, it insists, as does Williams, that all men are anti-heroic; that these figures, no more than others, are guilty of the human condition. In this context, Williams' catalogue of transgressors in search of salvation is a true symbolism—his anti-hero, the very present image of man.

Tennessee Williams
and the Predicament of Women

by Louise Blackwell

In a dozen plays written between 1945 and 1961, Tennessee Williams chose to feature women as major characters more often than men. This choice, in view of his unusual perception, has enabled him to display his talent in a remarkable succession of plays. After 1961, as Williams' doubts and fears about his own artistic powers have grown, his faith in sexual adjustment as the key to the meaning of life has waned; none of his more recent females attain happiness through lasting sexual relationships; some are not even concerned with such happiness; all suffer from physical or emotional mutilation (or both). For them, communication with another person in itself becomes more difficult and unattainable, or their restless search for a mate goes on without hope of fulfillment. Because of this shift in theme and characterization in the later plays, they have not been included in this short study.

Early in his career, the subtlety of Williams' themes and characterizations resulted in misinterpretation on the part of critics and audiences. From *A Streetcar Named Desire* (1947) through *The Night of the Iguana* (1961), however, Williams made his themes explicit by having major characters discuss them, but his purpose continued to be lost on some viewers and readers. As late as 1961, for instance, Hodding Carter wrote in the *New York Times Magazine* that he did not recognize the "Southern women-folk" portrayed by Williams. On the other hand, Signi Lenea Falk has called the playwright's female characters either Southern gentlewomen or Southern wenches. While it is true that many of Williams' characters speak with Southern accents, close scrutiny reveals that their problems are the old, universal ones of the human heart in its search for reality and meaning in life.

"Tennessee Williams and the Predicament of Women" by Louise Blackwell. From *South Atlantic Bulletin*, 35 (March, 1970), 9-14. Copyright © 1970 by *South Atlantic Bulletin*. A slightly revised version by the author is printed here by permission.

In the plays under consideration, Williams is making a commentary on Western culture by dramatizing his belief that men and women find reality and meaning in life through satisfactory sexual relationships. His drama derives from the characters' recognition of certain needs within themselves and their consequent demands for the "right" mate. Frustration is the surface evidence of the predicament of his female characters, but Williams is careful to distinguish the underlying reasons for their behavior. Analysis of the various plays reveals subtle differences in the cause of their frustration, so that there is not as much similarity among the characters as is often supposed.

One approach to the study of these characters is to categorize them according to their situation at the time of the action, so long as we allow for variations within each category. Four groups thus appear:

1. *Women who have learned to be maladjusted through adjustment to abnormal family relationships and who strive to break through their bondage in order to find a mate.*

In line with modern theories of psychology, Tennessee Williams believes that the individual learns to be maladjusted through living with and adjusting to maladjusted people. Alma Winemiller in *Summer and Smoke* (1948) is in this group. She is the only child of a rigid, scholarly, and self-righteous preacher and his wife who is described as "a spoiled and selfish girl who evaded the responsibilities of later life by slipping into a state of perverse childishness. She is known as Mr. Winemiller's 'Cross'." Of course, she is Alma's Cross, too, as is the father.

Mrs. Winemiller is not, as Professor Falk has written, simply "senile and mean." She has had a mental break with reality; and Alma has had to learn to live with this strange creature who is her mother. In this household, then, Alma has multiple roles to play. As a result of being, at once, the daughter of her father and mother, sister and parent to her mother, and social head of the household for her father, Alma has no role that she desires for herself.

In such a household there is a failure of meaningful communication so that the private needs of the daughter are never considered by the parents. The only way Alma can get out of the house for a date with John Buchanan is to grab her purse and rush out the door, leaving her father calling after her. Rash action is often the result of inadequate communication within family units, and the warning signals are present here.

Her mother's break with mature behavior presages a reversal in Alma's character. She does not, like her mother, regress to childhood and negate sexual relations, but she does abandon her previous moralistic approach to life for a profligate sex experience. Her later life is possible because she has learned from her mother how to reverse her life for more satisfying experiences

Blanche DuBois of *A Streetcar Named Desire* (1947) also belongs in this category. She was a dutiful child, remaining with her aged parents long beyond the marrying age for most women and later staying behind to try to save the family estate, while her sister, Stella, went out to find her place in the world. Since Blanche had adjusted to an abnormal family life, she was unable, when she had the opportunity, to relate to the so-called normal world of her sister. She was, in fact, following a family pattern when she became sexually profligate after the death of her parents. In a discussion of property matters, she says that the plantation was disposed of gradually by "improvident grandfathers and father and uncles and brothers" who exchanged the land for their "epic fornications."

In an earlier play, *The Glass Menagerie* (1945), Laura Wingfield has learned to be maladjusted from her mother, Amanda. In his notes on the characters, Williams states that Amanda Wingfield is "a little woman of great but confused vitality, clinging frantically to another time and place. ...She is not paranoiac, but her life is paranoia." Amanda's husband and son have long since deserted her, but Laura, who has been crippled since birth, has no escape open to her. She must adjust to her mother who is so unrealistic that she denies that Laura is crippled. According to the author, she has "failed to establish contact with reality, continues to live vitally in her illusions." Indeed, the only way Laura can survive is to retreat into her own delusions.

In *You Touched Me!* (1945), written in collaboration with Donald Windham, Williams depicts Emmie Rockley as having learned to distrust men and the idea of a mature sexual relationship from her spinster aunt, Matilda Rockley. This play ends happily for Emmie, but apparently life has not looked so simple to Williams since then, as he has not given us happy solutions for complicated problems.

2. *Women who have subordinated themselves to a domineering and often inferior person in an effort to attain reality and meaning through communication with another person.*

Stella Kowalski, in *A Streetcar Named Desire* (1947), is superior in background and personal endowments to her mate, but she subordinates herself to his way of life because they have a satisfying sexual relationship. When her sister Blanche cannot believe that Stella is happy with her crude husband, Stella tells her that "there are things that happen between a man and a woman in the dark—that sort of make everything else seem—unimportant." When Stella is willing to send her sister to a mental institution rather than believe that Stanley has raped Blanche we see just how far a seemingly gentle and attractive woman will go to defend her sexual partner.

In *Period of Adjustment* (1960), Dotty Bates will tolerate insult and abuse from her husband Ralph, so long as their sexual relationship is satisfying. She knows that he married her to please her wealthy father; and he frequently lets her know that she is so homely she might never have married if he hadn't come along. After a quarrel in which Ralph repeats all of the old insults, the two finally sit down to talk matters over. When their disagreements have been smoothed over, they go to bed together, this being the essential act in the vision of Tennessee Williams if Dotty is to maintain her grasp of reality and meaning in life.

Hannah Jelkes, in *The Night of the Iguana* (1961), is an example of the woman who has made the best of a relationship that is not so good as the true mating of a woman with a man. She is an unmarried artist who has travelled for years with her aged grandfather, a minor poet. In discussing her relationship to her grandfather she states:

> We make a home for each other my grandfather and I. Do you know what I mean by a home? I don't mean a regular home. I mean I don't mean what other people mean when they speak of a home, because I don't regard a home as a...well, as a place, a building... a house...of wood, bricks, stone. I think of a home as being a thing that two people have between them in which each can...well, nest— rest—live in, emotionally speaking.

When Reverend Shannon reminds her that birds build nests in relatively permanent locations "for the purpose of mating and propagating" the species, she responds that she is not a bird but a human being that needs to nest in the heart of another being. She then tells him that she has learned to believe in brief periods of understanding between two people. Never having had a mature sexual relationship, Hannah has sacrificed her life for her grandfather and she has managed to survive with fleeting and insignificant relationships.

Although she is not the major character in *Sweet Bird of Youth* (1959), Heavenly Finley is a vital character whose life is controlled by her crude and domineering father and the memory of Chance Wayne, with whom she fell in love as a young girl. Chance, after seducing Heavenly and giving her venereal disease, leaves town. He is a handsome *cad*, but because of her few intimate contacts with him, Heavenly wastes her life yearning for his return.

3. *Women who struggle to make relationships with men who are unable or unwilling to make lasting relationships*

In four plays, *Cat on a Hot Tin Roof* (1955), *Orpheus Descending* (1957), *Suddenly Last Summer* (1958), and *Period of Adjustment* (1960). Williams created a group of women who are remarkable for their sexual demands upon men who are either homosexual or otherwise inadequate to make a lasting relationship. In *Cat on a Hot Tin Roof* Maggie and Brick, presumably, had a satisfactory sexual relationship early in their marriage. Problems began to develop, however, when Maggie decided that Brick's close friendship with Skipper indicated homosexual tendencies. After the death of Skipper, Brick was so grieved over the loss of his friend that he became disgusted with Maggie and insisted upon sleeping separately. He would gladly have terminated the marriage, but Maggie would not leave him. In an effort to assuage his feelings, Brick began drinking heavily. Maggie finally bribes her husband to go to bed with her by locking up his liquor. Undoubtedly she is one of the most determined female characters in modern drama.

Lady Torrance, in *Orpheus Descending*, is a strong and decent woman who has been a hard-working and devoted wife to her husband, Jabe, whom she married for economic security. He is some years older than she. Actually Jabe was responsible for the death of her father when she was a young woman, but Lady does not know this until near the end of the play. Her yearning for the love of a man her own age is aroused when Val Xavier comes to town, carrying a guitar, and asks for a job in the Torrance store. Even though Jabe is dying of cancer in the family apartment up over the store, Lady arranges to sleep with Val in a small room at the back of the store.

When Val, who is a man with no lasting ties, decides to move on, he tells Lady that he will leave her a forwarding address. She replies:

Ask me how it felt to be coupled with death up there, and I can tell you. My skin crawled when he touched me. But I endured it. I guess my heart knew that somebody must be coming to take me out of this hell! You did. You came. Now look at me! I'm alive once more!

Through her sexual relationship with Val, Lady Torrance has attained reality and meaning in life. Although Val shows some remorse when he learns that Lady is pregnant, he is unwilling to assume responsibility for a permanent mate and he resumes his transient life.

In *Suddenly Last Summer*, Mrs. Venable and Catharine clash over a dead man, Sebastian. Sebastian was Mrs. Venable's son and Catharine her niece. Throughout his life Sebastian, a would-be poet and sexual misfit, was pampered, overprotected, and dominated by his mother. Catharine was in love with Sebastian and, at the request of his mother, she willingly agreed to travel abroad with him. Later, in spite of the threats of Mrs. Venable, she insisted upon telling the truth about how Sebastian was killed and partly devoured by a group of cannibalistic boys on a tropical island. The unique thing about Catharine is that she yearned for a sexual relationship with a man, her cousin, whom she knew to be weak and strangely perverted.

George and Isabel Haverstick, in *Period of Adjustment,* met in a veterans' hospital where George suffered from "the shakes" and Isabel was his nurse. Despite the fact that George is a weak man and Isabel knows that he shakes when he has to face certain situations in life, she expects him to be the model of composure on the first night of their honeymoon. He is not. It is on the second night after their wedding, when Isabel begins to mother and pet George again, as if she were his nurse, that the audience is led to believe the marriage will be consummated.

4. *Women who have known happiness, but who have lost their mates and who try to overcome the loss.*

The Princess Kosmonopolis in *Sweet Bird of Youth* (1959) is an aging actress who has known both happiness with a lover and popularity with audiences. After losing both, she failed in a comeback effort as actress and embarked upon a search for another lover who could return her to reality. She becomes attracted to Chance Wayne, a beach boy in Palm Beach. When he does not meet her needs, she dumps him in a Gulf Coast town where he must take his chances with some citizens who know him very well

because of his treatment of Heavenly Finley. The Princess will
continue her search in Hollywood.

The Rose Tattoo (1951) is one of Tennessee Williams' most
down-to-earth plays about the suffering of a woman who has
known and lost a mate who gave her complete sexual happiness.
Serafina delle Rose, an Italian-American living on the Gulf Coast,
is completely devastated upon learning that her truck-driver
husband has been killed in an automobile accident. In spite of the
needs of her children, she loses touch with reality, and life has no
further meaning for her. After three years of isolation, Serafina
is shocked back to reality when some of her neighbors tell her that
her husband had been killed while smuggling dope and that,
furthermore, he had had a mistress. Shortly afterwards, she finds
another mate.

Maxine Faulk in *The Night of the Iguana* (1961) has just lost
her husband when the play opens. She has known sexual happiness
with him, and having known reality and meaning in life through
her happy relationship, Mrs. Faulk is one of those women who will
waste no time in trying to re-establish a satisfying sexual relationship. It is apparently accidental that the Reverend Shannon, a
guide for a group of women, should stop at Mrs. Faulk's hotel at a
time when she is most in need of a mate. She has known Shannon
for some years and she knows him to be a weak man, leaning
toward alcoholism. But in her lonely state, she will gladly provide
the strength, to say nothing of the financial support, for a relationship with him.

Regardless of whether one agrees with the earlier thesis of
Tennessee Williams that most people find reality and meaning
in life through satisfactory sexual adjustment, one has to acknowledge that his major female characters, in the plays written
through *The Night of the Iguana*, fight a continuous battle to find
a mate or to keep the mate they have already found. Even though
Williams has experienced despair in recent years, and many of
his plays after 1961 appear to reflect his own increasing pessimism, the plays studied in this essay demonstrate his more
positive view that women willingly make sacrifices in their un-
ceasing search for a congenial and lasting mate.

Tennessee Williams' Fugitive Kind

by Donald P. Costello

Orpheus Descending, a play produced precisely in the middle of the career of Tennessee Williams—seven published full length plays before it and seven after it—provides us with a vocabulary for an interpretation of his whole body of dramatic work. Although all Williams' plays sound like Tennessee Williams, the inadequately regarded *Orpheus Descending*, a 1957 Broadway failure which lasted only 68 performances at the Martin Beck, sounds like *all* of Tennessee Williams. That is probably its trouble. It is the most obvious statement of his major theme, and it is jam-packed with his favorite devices. It concentrates—in obvious imagery and precise language—the thematic and formal concerns which have become almost obsessive with him over the period of his life's work. This play is unmistakably Tennessee Williams: Four sensitive human beings in a Southern town are lonely fugitives trying to escape earthly corruption. The basis of the corruption is that the earthly representatives treat human beings as objects. The dramatic technique used to communicate this corruption is a vivid theatricality of violence and horror, overlaid with a mystical non-realism made heavy with symbolism. Light-dark imagery helps to separate the unearthly fugitives from the earthly corrupted. The fugitives' attempts to escape corruption are marked by the retaining of a childlike, free or wild nature, by attempts to recapture a lost past of innocence, by sacramental purification of fire and water, by attempts to escape into artistic visions or sex, by attempts to counter barren death with fruitfulness, and by seeking as a symbol of hope some pure natural object which has risen above earthly taint.

The basic given in a Tennessee Williams play is that the earth is

"Tennessee Williams' Fugitive Kind" by Donald P. Costello has been somewhat abridged by the author for this volume. It was originally published in *Modern Drama*, 15 (May 1972), 26-43. Copyright © 1972 by A. C. Edwards. Printed by permission of the author, A. C. Edwards, and *Modern Drama*.

a corrupting place. The word "corruption," which he uses throughout *Orpheus Descending*, is his favorite word for the earthly world of men. Williams' Orpheus is Val Xavier, now a fugitive from that world of men in which he has in the past "lived in corruption." He has not yet been "branded" by the corruption represented by the chorus-people of Two River County, but he wants to be permanently out of its reach. So far he has escaped permanent corruption by means of his Orphic Voice, his music which "washes me clean like water when anything unclean has touched me."[1] In his early short play, *Auto-Da-Fé*, Williams has the boy Eloi describe the earth to his mother: "You harp on purity, purity all the time, and yet you're willing to stay in the midst of corruption."[2] When Eloi's mother admits the prevalence of corruption but insists that she never allowed it to touch her, Eloi denies that escape from corruption is possible: "It gets in our nostrils and even goes in our blood." (109) Similarly, Brick, in *Cat on a Hot Tin Roof*, sees the pervasiveness of corruption. He sees "the whole, the whole—thing" as a world of mendacity, of lying and liars (91); and it is "the conventional mores" (104) of that earth which has corrupted his "incorruptible" (42) love for Skipper. The notion of the pervasiveness of this evil, whatever names he gives to it, is as common throughout Williams as it is in *Orpheus Descending*. Serafina tells Alvaro in *The Rose Tattoo*, "There are some people that want to make everything dirty." (102) And Eloi complains to his mother in *Atuo-Da-Fé*, "Your broom and your dust-pan wouldn't accomplish much. Even the air in this neighborhood is unclean." (108) In Williams' latest play, *Kingdom of Earth*, which played on Broadway as *The Seven Descents of*

[1]Tennessee Williams, *Orpheus Descending with Battle of Angels* (New York: A New Directions Book, 1955, 1959), p. 37. All citations from Williams' plays will be identified in the text by page numbers. All quotations will be from New Directions texts, in the following editions:

Baby Doll (The Script for the Film). 1956; *Cat on a Hot Tin Roof.* 1955; *The Eccentricities of a Nightingale and Summer and Smoke.* 1948, 1964; *The Glass Menagerie*, New Classics Edition. 1949; *Kingdom of Earth.* 1967, 1968; *The Milk Train Doesn't Stop Here Anymore.* 1964; *The Night of the Iguana.* 1962; *Orpheus Descending with Battle of Angels.* 1955, 1959; *Period of Adjustment.* 1960; *A Streetcar Named Desire.* 1947; *Suddenly Last Summer.* 1958; *Three Plays of Tennessee Williams* ("The Rose Tattoo," "Camino Real," "Sweet Bird of Youth.") 1948, 1950, 1951, 1953, 1964; *27 Wagons Full of Cotton and Other One-Act Plays by Tennessee Williams.* 1945, 1953.

[2]"Auto-Da-Fé from *27 Wagons Full of Cotton and Other One-Act Plays*, pp. 108, 109. All quoted one-act plays are from this text, and, in the future, will be cited with only the page number.

Myrtle, Chicken asks Myrtle, "You know what life is made out of?" and she answers clearly and simply, "Evil, I think it's evil." (92) In *Baby Doll*, Silva gives the spreading evil many names. He tells Baby Doll, "Spirits of violence—and coming—malevolence—cruelty—treachery—destruction....They're evil spirits that haunt the human heart and take possession of it, and spread from one human heart to another human heart." (78) The evil is not only spreading, it is part of a wasting process. In *The Last of My Solid Gold Watches*, the 78-year-old salesman, Mister Charlie, exclaims about "Deterioration!" That word sets the symbolic theme of the whole: "Everything's going downhill around here lately!" And the Negro choral figure echoes: "Yes suh, dat's de troof, Mistuh Charlie, ev'ything's goin' downhill." (76) And John Buchanan, in *Summer and Smoke*, sees himself as deteriorating: "Did anyone ever slide downhill as fast as I have this summer?" (240) And Marguerite Gautier in *Camino Real* talks about the earth as "this place where there's nothing but the gradual wasting away of everything decent in us." (240) As he does in *Orpheus Descending*, Williams often tells us of the corruption of the world symbolically as well as directly. Cancer is an obvious symbol of corruption, both spreading and deteriorating. Jabe in *Orpheus Descending*, Mother in *The Long Goodbye*, and Big Daddy in *Cat on a Hot Tin Roof* all suffer from cancers which are signs of the larger moral cancer devouring the earth: Gooper is graphic in his description of the spreading corruption: "Big Daddy is dying of cancer, and it's spread all through him and it's attacked all his vital organs including the kidneys and right now he is sinking into uremia, and you all know what uremia is, it's poisoning of the whole system due to the failure of the body to eliminate its poison." Maggie makes the symbolic connection for the audience: "Poisons! Poisons! Venemous thought and words! In hearts and minds!—That's poisons!" (136) Another favorite symbol for the spreading corruption of the earth is what Williams calls in *The Night of the Iguana*, "the encroaching jungle." (5) Shannon's flight is to escape that jungle, for, as he tells Maxine, "I don't want to rot." (81) The scene description in *Auto-Da-Fé* is similar: "There is an effect of sinister antiquity in the setting, even the flowers suggesting the richness of decay." (107) The setting of *Suddenly Last Summer* combines the corrupting jungle imagery with the Williams symbol of devouring: The Venable garden is "like a tropical jungle....There are massive tree-flowers that suggest organs of a body, torn out, still glistening with undried blood; there are harsh cries and sibilant hissings and thrashing sounds in the garden as if it were inhabited by beasts, serpents and birds all of a savage nature." (13) It is against this setting that life on the earth as "flesh-eating" (20) and as "long, long trails of debris with nothing to clean it all up" (27) and as "destruction" (74) is revealed.

What is man to do if he has to live on that kind of earth? He can either be of that earth, or he can be a fugitive from it. In a New York *Times* article about *Orpheus Descending*, Tennessee Williams told his readers that his play is about those two kinds of people, those who are of the earth, who accept the "prescribed answers that are not answers at all," contrasted with his four protagonists, those who "continue to ask" the "unanswered questions that haunt the hearts of people,"[3] those who are—in a key phrase of the play—"the fugitive kind." (117) So central was that phrase to Williams that he had called a very early unpublished play *Fugitive Kind;* and, in 1960, the film version of *Orpheus Descending*, written by Williams in collaboration with Meade Roberts, lifted that phrase from the text and took it as the title of the film: *The Fugitive Kind.* To surrender to the evil earth is, to Williams, man's major sin; to continue the fugitive flight is what Williams asks. The classic Williams plea: continue the quest. Lady Torrance, in *Orpheus Descending*, speaks for all the Williams fugitives: "I don't know the answer, I just know corruption ain't the answer." (49) And so the fugitive kind move on, away from corruption. "The fugitive kind," Carol Cutrere says at the end of *Orpheus Descending*, as she moves on, ignoring the Sheriff's command to stop, "The fugitive kind can always follow their kind." (117) From early plays to late, Williams images fugitives from the corrupting earth. He never fails to make his protagonist a fugitive. His lesser people accept the earth. A quick survey of all his plays shows the startling consistency of this Williams image, and the variety with which he works it. In 1940, in *Battle of Angels*, Cassandra, the early version of Carol Cutrere, tells Val: "You an' me, we belong to the fugitive kind. We live on motion. Think of it, Val. Nothing but motion, motion, mile after mile, keeping up with the wind, or even faster!" (213) Several of the short plays in *27 Wagons Full of Cotton and Other One-Act Plays* published in 1945, continue the fugitive image and play variations on it.... In *The Glass Menagerie*, in 1945, none of the three main char-

[3]"The Past, the Present, and Perhaps," *New York Times*, reprinted in *Orpheus Descending with Battle of Angels*, p. vi.

acters is at home on the earth. Amanda lives in the past; Laura "lives in a world of her own—a world of—little glass ornaments" (59); Tom is "always so restless," and identifies himself in his imagination with the sign of the "sailing vessel with jolly roger." (39) In 1947, Blanche DuBois, the consummate fugitive of *A Streetcar Named Desire,* is likened to a moth. (12) And she wants to "make myself a new life." (74) Even physically, in the plot, she is a fugitive, seeking "sanctuary," (69) staying unwanted in her sister's house, promising, "I won't stay long! I won't, I *promise.*" (92) She wants Mitch because: "I want to rest! I want to breathe quietly again!" (94) At the end, Blanche tells the men, symbolically, "I'm only passing through." (165) Eunice, a choral figure, sums up the situation of Blanche: "She couldn't stay here; there wasn't no other place for her to go." (168) In 1948, Alma, of *Summer and Smoke,* like all the fugitives of Williams, reaches for something beyond the earth. She sees the Gothic cathedral as the symbol of questing man: "Everything reaches up...everything seems to be straining for something out of the reach of stone.... To me—well, that is the secret, the principle back of existence— the everlasting struggle and aspiration for more than our human limits have placed in our reach." (189) In 1950, in *The Rose Tattoo,* Serafina's heart will not stay where she put it, in the marble urn with the ashes of her husband. Instead, in the image of Alvaro, her heart "has broken out of the urn and away from the ashes," and—familiar image—is like a bird seeking a new resting place. (112) In 1953, the quintessential fugitive in literature, Don Quixote, makes an appearance along *Camino Real.* In this play, Williams gives us a parade of fugitives who refuse to face the realities of earth. ...Kilroy is the standard fugitive, the unknown person of "Kilroy Was Here," with date and place of birth unknown, whose address is that of a traveler and whose parents are anonymous. (279, 280) His only plans are "—going *on* from— *here!*"(327) In the same play, Lord Byron tells Marguerite Gautier, *"Make voyages!—Attempt them!—*there's nothing else." (246) In 1955, Williams makes his instructions for the stage design of *Cat on a Hot Tin Roof* symbolic: "The designer should take pains to give the actors room to move about freely (to show their restlessness, their passion for breaking out." (xiv) The play starts when Brick has given up the fugitive's role: "He has the additional charm of that cool air of detachment that people have who have given up the struggle." (3) Maggie defines herself in opposition to such giving up: "My hat is still in the ring, and I am determined to win!—what is the victory of a cat on a hot tin roof?—...Just staying on it, I guess, as long as she can." (15) In 1956, in the film *Baby Doll,* Silva views the world as a world of fugitives: "People come into this world without instructions of where to go, what to do, so they wander a little and...then go away.... *Drift*—for a while and then...*vanish."* (58) Aunt Rose Comfort's situation, wandering forlornly with her ancient suitcase, is seen as the human condition. Baby Doll says, "I feel sorry for poor old Aunt Rose Comfort. She doesn't know where to go or what to do".... In 1958, in *Suddenly Last Summer,* the world will not face Catharine's clear view of the cannibalistic nature of man on the earth —"the true story of our time and the world we live in." (47) So the world makes Catharine into a fugitive: she is put into an asylum; she is threatened with a lobotomy; she, instead of society, is made the one who is "perverse." (47) In 1959, in *Sweet Bird of Youth,* Chance Wayne and Princess Kosmonopolis are both fugitives. In the last act "the lamentation music" plays for them and the Princess interprets it: "All day I've kept hearing a sort of lament that drifts through the air of this place. It says, 'Lost, lost, never to be found again'...places of exile from whatever we loved....Oh, Chance, believe me, after failure comes flight. Nothing ever comes after failure but flight." (431) In 1960, in his only comedy, *Period of Adjustment,* Williams can gently mock the fugitive's condition. Isabel performs as the Tennessee Williams heroine: "*What* is life for us *all*? (She sighs.) My philosophy professor at the Baptist college I went to, he said one day, 'We are all of us born, live and die in the shadow of a giant question mark that refers to three questions: Where do we *come* from? *Why? And where, oh where, are we going?'"* (22) George's fugitive dream is the classic American dream of the free and unspoiled West, complete with longhorn cattle, buffalo, and even some dignity. (71) And Ralph wants to get even further away from corrupting earth: "Oh, I wish I could be the first man in a moon rocket! No, not the moon, but Mars, Venus!" (73) In 1961, in *The Night of the Iguana,* Hannah Jelkes appears as a classic fugitive, unreal as Carol Cutrere, wheeling her grandfather from country to country: "Nobody would take us in town, and if we don't get in here, I would have to wheel him back down through the rain forest, and then *what, then where?*" (34) She tells Shannon that humans need to cultivate endurance, just to be able "to keep on going." (105) In 1963, in *The Milk Train Doesn't Stop Here Anymore,* Christopher Flanders wanders into the action of the play.

Like Val Xavier, his physical description shows him to be a fugitive: "His appearance is rough and weathered; his eyes wild, haggard. He has the look of a powerful, battered, but still undefeated, fighter." (17) He has "climbed a mountain and fought off a wolf pack" to see Mrs. Goforth simply because there is "no where else to go." (27)...And, finally, in *Kingdom of Earth,* the 1968 published version of *The Seven Descents of Myrtle,* all three characters are fugitives. Myrtle herself seeks a home throughout the play: "the little animal has to make a home of its own" (8 and *passim*) is her refrain....

Williams need take no special pains to draw the opposite kind of character, the kind who is of the earth. That is the common lot of men, so he need not insist on it. Whoever is not a fugitive has made his peace with the corrupting earth. In a few plays, for contrast, Williams does specifically identify the non-fugitives. Thus, in *Streetcar,* Blanche accuses Stella: "You've given in." (74) And, in *Summer and Smoke,* John Buchanan admits to Alma, "I've settled with life on fairly acceptable terms." (232) In *The Night of the Iguana,* Maxine tells Shannon that she is ready to give up the fugitive's life: "We've both reached a point where we've got to settle for something that works for us in our lives—even if it isn't on the highest kind of level." (81) Shannon gives in: he compromises, the only Williams protagonist to do so.

Williams variously describes the corrupting earth from which flight becomes necessary. As in *Orpheus Descending,* the components are human greed; social injustice, especially against the blacks; and various forms of violence and human exploitation. A favorite Williams device is to generalize these corruptions into a single metaphor: human beings treat other human beings not as persons but as objects. Sometimes this metaphor, especially in *Orpheus Descending,* takes on a mercantile basis. Thus, early in the play, Beulah tells us the relationship between Lady Torrance and her husband: "Jabe Torrance bought that woman." (5) Later, Val extends Jabe's behavior to the general behavior of the human race: "I'm telling you, Lady, there's people bought and sold in this world like carcasses of hogs in butcher shops...there's just two kinds of people, the ones who are bought and the buyers." (41) Lady's experience has told her the same thing: "You ain't tellin' me nothin' I don't know." (41) And she even confirms what we already have been told, that as one of the fugitive kind she is one of those that are bought: "I sleep with a son of a bitch who bought me at a fire sale." (42) The buying and selling of people is not new to Lady. She accuses David, her former lover who abandoned her to marry a woman with money just before Lady herself married Jabe Torrance's money: "You sold *yourself. I* sold *my* self. *You* was bought *I* was bought. You made whores of us both!" (61) And Lady fears that Carol is one of the buyers too. She warns Carol about Val: "This boy's not for sale in my store!" (56) In other Williams plays, the buying and selling goes on. In *Sweet Bird of Youth*, Boss Finley had tried to sell his daughter to "a fifty-year-old money bag." (326) And, in the same play, Princess had purchased Chance for love-making. (372) In *Suddenly Last Summer*, Catharine reveals that Sebastian had "used" first his mother and then, after her disfiguring stroke, had "used" Catharine as mere objects to attract male companions. ...To make more shocking the metaphor of human beings treating other human beings not as persons but as objects, Williams extends the metaphor from buying and selling into cannibalism, clarifying Val Xavier's comments about people becoming carcasses of hogs in butcher shops. This cannibalism is central to *Suddenly Last Summer*, for Sebastian becomes an object, used for food by the bird-like boys of Cabeza de Lobo, just as the turtles had been devoured by the flesh-eating birds of the Encantadas, all as a mirror of the way Sebastian had used his mother and Catharine. In the second act of *Sweet Bird of Youth*, Princess realizes that her using of Chance has made her into "a monster" who lives in "the country of the flesh-hungry," and "blood thirsty." (426) And even at the beginning of Williams' career, in the one-act, *The Strangest Kind of Romance*, the prophetic Old Man denounces men of the earth, especially the "stupidity and cupidity" of commercial and industrial society: "Feed on, Feed on! You race of gluttons! Devour the flesh of thy brother, drink his blood! Glut your monstrous bellies on corruption!" (151)

The imagery of light-dark, of water, and of fire, is used predominantly in *Orpheus Descending*, and helps in many other Tennessee Williams plays to identify the corrupting earth and to symbolize the flight from it. The obvious, recurrent, and even obtrusive use of this imagery helps to keep the plays non-realistic, and helps, through ritualizing and through sacramental suggestions, to show that Williams is talking about the human condition in eternal terms and not as mere local Southern gothic.

Mrs. Venable, in *Suddenly Last Summer*, describes her life with Sebastian in precisely the same terms that Vee used in *Orpheus Descending* to describe the conventional society of the non-fugitives: Vee had told Val, "We *live* in, a world of—*light* and—shadow." (92); Mrs. Venable tells the Doctor, "We—still lived in a—world of light and shadow." (22)...And the darkness is the despair in the heart of Blanche DuBois in *Streetcar,* a darkness that prevents her from finding her way. She tells Mitch that the despair began with the death of Allan: "Then the searchlight which had been turned on the world was turned off again and never for one moment since has there been any light that's stronger than this—kitchen—candle. ..." (113)

Water and fire in *Orpheus Descending* are cleansing, purifying. The fugitive kind have been cleansed in a kind of eternal sacramental stream, and thus: "The fugitive kind leave clean skins and teeth and white bones behind them." (117) Early in the play, Carol refuses to touch the breastbone of the bird used in the primitive ritual of the Conjure Man. It is "still tainted with corruption" (16) because "there's still some flesh clinging to it." (15) Only fire and water can clean away corrupting flesh, the taint of the earth: "Leave it a long time on a bare rock in the rain and the sun till every sign of corruption is burned and washed away from it, and then it will be a good charm." (16) Williams then makes the cleansed bone partake in the light-dark imagery: when it is cleansed, says Carol, it will be "a white charm, but now it's a black charm." (16) The movie carries through this sacramental pattern more fully than the play. Where in the play Val is killed by the fire of a lynch-mob's blow-torch, in the movie he is killed by *both* fire and water. ...as the firemen turn their hose on Val, the water pushes him into the engulfing flames. As he is killed, in both play and movie, he is purified finally from the corrupting earth, becoming eternally a fugitive kind, leaving his snakeskin jacket behind him and becoming a fugitive symbol for others to follow.

In other plays, Williams works variations on the basic water symbol. A short play very similar in mood to *Orpheus Descending* is *Talk to Me Like the Rain and Let Me Listen.* The title establishes the water image which is the play's central symbol, rich with sacramental suggestions. The play is a ritual of a Man's confession and a Woman's dream of escape into non-earthly purity. The ritual begins as the Man and the Woman (those are the only names Williams gives them, establishing their universality) share a glass of water. As he recites "the litany of my sorrows," a mandolin is heard (again much like *Orpheus Descending),* and they seek communion: "Let's find each other and maybe we won't be lost." (214) Four times he asks her to "talk to me like the rain and I will lie here and listen." (215) And so she begins her long monologue of escape through ritual cleansing: "The room will be shadowy, cool, and filled with the murmur of...Yes. Rain....Then I'll dress in white." (216) This cleansing will be an escape: "I won't have any idea of what's going on in the world." Then the whiteness imagery builds up still more strongly: "I will look in the mirror and see that my hair has turned white. As white as the foam on the waves." Like the pure bird in *Orpheus Descending* which never touches the corrupting earth, she will become "transparent." (217) At last "the white clean wind that blows from the edge of the world" will so purify her that "finally I won't have any body at all." (218) The perfect pure state for Williams is to be thus bodyless, with no touch of the earthly. That is the object of the quest. Water is used as encouragement for continuing the quest in *Camino Real.* In Block Sixteen, as everyman Kilroy is about to despair about continuing to walk the road that used to be royal, Don Quixote talks him into "going *on* from—here!" And at that point, the dry fountain, in approval, begins to flow with clear water. (327) Throughout *A Streetcar Named Desire,* Blanche seeks the still waters of her bath, and in the moving final scene, she seeks the purity both of water and of fire. She asks repeatedly if the grapes are washed, and then falls into her final fantasy: "the rest of my time I'm going to spend on the sea. And when I die, I'm going to die on the sea. ...And I'll be buried at sea sewn up in a clean white sack and dropped overboard—at noon—in the blaze of summer." (162, 3) The sea is a favorite Williams water symbol, not only as purity but, more basically, as the beginning of life, a beginning before corruption. ...Williams also uses rain as a significant water symbol. Rain is the vehicle of purification that gives the short play *The Purification* its title. ...In *The Night of the Iguana,* Williams makes rain the symbol of the un- attainable God, the purity above the corruption which the fugi- tives seek but can never reach. Shannon has claimed that his God is in the storm, and as it finally starts to rain, Hannah tells him, "Here is your God, Mr. Shannon."...

Fire is the most powerful purifying and sacramental symbol in several Williams plays, as it is in *Orpheus Descending.* The sym- bol that gives meaning, and the title, to the short play *Auto-Da- Fé* is purification by fire. Eloi's speeches are explicit: "All through the Scriptures are cases of cities destroyed by the justice of fire when they got to be nests of foulness!...Condemn it, I say, purify it with fire!" (110) Eloi wants to burn the pornographic pictures, his house, the whole corrupt earth, "because there needs to be burning!...For the sake of burning, for God, for purification!" (114) Serafina, in *The Rose Tattoo,* feels so deeply the purifying power of fire that she defies the Church by having her husband cremated. Alvaro confirms her wisdom: "The body would've decayed, but ashes always stay clean." (101) The horrible ritual of the devouring of Sebastian, in *Suddenly Last Summer,* is pushed beyond realism, into the sacramental, by the insistent, rhythmic fire imagery in Catharine's long monologue:

> It was all white outside. White hot, a blazing white hot, hot blazing white.... As if a huge white bone had caught on fire in the sky and blazed so bright it was white and burned the sky and everything under the sky white. ...

In *Camino Real,* Lord Byron's description of the sacramental purification-by-fire of the body of the poet Shelley shows both the corruption of the fleshly and the purity to which fugitive man aspires....

The paths which the Williams fugitives follow as they seek to avoid the corruption of the earth are those paths which are clearly delineated in *Orpheus Descending.* They attempt to retain or regain a childlike innocence of the past, they desperately seek freedom or wildness, or they seek escape through art or sex.

Nostalgia is a major Williams mood. The sadness of the lost past hovers over his fugitives. The "lonely children" image that is carefully applied to each of the four fugitives in *Orpheus Descending* (13, 19, 23, 40, 43, 47, 57, 91, 92) appears continually in other plays, always describing a sweet state that is forever lost. Williams describes the attempt of Sarafina and Alvaro to come together in *The Rose Tattoo:* "Their fumbling communication has a curious intimacy and sweetness, like the meeting of two lonely children for the first time." (100) And the short play, *This Property is Condemned,* has as its entire meaning a meeting of two lonely children caught in a corrupting world that will soon condemn them. (197-207) "What happens to kids when they grow up?" is the haunting question of *The Long Goodbye* (169) and of much of Williams. And therefore many of the fugitives refuse to grow up or they try to recover a lost past: like Lady Torrance who tries to re-establish—in the confectionery of her store—the wine garden of her father, the only place where she was free and happy, in the time of young love and song; and like Baby Doll asleep in her crib with her thumb in her mouth (47); and like Brick in

Cat on a Hot Tin Roof who breaks his leg trying to get back to the simpler world of the high school athlete and who is, in Maggie's words, "scared to grow up" (106); and like Mrs. Venable and Sebastian who for a time hold off the world in *Suddenly Last Summer* by refusing to grow old; and like Amanda Wingfield in *The Glass Menagerie* who is described as "a little woman of great but confused vitality clinging frantically to another time and place" (vii), and like fragile Laura playing with her glass animals; and like Blanche DuBois in *Streetcar* whose memory brings back her old beau, Shep Huntleigh, when she finds herself finally trapped at Stanley's (147); and like Ralph and George in *Period of Adjustment* who live now in the reflection of "past glories." (95) The sadness of lost youth and innocence gives *Sweet Bird of Youth* its title; and, in that play, Aunt Nonnie explains to Chance his fruitless quest: 'What you want to go back to is your clean, unashamed youth. And you can't." (411) *Camino Real* strikes the same note: Lord Byron announces his desire to make a departure, "from my present self to myself as I used to be!"; but Gutman knows the hopelessness of that desire and replies, "*That's* the *furthest* departure a man could make!" (241, 242)

The wildness of the fugitives in *Orpheus Descending* is also reflected in other Williams plays. Carol had been a "wild animal" (53); Val, with his "wild beauty," is twice summoned into the play by the primitive Choctaw cry of the Conjure Man. (16, 102) And Carol connects the wildness of Val with the past and with a sweetness: "This country used to be wild, the men and women were wild and there was a wild sort of sweetness in their hearts." (103) In *Camino Real,* Jacques Casanova repeats to Kilroy the code of the earthly creatures: "You have a spark of anarchy in your spirit and that's not to be tolerated. Nothing wild or honest is tolerated here!" (225) The trapped figures long for freedom: Maggie the Cat would "love to run with dogs through chilly woods, run, run, leap over obstructions" (*Cat,* 20); Chance Wayne would rather die than be tied by an "invisible loving steel chain." (*Sweet,* 442) The Mother in *The Long Goodbye* most clearly states this Williams theme: "Freedom's the big thing in life. It's funny that some of us don't ever get it until we're dead." (171) Williams has written, in a *New York Times* article reprinted as the "Foreword" to *Camino Real,* that he himself is always trying to pass on his "own sense of something wild and unrestricted that ran like water in the mountains." (160)

Another attempted path to escape is the path of artistic vision.

Val Xavier and Vee Talbott try this road, and so do other Williams fugitives. Vee, the primitive painter in *Orpheus Descending*, "couldn't *live* without visions!" (65) And, through her art, she has "made some beauty out of this dark country." (68) The artist knows that his world is not the earthly one. Indeed, the poet's world is "a dream," is "illusions." (*Glass*, 122) Christopher Flanders in *Milk Train* is probably most like Vee Talbott in actively seeking visions. His program is to "look and look and look, till we're almost nothing but looking, nothing, almost, but vision...." (106) Yet this illusory and visionary world can, in Blanche DuBois' view, give "new light" (*Streetcar*, 83) and it can protect: "A poet's vocation is something that rests on something as thin and fine as the web of a spider, Doctor. That's all that held him *over!* out of destruction." (*Suddenly*, 73) Lord Byron, in *Camino Real*, believes that the "poet's vocation" can save not only himself from destruction but others as well, by working "to influence the heart," to "purify it and lift it above its ordinary level." (235) Williams tells us that he sees his own art as less hopeful and helpful than that, as, instead, at best the temporary escape from reality which most of his characters find it to be: "At the age of fourteen I discovered writing as an escape from a world of reality. ...It immediately became my place of retreat, my cave, my refuge."[4]

The attempt to escape the earth through the refuge of sex is perhaps the most obvious of the possible paths which seem to lie open to Williams' fugitives. But, as in *Orpheus Descending*, sex in all of Williams is only the temporary "make-believe answer." (48) Although Serafina in *The Rose Tattoo* and, in fantasy, the mad loveless old lady in *Portrait of a Madonna* do exult, as does Lady Torrance, in the hope that their fruitfulness will mean that pure new life is possible, sex is, finally, in Williams, connected rather with desperate and unsuccessful attempts at human contact, with protection, and with distraction. Blanche DuBois uses sex as a substitute for a deeper human need: "After the death of Allan—intimacies with strangers was all I seemed able to fill my empty heart with." (*Streetcar*, 140) Similarly, Shannon, in *The Night of the Iguana*, knows that the motive behind his hopeless and trivial sexual adventures is that "people need human contact" (20); and John Buchanan, in *The Eccentricities of a Nightingale*, tries to explain to Alma that he has discovered over the years that

[4]Tennessee Williams in an article in the *New York Times*, March 8, 1959, reprinted as "Foreword" to "Sweet Bird of Youth" in *Three Plays*, p. 333.

"'propinquity,' as you call it—just propinquity—sometimes isn't enough." (93) And Marguerite Gautier, in *Camino Real,* summarizes the motive behind human love-affairs: "We stretch out hands to each other in the dark that we can't escape from—we huddle together for some dim-communal comfort—and that's what passes for love on this terminal stretch of the road that used to be royal." (265) Through sex, Blanche DuBois is looking for both human contact and for "protection." (*Streetcar,* 141) Sounding much like Carol Cutrere, Princess tells Chance in *Sweet Bird of Youth:* "I have only one way to forget these things I don't want to remember and that's through the act of love-making. That's the only dependable distraction." (372) Sex is the satisfactory answer to man's quest only to the non-fugitive, to the man who belongs to the earth. The most articulate spokesman for the earthly position is Chicken, the most recent creation of Williams, from the play *Kingdom of Earth.* To him, sex is a possible path; it is everything: "There's nothing in the world, in this kingdom of earth, that can compare with one thing, and that one thing is what's able to happen between a man and a woman, just that thing, nothing more, is perfect. ... That's how I look at it, that's how I see it now, in this kingdom of earth." (107) But the Williams kingdom is clearly not an earthly kingdom.

The Williams theme and manner are most clearly seen in his frequent attempts to symbolize the fact that his kingdom is not of this earth. In *Orpheus Descending,* the theme statement about escaping corruption is encapsulated in a controlling symbol: the free little bird who is not corrupted by the earth, who escapes the earth by never touching it except to die, who is transparent, the color of the sky, who sleeps on the wind. Lady wants to be one of those birds, and Val echoes her: "Lots of people would like to be one of those birds and never be—corrupted." (42) Later, Carol is brought into the bird symbolism: "Little girl," Val says to her in a continuation of the child imagery which fills the play, "Little girl, you're transparent," and, "Well, then, fly away, little bird, fly away before you—get broke." (58) Lady clearly connects Val with the bird: "I was touched by your—strangeness, your strange talk. —That thing about birds with no feet so they have to sleep on the wind?—I said myself, 'This boy is a bird with no feet so he has to sleep on the wind.'" (79) And the very last scene of the play reminds us again of the bird, God's "one perfect creature," (42) who remains uncorrupted because he remained above the corrupting earth. As he does with this transparent-bird symbol, Wil-

liams often finds a central non-earthly symbol for the pure. Indeed, the bird—flying, freed from the earth—is a natural symbol
for the Williams theme, and it becomes his favorite one. Thus, in
Suddenly Last Summer, the jungle noises which, as in *The Night
of the Iguana,* represent the corruption of rotting earth, are contrasted with the pure song of a bird. At the climax of scene four,
when Catharine, by now clearly identified with the fugitives and
not with the earthly jungle, begins the true story of what happened "last summer," the stage direction sets the mood with the
symbol, the first sound in opposition to the jungle: "There is a
long pause. The raucous sounds in the garden fade into a bird-
song which is clear and sweet." (70) Similarly, the first sound
heard in *Sweet Bird of Youth,* which is a play about two aging
fugitives seeking escape from corruption, is this: "Outside the
windows there is heard the soft, urgent cries of birds." (341) And
the urgent cries of Chance and Princess continue throughout the
play. In *The Purification,* The Rancher tells of birds escaping
corrupting earth on purifying rain:

> The birds already, the swallows,
> before the rainstorm ceased,
> had begun to climb
> the atmosphere's clean spirals.   (55)

The sky and a star are the non-earthly symbols for the pure that
Williams uses in *This Property is Condemned.* Throughout this
strange little mood piece, the two doomed children muse about
the whiteness of the sky—"white as a clean piece of paper"—(199,
204, 206, 207) and sing about "the only star/ In my blue hea-ven."
(203, 204, 205, 206, 207) Other heavenly symbols of escape from
earth are used in both the early play, *The Strangest Kind of
Romance,* and in the latest play, *Kingdom of Earth.* The anonymous Old Man is saved from corrupting earth only by the cords
that tie him to heaven: "The roof is thin. Above it, the huge and
glittering wheel of heaven which spells a mystery to us. Fine—
invisible—cords of wonder—attach us to it. And so we are saved
and purified and exalted." (150) And Myrtle sings the words to
the song that, according to the stage directions in *Orpheus
Descending,* Val sings to himself several times in that earlier
play. The song is called *Heavenly Grass,* and is a lament in which
the singer tells of once, in daylight, walking in heavenly grass
although now, in nighttime, his feet can only "walk the earth."
The song, written by Tennessee Williams and set to music by

Paul Bowles, tells of the desire to escape again to heaven. (62)
It, of course, fits Val Xavier as well as it fits Myrtle. In *Milk
Train,* Williams turns to the mythical griffin for his non-earthly
symbol. We are told at the beginning of that play that the griffin,
"half lion, and half eagle," (5) an earthly animal trying to be a
heavenly one, is the "personal emblem" (6) of Mrs. Goforth, who,
like all of Williams' fugitives, is trying to go-forth. Her attempt
to escape has the power of the griffin: "a force in life that's almost
stronger than death." (66) And it is precisely in the non-earthly
that Mrs. Goforth seeks her release; in a trance she shouts: "Wind,
cold wind, clean, clean! Release! Relief! Escape. ..." (56) The
one Williams play which compromises, which makes its peace with
the corrupting earth, uses a non-earthly symbol in a different way
from the other plays. It is not quite non-earthly. Nonno's poem
at the climax of *The Night of the Iguana* tells of an orange branch
which observes that winter is coming and that it thus soon must
fall to the corrupting earth. Finally the branch does plummet
down and then begins

> An intercourse not well designed
> For beings of a golden kind
> Whose native green must arch above
> The earth's obscene, corrupting love.

Year after year new branches face the same fate, but with an existential courage. Nonno sees this as man's fate, to fall to earth—and,
like Shannon, comes to accept it. (123)

   To the Williams hero no happy escape from the earth is possible, and so most of the fugitives remain, questing and lonely;
or they find madness or despair or death. *Orpheus Descending,*
which records a quest, is, in its several versions and in its reflections in all of Williams' work, itself a quest. It is a key part of
that larger search which Williams contends is the very purpose of
both life and of the theater:

> I would say that there is something much bigger in life and death
> than we have become aware of (or adequately recorded) in our
> living and dying. And, further, to compound this shameless ro-
> manticism, I would say that our serious theatre is a *search* for that
> something that is not yet successful, but is still going on.[5]

---

[5]*Ibid.,* p. 337.

Tennessee Williams:
A Desperate Morality

by Arthur Ganz

"Moralist" may seem a perverse appellation for a playwright whose works concern rape, castration, cannibalism, and other bizarre activities, but in examining the plays of Tennessee Williams it is exactly this point—that he is a moralist, not a psychologist—that should be borne in mind. Williams' powers of characterization are real, but they are not his central gifts: witness *Cat on a Hot Tin Roof* which contains Big Daddy, one of Williams' most striking characterizations, but which fails nonetheless because in this play Williams' moral vision becomes blurred, and it is in the strength of that moral vision that his power as a playwright lies.

Admittedly, Williams' morality is a special one, but it is a consistent ethic, giving him a point of view from which he can judge the actions of people. Yet to say that Williams rewards those who, by his standards, are virtuous and punishes those who are evil is to oversimplify, for in the world of Williams' plays, good often has a curious affinity with evil. Beneath the skin of the Christlike martyr destroyed by the cruel forces of death and sterility lies the disease, the transgression that had made the author destroy him, while the character most fiercely condemned may at the same time be the one for whom pardon is most passionately demanded. From the self-lacerating desire simultaneously to praise and to punish stems the violence that agitates so many of Williams' plays.

To understand this violence in Williams' work we must first look at his gentlest plays, those in which the virtuous are rewarded, for here is most directly revealed the morality by which the guilty are later so terribly condemned. Surprisingly, one of Williams' most significant plays is an indifferent and undramatic one-acter about the death of D. H. Lawrence, only slightly redeemed by the audacious title, *I Rise in Flame, Cried the Phoenix*. It gives us the central fact we must have to understand Williams' work, the nature of his literary parentage. In art, a son must seek out a father who will give him what he needs. Williams needed a rationale for the sexual obsessions that dominate his work, and this Lawrence seemed to give him.

Whether or not Williams assesses Lawrence correctly is, for an understanding of Williams' own work, irrelevant. What does matter here is that at a very early point in his career (*I Rise in Flame* dates from 1941) Williams saw Lawrence as the great writer who "celebrates the body" and himself apparently as that writer's disciple. A disciple, however, is not invariably the best advocate of his master's doctrine; Williams began his career as a neo-Lawrencian writer by basing a very bad play on one of Lawrence's short stories. Called *You Touched Me* (also the title of Lawrence's story), this early work (copyrighted in 1942) is indeed of slight interest in itself, but it is revelatory in the distortions it introduces in transforming the original material and additionally important for establishing the structural pattern of two of Williams' more attractive plays, *The Glass Menagerie* and *The Rose Tattoo*.

Williams' play (written in collaboration with Donald Windham) becomes a stunning vulgarization of Lawrence's tale as the younger sister of the story, Emmie, is changed into a frigid maiden aunt representing "aggressive sterility," and the heroine, Matilda, a thin, large-nosed woman of thirty-two in Lawrence's version, is turned into a pale girl of twenty, the cliché of the frail, sheltered maiden. Hadrian, in the story a neat, scheming little soldier with a common-looking mustache, is transformed into "a clean-cut, muscular young man in the dress uniform of a lieutenant in the Royal Canadian Air Force," much given to speeches about faith and the glories of the future. And finally, the elderly pottery manufacturer is turned into a spry, if alcoholic, old sea captain. Given this set of popular-magazine characters, the play has no trouble reaching its predictable conclusion as the captain helps the handsome airman defeat the aunt and win the shy Matilda.

What is significant is not that Williams, working with unfamiliar material at this early stage in his career, should write a poor play, but that, while retaining the essential Lawrencian theme, he should so alter Lawrence's material as to produce an unmistakable Tennessee Williams play. The light but subtle characterizations around which Lawrence built his story are in the play coarsened to the point where the characters are obviously broken down into good guys (those in favor of sexuality—Hadrian, Matilda, and the captain) and bad guys (those opposed to it—the frigid Emmie and her suitor, an impotent clergyman). Williams here is very little of a psychologist; rather he is a moralist, a special kind of sexual moralist, whose creations are judged virtuous only if they owe their allegiance to the sexual impulse. Though Williams distorted and sentimentalized Lawrence's story, its central action, the awakening to life, and particularly to sexual life, of one who had previously been dead to it, was one that Williams, with an unquestioning faith in Romantic vitalism, saw as profoundly good, developed roughly in *You Touched Me*, and then placed at the center of two of his most pleasing works, *The Glass Menagerie* and *The Rose Tattoo*.

In each of these plays a woman who has retired from life is confronted by a man, like Hadrian (named for the conquering emperor from the warm south) the sexual force designed to release her from bondage. But although he succeeds in one case, in the other he fails. The reasons for this difference are worth noting.

The figure of Laura in *The Glass Menagerie* has clearly been developed from that of Matilda of *You Touched Me*, who is described by Williams as having "the delicate, almost transparent quality of glass." Both are shy, fragile creatures, remote from the life around them. But whereas Hadrian awakens Matilda to life, Laura's gentleman caller gives her only a momentary glimpse of normal existence before she drifts back into the fantasy world of glass animals. Though in Williams' moral system the rejection of life is a crime demanding punishment, Laura is adjudged innocent; she is not frigid and hostile; she does not reject but rather is rejected, not because of her limp, which does not exist in "Portrait of a Girl in Glass," Williams' own short story upon which he based his play, but because she is the sensitive, misunderstood exile, a recurrent character in Williams' work, one of the fugitive kind, who are too fragile to live in a malignant world.

The vigorous Serafina Delle Rose of *The Rose Tattoo*, however, openly rejects life after the death of her husband, leading an existence as solitary and sterile as that of Laura among the glass animals. Only when the truck driver Alvaro Mangiacavallo, who has the face of a clown but the body of her husband, appears does she disclaim her rejection and return to the world of life and sexuality. Again it was to this theme of the acceptance of life that Williams turned when he converted his one-acter *27 Wagons Full of Cotton* into the script for the film *Baby Doll*. The vengeful sadist Vicarro becomes in the film the Lawrencian lover Vacarro who awakens the virginal heroine to sexual life.

A later and less likable work *Period of Adjustment* belongs with this group of gentle dramas, for at its conclusion the two couples achieve sexual harmony as the phallically named community of High Point sinks further into the cavern beneath it. But before the playwright allows these consummations, each of the two men who are its central figures is humiliated and forced to admit his weakness. They have been great fighters and war heroes, but one has abased himself to marry for money and must be bullied by his father-in-law and forced to accept his unattractive wife before he can be forgiven. The other, who has rejected his homosexual nature or at least pretended to a virility he does not possess, must publicly admit his weakness before he is bedded down, blissfully it is assumed, with his hysterical bride. Ultimately the play falls apart because the author, vaguely hostile to his masculine characters, cannot decide whether they are to be forgiven or to be punished.

Though the impulse to forgive has produced attractive plays in Williams' work, the need to punish has led to his most powerful dramas. Invariably, the central crime in Williams' moral code has been that from which Matilda and Serafina were preserved, the rejection of life. The theme of punishment for an act of rejection is at the center of a group of plays very different from that already examined, but it is expressed most explicitly in a short story, "Desire and the Black Masseur," from the volume *One Arm and Other Stories.* In this story the central character, Walter Burns, who has yielded to the loveless life around him, is haunted by a nameless desire that is fulfilled only by the manipulations of a gigantic black masseur who first beats Burns and then, as the story veers toward fantasy, kills him and proceeds to eat his body in the atmosphere of a sacred ritual. Bizarre and perhaps a little ridiculous, the story nevertheless reveals much about the cast of mind of its author. For him, Walter Burns is a broad symbol of human guilt and desire for atonement. Williams claims that the sins of the world "are really only its partialities, its incompletions, and these are what sufferings must atone for." His ritual treatment of "the principle of atonement, the surrender of the self to violent treatment by others" suggests a wider vision comprehending the world and the place of suffering in it. "And meantime," Williams concludes, "slowly, with barely a thought of so doing, the earth's whole population twisted and writhed beneath the manipulation of night's black fingers, and the white ones of day with skeletons splintered and flesh reduced to pulp, as out of this unlikely problem, the answer, perfection, was slowly evolved through torture."

We need not believe that anything like perfection could be evolved from the process here described (nor linger over the element of erotic gratification in these images) to see its significance in relation to Williams' major work. The story concerns an elaborate, ritual punishment of one who has rejected life, and, more specifically, rejected sexuality. A whole group of Williams' plays including some of his most remarkable—*A Streetcar Named Desire, Summer and Smoke, Cat on a Hot Tin Roof* and *Suddenly Last Summer*—is centered on this idea of the terrible punishment visited on one because of an act of sexual rejection.

The stage action of *A Streetcar Named Desire*, still Williams' finest play, consists almost entirely of the punishment that its heroine, Blanche DuBois, endures as atonement for her act of rejection, her sin in terms of Williams' morality. Since Williams begins the action of his play at a late point in the story, the act itself is not played out on stage but only referred to. Not realizing that she is describing the crime that condemns her, Blanche tells Mitch of her discovery that her adored young husband was a homosexual and of the consequences of her disgust and revulsion:

> *Blanche.* ...He'd stuck the revolver into his mouth, and fired—so that the back of his head had been—blown away! *(She sways and covers her face.)* It was because—on the dance floor—unable to stop myself—I'd suddenly said—"I saw! I know! You disgust me..." And then the searchlight which had been turned on the world was turned off again and never for one moment since has there been any light that's stronger than this—kitchen—candle....

While Blanche delivers this speech and the ones surrounding it, the polka to which she and her husband had danced, the Varsouviana, sounds in the background. At the end of the play, when Blanche sees the doctor who is to lead her off to the asylum, her punishment is complete and the Varsouviana sounds again, linking her crime to its retribution. As Blanche flees from the doctor, "the Varsouviana is filtered into a weird distortion accompanied

by the cries and noises of the jungle." These symbolize simultaneously Blanche's chaotic state and the instrument of her
destruction, Stanley Kowalski, the complete sensual animal, the
equivalent in function to the black masseur.

Although Kowalski's primary function, to destroy Blanche, is
clear, there are certain ambiguities evoked by this role. By becoming Blanche's destroyer, Kowalski also becomes the avenger
of her homosexual husband. Although he is Williams' exaggeration of the Lawrencian lover, it is appropriate from Williams'
point of view that Kowalski should to some degree be identified
with the lonely homosexual who had been driven to suicide, for
Williams saw Lawrence not only as the propagandist of sexual
vitality but as the symbol of the solitary, rejected exile. (In the
poem "Cried the Fox" from Williams' collection, *In the Winter
of Cities*, Lawrence is seen as the fox pursued by the cruel hounds.)
But however gratifying it may be to identify the embodiment of
admired male sexuality with the exiled artist and thus by implication with the exiled homosexual, the identification must remain
tenuous.

Kowalski, though an avenger, is as guilty of destroying Blanche
as she is of destroying her husband. For Blanche, who has lost
the plantation Belle Reve, the beautiful dream of a life of gracious
gentility, is an exile like the homosexual; her tormentor, the ape-
like Kowalski, from one point of view the representative of Lawrencian vitality, is from another the brutal, male torturer of a
lonely spirit. However compassionately Blanche is viewed, she
nevertheless remains a woman who, in effect, has killed her husband by her cruelty, and her attempts to turn away from death to
its opposite—"the opposite is desire," as Blanche herself says—
are fruitless. Even as she tells Mitch about her promiscuity, a
Mexican woman stands at one side of the stage selling flowers for
the dead. *"Flores para los muertos,"* she calls, *"flores—flores."*

A variant on the act of rejection is performed in Scene Six of
Summer and Smoke. The characters are similar to those already
encountered: the frail, spinsterish Southern girl with her sen-
sualtiy repressed by a puritanical background; the man who is
seeking spiritual relief through a sexual union. Like many of
Williams' characters he needs love as relief from solitude. At
one point, while giving Alma an ironic anatomy lecture, he shouts,
"This part down here is the sex—which is hungry for love because it is sometimes lonesome." At the crucial moment she rejects his advances and rushes off. Like Blanche, Alma has

committed the sin of rejection, is condemned to be tormented by the very urges she had fled from, and turns to promiscuity. Yet because her sin has been somewhat mitigated by her realization of it, there is a suggestion at the end of the play that the traveling salesman she has picked up may lead her to salvation rather than destruction.

A later play, *The Night of the Iguana* (a reworking of Williams' short story of the same title), has, like *Summer and Smoke*, affinities with both the severity of *Streetcar* and the gentleness of *The Glass Menagerie.* Its heroine, Hannah Jelkes, a New England spinster artist, is placed in a position that closely parallels that of Blanche DuBois. But unlike Blanche, when confronted by an appeal for help from one with abnormal sexual inclinations (a homosexual in the original story, but converted for stage purposes to an unfrocked minister with a taste for pubescent girls), instead of driving him to suicide, she offers him what help she can. That help, however, is limited. When he asks to be allowed to travel with her, she cannot accept him. Because like Laura and Alma she is too delicate and repressed to take on a full emotional relationship, Shannon's rescue is finally left to the sexually vital hotel proprietor, while Hannah must continue in loveless solitude. By her sympathy for Shannon and for the pathetic fetishist she had previously aided, she has earned, however, a fate far gentler than the breakdown meted out to Blanche and to her own predecessor in the original story.

In *Cat on a Hot Tin Roof,* however, Williams produces something much nearer the pattern of *Streetcar.* In fact, from one point of view *Cat* is simply a reworking of the materials of the earlier play, but with a crucial change that made it almost impossible for Williams to bring his play to a reasonable conclusion. Again we are presented with a work in which the motivating figure does not appear, and again that figure is the rejected homosexual. But because the rejector, the sinner who must atone, is not a woman but a man, certain problems arise. The audience, although it sympathizes with Blanche, can accept her as guilty. She could not only have given her husband love instead of contempt but at least the possibility of a heterosexual life. But, confronted with Skipper's telephoned confession of a homosexual attachment, Brick has fewer possibilities before him. The audience is likely to feel that sympathetic understanding is the most that Brick can offer—short of admitting to a similar inclination. Yet Williams, although he is ambiguous about several points in this play, is not ambiguous about Brick's guilt. Big Daddy himself, who despises mendacity, condemns his son. "You! dug the grave of your friend," he cries, "and kicked him in it!—before you'd face the truth with him!" But it is beyond Big Daddy's power to explain how Brick was to do so.

Yet in a play designed for the commercial theater, Williams could not then openly punish Brick for failing to be an honest homosexual. When he showed *Cat* to the representative of that theater, Elia Kazan, and Kazan suggested certain changes, Williams accepted his advice. As a result, the comparatively optimistic third act performed on Broadway contains the shift in Brick's character that leads to the suggestion that his castration, symbolized obviously enough by his broken ankle, will not be permanent. There is no reason to disbelieve Williams' claim that he had agreed to Kazan's suggestions to retain his interest, but it is worth noting that by mitigating Brick's punishment, Williams was relieved of the necessity of asking his audience to agree that Brick deserved castration for an act much of that audience would not have considered criminal.

Although the tentativeness of Williams' condemnation of Brick makes it difficult to know whether Brick was so condemned for rejecting his homosexual friend or for rejecting his own homosexual nature, in *Cat*, at least, homosexuality itself carries no stigma. Although Big Daddy is a man of almost ostentatious virility (the latent anti-feminism in his sexual revulsion from Big Mama is not stressed) as well as the most powerful and sympathetic figure in the play, he had served and respected the two idyllically conceived homosexuals Straw and Ochello, and received his land from them as a kind of benediction. Yet in *Suddenly Last Summer,* a later play of what may be called the "punishment" group, Williams has produced a work in which the homosexual— so often for him the symbol of the lonely, rejected exile—becomes the rejector, the sinner who must be punished.

But neither this shift in Williams' usual pattern nor the *bizarrerie* of the play's atmosphere should conceal the fact that *Suddenly Last Summer* follows closely the structure of the other plays in this group. Once more the pivotal figure, the exiled homosexual, has met a violent death before the opening of the play. As the sterile Brick is contrasted with Big Daddy, the life-giving father of *Cat,* so the cruel Sebastian is played off against the loving and merciful Catharine who gives herself not, it seems, out of desire but as an act of rescue. "We walked through the wet grass to the great misty oaks," she says, "as if somebody was calling us for help there." If we remember that this act of rescue is exactly what Blanche, Alma, and Brick failed to perform, we realize that Williams means us to accept Catharine as entirely good. Although Sebastian is, as we expect him to be, the loveless rejector who is punished for his sins, there is a surprising similarity between his vision of a world dominated by remorseless cruelty — as expressed in the description of the Encantadas, the Galápagos Islands, where baby sea turtles are killed and devoured by carnivorous birds of prey — and the vision of a world undergoing perpetual punishment expressed in "Desire and the Black Masseur." However, in punishing Sebastian, Williams is not disclaiming this vision. Sebastian's sin lay not in perceiving the world as, for Williams, it is, but in his believing, with a pride bordering on *hubris,* that he could exalt himself above his kind, that he could feed upon people like one of the devouring birds of the Encantadas. As always in Williams, the punishment monstrously fits the crime. As Sebastian had cruelly watched the turtles being eaten, as he had fed the fruit flies to the devouring plant, so he is fed to the band of children whom he has perverted and is devoured by them.

Sebastian's crime then is the very one committed by Blanche, Alma, and by Brick. He has turned away from his suffering fellow creatures and, instead of offering love, has offered hate. And yet there is a difficulty for the spectator in accepting the nature of Sebastian's punishment, however fierce he knows Williams' morality to be. It is not merely that Sebastian's fate is so violently grotesque but that, unlike Blanche and Brick, he has not performed a specific act that brings his punishment upon him; he is punished for what he is rather than for what he does. He is not only a rejector but also a homosexual, always in Williams' work an object simultaneously of sympathy and of revulsion. There is an intimate connection between the guilty rejector and the martyred homosexual; the punishment visited on the former regularly echoes the fate of the latter, so that the two characters are not always distinguishable. In *Streetcar* the rejector and the homosexual victim were separate, but both met desperate ends. In the ambiguous Brick these figures began to converge, and in *Suddenly Last Summer* they have completely coalesced.

They remain linked in *Kingdom of Earth* — called the *Seven Descents of Myrtle* in its New York acting version — in which the sickly and effeminate Lot Ravenstock (in his search for an elegantly Southern name with sinister connotations Williams skirts dangerously close to Gaylord Ravenal) attempts to keep his property from falling into the hands of Chicken, his virile half brother. That Chicken is half black and that his domain is a rough kitchen are evident signs of an irresistible earthiness. Thus Lot's pathetic effort to keep the land from Chicken through his unconsummated marriage to an amiable hysteric named Myrtle is an ultimate denial of life. As the procreative flood sweeps over the farm, however, Chicken easily takes over wife and land while Lot expires of tuberculosis after dressing himself in the clothes of his adored mother. Though Chicken is a mere caricature of virility, Lot, the despairing transvestite, reveals a certain complexity, for he is at once ineffectual victim and cruel life-denier.

Once again we see the ambiguity in the vision of corruption pervading so much of Williams' work. Not only must retribution be visited on the cruel rejector of the homosexual victim, but the homosexual himself—sterile and guilty—must be punished as well. Again and again in Williams' plays those whom he most desperately wishes to perceive as innocent—whom he sometimes does so perceive—are ultimately adjudged guilty. A group of Williams' plays—*Camino Real, Orpheus Descending,* and *Sweet Bird of Youth*—develop this vision of pervasive corruption through the story of a wanderer, usually only dubiously innocent, who enters a world of blatant evil and is destroyed by it.

Williams has said flatly that the sinister fantasy world of the Camino Real "is nothing more nor less than my conception of the time and world that I live in." It is a time in which greed and brutality are the ruling forces and a world in which those pathetic souls who attempt to show some affection for their fellow creatures are remorselessly crushed and then thrown into a barrel and carted away by the street cleaners. Although admittedly a nightmare world, it does not differ in any essential way from the American South as it appears in *Orpheus Descending* and *Sweet Bird of Youth.* Here too is a nightmare world where greed, brutality, and sterility rule, and where those who love are castrated or burned alive. As an epigraph to *Camino Real* Williams has selected the opening lines of Dante's *Inferno;* the setting of the play is the place to which Orpheus descended.

As we would expect, the ruler of hell is Death; more specifically, he is the god of sterility. In *Camino Real,* Gutman, the proprietor of the Siete Mares hotel, is cruel and sinister enough, but he always remains a little remote from the action. Had Williams personified the evil of the place in a single powerful figure, he might have been less able to end the play with its suggestion (however unconvincing) of optimism. Like Gutman, Jabe Torrance, the proprietor of the mercantile store in *Orpheus Descending,* takes little direct part in the action, but he is a far more heavily drawn figure and a far more violent antagonist. The evil creature who destroys life wherever he can find it is, as Williams describes him in a stage direction, "death's self and malignancy." He is not only "death's self," but the personification of sterility and impotence. Nurse Porter, who seems to have supernatural perception, can tell at a glance that Lady is pregnant and that Jabe is not the father. As he had burned the wine garden of Lady's father where the fig tree blossomed and true lovers met, so he calls upon the fires of the hell of impotence to burn her and her lover. (It should be noted that while Williams' work has changed in tone from the gentleness of *You Touched Me,* where the impotent clergyman was a figure of fun, it has not shifted in point of view.) Even more heavily than Jabe, however, Boss Finley of *Sweet Bird of Youth* is drawn as the symbol of malignant impotence. Miss Lucy, his mistress, has scrawled in lipstick across the ladies' room mirror, "Boss Finley is too old to cut the mustard." By implication, at least, he had presided over the castration of an innocent Negro and, as the play ends, is about to preside over that of its hero, Chance Wayne. (The treatments of racism here and of Nazism in *The Night of The Iguana,* both largely irrelevant to the drama, are calculated to appeal to a liberal New York audience.)

When Boss Finley's impotence is contrasted with Chance's attitude toward the emasculation of the Negro, the natures of the opposing forces in the play become clear. "You know what that is, don't you?" Chance cries. "Sex-envy is what that is, and the revenge for sex-envy which is a wide-spread disease that I have run into personally too often for me to doubt its existence or any manifestation." Boss Finley, Chance says, "was just called down from the hills to preach hate. I was born here to make love." Each of the three wanderers, Kilroy, Val, and Chance, had been born to make love, but each has been wounded by a hostile world. Kilroy's heart condition prevents him from continuing as a prizefighter or from staying with his "real true woman." Of the three he is the only true innocent and, significantly, the only one who is alone. Val and Chance both speak of the corrupt lives they have lived and of the waning of their youths, but in reality each is bound not by time or by his past but by his relationship with an older woman.

Williams' sense of the symbolic corruption embodied in such a relationship is most clearly suggested in his novella, *The Roman Spring of Mrs. Stone.* In that book a once beautiful actress, who had married lovelessly "to escape copulation," finds herself an aging widow reduced to buying sexuality from the lowest and most sinister of gigolos. What is most striking here is not the familiar punishment-for-rejection pattern but the fact that Mrs. Stone's real inclinations are toward lesbianism. Her most vivid sexual experience had been an abortive moment with a school-girl friend. In addition, during a brief affair with a young actor, she had enveloped him in an embrace "in a manner that was more like a man's with a girl, and to which he submitted in a way that also suggested a reversal of gender."

If the suggestion of homosexuality that underlies the relation-ship between the older woman and the younger man in *The Roman Spring of Mrs. Stone* is extended to *Orpheus* and *Sweet Bird* (in each case the ostensible woman is an older person having a forbidden affair with a beautiful young man), these works fit very easily into the pattern of ambiguity we have observed in the "punishment" group. From one point of view we have the wander-ing love-giver—Val, whose phallic guitar is an obvious symbol, and Chance, who has a speech about his vocation as a love-maker —who enters the nightmare world of Hades in *Orpheus* and of what the Princess in *Sweet Bird* calls "the ogre's country at the top of the beanstalk, the country of the flesh-hungry, blood-thirsty ogre." There he attempts to rescue a lover, and in the at-tempt he is brutally destroyed by the giant. (Since "Jack and the Beanstalk" is a classic Oedipal fantasy, in which a boy destroys a father symbol and thereafter possesses his mother undisturbed, the imagery here has an extra level of appropriateness.) In a special variation of the wanderer material, *The Milk Train Doesn't Stop Here Anymore,* the beautiful young man comes to a ruthless but vital older woman not to rescue her through love but to preside benignly over her death.

From another point of view, however, the wanderer is not innocent but corrupt. Beneath the apparent heterosexual re-lationship lies one that is homosexual (the "eccentric" were among Chance's lovers), and from it spreads an aura of guilt that pervades the plays. Chance calculates his age by the level of rot in him, and Val, who has been "on a party" in the bars of New Orleans since he was fifteen, is trying vainly to flee from his past. As before, the seeming-innocent is himself guilty and must be hideously punished. Once his moral sense has been appeased, however, Williams can allow himself the luxury of a sentimental apotheosis. *Orpheus* and *Sweet Bird* take place at Easter, and in both plays there is a suggestion that the dead wanderer should be viewed as a martyred Christ figure whose spirit is resurrected in Carol Cutrere and the Princess. (Whereas the suggestion of resurrection is not incredible in *Orpheus,* the idea that the pathetic gigolo of *Sweet Bird* could be a Christlike martyr is merely bizarre, as is the notion that the significantly named Christopher in *Milk Train* could be an "Angel of Death" who would "mean God" to the dying Mrs. Goforth.) Yet, whatever the wanderer's ultimate state as an object of reverence, he is allowed to reach that exalted condition only after he has been punished and destroyed.

The absence of this conflict between the need to condemn and the desire to pardon is what distinguishes Williams' later plays and what, more than anything else, accounts for their weaknesses. Several of them—*In the Bar of a Tokyo Hotel, Small Craft Warnings,* and *Out Cry*—are indeed rambling discourses with little or no sense of movement toward a climax. (One is sometimes tempted to wish that playwrights might be forbidden by law from reading *Waiting for Godot* or the third act of *Man and Superman.*) Moreover, *The Mutilated* and *Gnädiges Fräulein* are attempts to use elements of the absurdist style, one for which Williams has no essential affinity. But these miscalculations in technique and style are merely symptoms of an underlying problem. For whatever reason, in these plays Williams has ceased to project the opposing elements of his consciousness outward into self-sustaining dramatic entities, characters who stand in conflict with each other and whom Williams judges to be innocent or guilty. Now all are innocent. All significant characters are pathetic victims—of time, of their own passions, of immutable circumstances—and all receive the playwright's sympathy in unbounded measure. But since these characters are so recognizably close to Williams and his concerns, the pity extended to them is ultimately self-pity, an emotion of very limited dramatic appeal.

The most obviously personal, and even self-indulgent, of these late plays is *Out Cry,* in which a brother and sister (suggestive of the figures in *The Glass Menagerie*), the leaders of a traveling acting company, find themselves immured alone in a mysterious foreign theatre. There—on a stage dominated by a terrifying black statue, the symbol of their psychic torments—they act out a play about a brother and sister immured alone in a house dominated by ghosts of a past domestic tragedy. Unfortunately the Pirandellesque element of the play within the play is handled without theatrical flair, and the obsessive concern with fear and retreat becomes stultifying. Even less appealing is the distracted artist of *In the Bar of a Tokyo Hotel,* whose madness makes him the easy victim of his cruelly vital wife, herself a victim of passing time. This contrast between inert pathos and comparative vitality, regularly presented though pairs of women in the later works (Celeste and Trinket in *The Mutilated,* the Molly-Polly figures and the Fräulein in *Gnädiges Fräulein,* Leona and Violet in *Small Craft Warnings*), runs through Williams' other plays of the late sixties and early seventies. But whereas this motif was handled with evocative complexity in Williams' earlier work (Amanda and Laura, Stanley and Blanche, Maggie and Brick are the most obvious examples), here everything is awash in a flood of sentimentality that invites, though it cannot induce, total sympathy for the suffering victims.

But Williams' best work derived its force from the strength of his moral temper, which led him to censure even what he most wished to exalt. Williams remains committed to the Romantic dictum inherent in his neo-Lawrencian point of view, that the natural equals the good, that the natural instincts welling up out of the subconscious depths—and particularly the sexual instinct, whatever form it may take—are to be trusted absolutely. But Williams was far too strong a moralist, far too permeated with a sense of sin, to accept such an idea with equanimity. However pathetic he made the martyred homosexual, however seemingly innocent the wandering love-giver, the moral strength that made him punish the guilty Blanche also impelled him to condemn Brick and Chance. Because he was condemning what he most desired to pardon, in order to condemn at all he sometimes had to do so with ferocious violence.

This violence, however grotesque, was never in itself the real problem in Williams' work. Nor were the disguises, transpositions, even evasions in his handling of the theme of homosexuality. They were, in fact, arguably a source of his strength, for they protected him from over-simplifications and encouraged the genuine ambiguity and complexity of his attitude to take symbolic form in his plays. Williams' problem is not that he dealt obliquely with homosexuality (the oblique view, after all, often reveals things that are invisible when the object is contemplated directly) but that he has expressed all too openly, especially of late but to some degree from the first, the impulse to sentimentalize. One of the central dangers confronting a Romantic writer is that his commitment to the idea of natural innocence will lead him not only to see this quality as inherent in the child or man in a state of nature (Kowalski is a curious late variant on the Noble Savage), but to affirm its existence in characters who have lived all too fully in the fallen world of mortal corruption. When this easy sympathy is extended without qualification, Williams' work slips over the edge of control into the maudlin just as it slips over the opposite edge into hysteria when the opposing impulse to punish —the self or others—is dominant. When these conflicting impulses are held in some degree of balance and Williams and judge his characters with perception, he is a moralist of some force, a playwright of some distinction.

The Search for God in the Plays
of Tennessee Williams

by Thomas P. Adler

In Tennessee Williams' *Suddenly Last Summer* (1958), Catharine Holly—whose surname we associate with the Christmas celebration of God's revelation of Himself to man—remarks: "Somebody said or wrote, once: 'We're all of us children in a vast kindergarten trying to spell God's name with the wrong alphabet blocks!'" As John J. Fritscher has noticed, Williams' characters oftentimes arrange their alphabet blocks so that they spell "God of Wrath." Fritscher accounts for this tendency not by anything inherent in the characters themselves, but attributes it instead to the psychic wounds left by the playwright's "own experience of wrath and love": "The God-image, in short, becomes delineated in terms of the father-image as experienced in early childhood. ...Thus as a personal unresolved Oedipus complex becomes... projected on the word *God*, it is small wonder that the word receives angry connotations of alienation and violence." But as Fritscher also suggests, there is sometimes an arrangement of the blocks so that they read "God of Love"; for Williams this second spelling is the favored one, since the way we conceive of God is also the way we will see our neighbor and ourself. So "sin in Williams" is "not so much an offense against some God, but an establishment of alienation between people which keeps them from meaning God to each other," which prevents "person-to-person god-ness." It is Fritscher's contention, however—again indulging himself in some psychologizing about Williams—that to live under "a New Testament God of Love offering a cycle of need-submission-communication-salvation," demanding as it does "surrender of the creature," is potentially as psychologically

"The Search for God in the Plays of Tennessee Williams" by Thomas P. Adler. From *Renascence*, 26 (Autumn 1973), 48-56. Copyright © 1973 by *Renascence*. Reprinted by permission of the author and the publisher.

crippling as living under "an Old Testament God of Wrath ruling over a semi-Calvinistic cycle of guilt-submission-atonement-uncertainty": "To surrender the ego, a problem not only Oedipally difficult, but also dangerous because of the advantage it gives the other, is the only route Williams sees to balanced creature-Creator relations." (John J. Fritscher, "Some Attitudes and a Posture: Religious Metaphor and Ritual in Tennessee Williams' Query of the American God," *Modern Drama*, XIII, September 1970.)

If we prescind, however, from reading Williams' major plays as reflections of the author's own psyche and focus instead on the characters' motivations, we discover that the self-effacement ordinarily involved in meaning God to another person, while "difficult" since it requires not using or abusing the other for one's own aggrandisement, is never really "dangerous." Abnegation of self is, paradoxically, the only avenue to fulfillment of self and, at the same time, transcendence of self. As the Doctor explains to the priest in *The Rose Tattoo* (1951), people "find God in each other. And when they lose each other, they lose God and they're lost." Only through such a reciprocal dependency can a person escape that solipsistic obsession with self which Williams has defined as hell: "Hell is yourself. When you ignore other people completely, that is hell" (quoted in "The Angel of the Odd," *Time*, LXXIX, March 9, 1962, 53).

One reason why Williams characters frequently close their eyes to the needs of others is that they find some trait in those around them that disgusts them. In order to mean God to the other, one must be able to say, along with Hannah Jelkes in *The Night of the Iguana* (1961), "Nothing human disgusts me unless it's unkind, violent." If one has such limitless compassion, he will never become so obsessed with the evil in himself or others that he denies the possibility of the good, nor will he be deliberately cruel to the other or sit in judgment upon him. So Hannah does not succumb to disgust or despair when she hears Shannon's story about an isolated incident of coprophagy, just as earlier she maintained her equanimity when the underwear fetishist requested a piece of her clothing. Sympathetic to all human needs, she understood his request not as something "dirty"—as Shannon would name it—but rather as "a love experience," since it called for a response on her part to a "degree or depth of loneliness" she had never before encountered in one of God's creatures. For in Williams, outcries for help require diverse responses, governed not by any preconceived notions of ethical behavior but instead by human need, our own or that of others. So in *Confessional* (1970) —revised under the title *Small-Craft Warnings* for its 1972 New York production—it is the need for a furtive touch under the table between Violet and Monk; Leona feels "it's a pitiful thing to have to reach under a table to find some reason to live," and yet, at the same time, understands that by doing so Violet is "worshipping her idea of God Almighty in her personal church." Or the response, on a different level, might be Kilroy's decision, recounted in *Camino Real* (1953), to leave his wife and sacrifice the warmth of "some one you're used to. And that you KNOW LOVES you," in order to protect his wife from the anguish of being tied to "a broken-down champ," with "the earth still turning and her obliged to turn with it, not out—of dark into light but out of light into dark."

The motifs of allowing disgust for something human to prevent one's aiding another in time of need, as well as the possibility of bringing God to the other, are both evident in Williams' plays as early as *A Streetcar Named Desire* (1947). The event in the past most responsible for Blanche's present instability was her rejection of her young husband when she discovered his homosexuality. Her judgment, "You disgust me,"—albeit impulsive and hardly an act of deliberate cruelty—drove him to suicide. That she is still hounded by guilt over her failure is suggested musically by the strains of the Varsouviana which still haunt her. Like Nina Leeds in O'Neill's *Strange Interlude*, Blanche tried unsuccessfully to alleviate her guilt by a string of promiscuities, which she regarded as chances not to fail others as she had her husband. She enters the play in need of someone to love and reassure her, of someone to mean God to her by helping her refind a belief in her own humanity. Blanche thinks she has found that person in Mitch, and "sometimes—there's God—so quickly!" But just as she failed Allan in passing judgment upon him, so, too, Mitch rejects Blanche when he learns of her debaucheries, destroying any hope, however slight, that she might regain her mental stability.

This pattern of Blanche's rejection of Allan and Mitch's rejection of Blanche is repeated in Brick's rejection of Skipper, recounted in *Cat on a Hot Tin Roof* (1955). Fearing that Skipper's words would destroy an ideal friendship by turning it into something unnatural and dirty, Brick refused to listen and hung up the phone just before Skipper's suicide. Now Brick, like Blanche before him, feels a persistent guilt over his failure to have had the necessary openness to respond to the plea of another even at cost to himself, and he assuages his guilt with alcohol. He is more fortunate than Blanche, though, in finding someone stronger than Mitch who can restore to him his sense of worth and self-respect. Brick's wife Maggie, like Hannah, realizes that what "you weak, beautiful people who give up with such grace...need is someone to take hold of you—gently, with love, and hand your life back to you, like something gold you let go of—and I can!"

Blanche and Brick, lacking the wisdom of a Hannah or a Maggie, each assumed the role of a wrathful God and passed judgment upon another person; now both of them need some assurance that a loving God exists. Since Williams conceives of God as anthropomorphic, made in man's own image and likeness, the assurance that Blanche and Brick crave can come only from another person who reaches out to them with love.

There are three male characters in Williams who become so obsessed with the evil in themselves and in those around them that they transfer this evil to God, creating a God devoid of any goodness or love. Two of these characters, Sebastian Venable in *Suddenly Last Summer* and Chicken Ravenstock in *Kingdom of Earth* (1968), deny themselves the possibility of redemption because of their own distorted vision of God; the third, T. Lawrence Shannon in *Night of the Iguana*, is saved because Hannah helps him perceive just how distorted his vision of God really is.

Suddenly Last Summer is a modern morality play, revealing not what the good is, or what God is, but rather what evil is, and what God is not. Sebastian went looking for a clear image of God in the Encantadas islands, and thinks he found the desired image in the birds of prey devouring the newborn turtles. Since Sebastian himself lives a basically predatory life, using his mother Violet as a crutch for his poetic efforts and both his mother and his cousin Catharine as procurers for his homosexual liaisons, he mistakenly, yet understandably, equates his savage vision with a cruel God who created a hideous world where men attack their fellowmen. Instead of entering into communion with other people, Sebastian inverts the normal flow of love, turning it back in upon himself. As a poet, also, he fails to communicate, for he is essentially a private poet whose only audience is his mother. Sebastian finally sacrifices himself to his personal image of God the devourer as the "children that looked like a flock of plucked birds" cannibalistically consume him in a sort of black sacrament. This is Williams' clearest warning that the worst possible evil is to become so obsessed with evil that you lose belief in any good or love, and thus risk being destroyed by your own vision of evil. As Paul J. Hurley concluded in his excellent article on *Summer:* "What his drama proclaims is that recognition of evil, if carried to the point of a consuming obsession, may be the worst form of evil. To look about oneself for manifestations of sinfulness and to become so overwhelmed by the viciousness of humanity that one begins to see cruelty and vulgarity as the only truths about human nature is...a fearful sin" (*"Suddenly Last Summer* as 'Morality Play,'" *Modern Drama*, VIII, February 1966, 393).

Kingdom of Earth, like *Summer*, demonstrates what results when one commits himself to a belief in a God devoid of mercy and love. Chicken Ravenstock accepts the Calvinistic doctrines of predestination: "I think there's a good deal of truth in the statement, the saying, that either you're saved or you ain't, and the best thing to do is find out which and stick to it." He believes that he is one of those people "just not cut out for [salvation]" because "You can't haul down your spiritual gates [on your lustful body] if you don't have any in you. I think that's the case in my case. I was just created without them." There is, he asserts, an absolute dichotomy between matter and spirit, damnation and salvation, the hard way and the soft way through life. In this, Chicken resembles O'Neill's Ephraim Cabot in *Desire Under the Elms*, who also believed in a "hard" God who must be emulated, though Cabot felt that endurance and obedience to his God would bring salvation. As Donald P. Costello has suggested in another context, "To surrender to the evil earth is, to Williams, man's major sin..." ("Tennessee Williams' Fugutive Kind," *Modern Drama*, XV, May 1972, 29). Chicken (whose animal name suggests his wholly instinctual nature) not only commits himself totally to the earth and "personal satisfaction," the only glory of the earth, but also pulls Myrtle, his half-brother Lot's wife, down with him. Halfway through the play (appropriately subtitled "The Seven Descents of Myrtle"), Myrtle sings a hymn about her descent from heaven—from her "religious," motherly devotion to the ethereal and effeminate Lot—to earth and the lustful Chicken: "'Then my feet came down to walk on earth,/ And my mother cried when she gave me birth./ Now my feet walk far and my feet walk fast,/ But they still got an itch for heavenly grass.'" Myrtle quickly loses any "itch for the heavenly grass," though, when, desperate for survival from the encroaching flood waters, she goes up onto the roof with Chicken, becoming the exemplum of Lot's earlier statement that "when people are desperate,...they only think of themselves." Myrtle comes to believe, along with Chicken, that life is "evil," and they therefore fittingly end the play waiting for the Old Testament destruction of the world by water to come again.

Myrtle's descent to earth is not unlike that of Alma Winemiller's "descent" from soul to body in *Summer and Smoke* (1948), another Williams morality play. Both plays demonstrate Williams' consistent notion that man is a blend of good and evil, spirit and matter. Dr. John Buchanan, whom Alma considers a "priest" since by vocation he quiets suffering and fear, sees through his microscope "a mysterious universe—part anarchy and part order," an analogy for passion and reason fighting for dominance within man. Alma, in turn, suggests that all nature's facets are ultimately contained in God when she says that the universe is "the footprints of God." Rather than see experience as fragmented into a succession of contrarieties—*either* this option *or* that option—Williams demands that his characters, and we, too, see "life steadily" and see "it whole," as a sequence of unities that must of necessity encompass *both* this alternative *and* that alternative. Nowhere in Williams is this point made more explicit than in *Streetcar*, where experience is presented in terms of polarities (such as present versus past, desire versus death, brute animal sexuality versus spiritual beauty, jazz versus cathedral bells, garish, brightly colored shirts versus a light shaded by a paper lantern), all of which reflect Blanche's habitual dichotomizing of experience into irreconcilable opposites. This polarizing tendency of Blanche's mind is symptomatic, to Williams, of fragmented modern man.

Alma, who begins *Summer* as a disciple of the spirit, and John, who begins as a seeker after bodily satisfaction, are each living only a half-truth. Ironically, they pass each other without ever meeting as they go in opposite directions: he, to integration of the body and the soul in his love for Nellie; she, to undue emphasis upon the flesh. Alma, like Blanche before her, is not wrong in her desire to keep alive human aspiration lest mankind backslide down the evolutionary ladder; she desires to emulate the Gothic cathedral which "reaches up...striving for something": "To me, well, that is the secret, the principle back of existence—

the everlasting struggle and aspiration for more than our human limits have placed in our reach." Where Alma is wrong, though, is in her mistaken belief that such upward striving requires absolute denial of the flesh and matter. In *Night,* Hannah is described as "ethereal, almost ghostly....a Gothic cathedral image of a medieval saint," and yet she, unlike Alma, never sacrifices her humanity in exchange for a place in a stone niche. At the beginning of *Summer,* Alma is like the central prop on the stage, the statue of the angel named ETERNITY, become stone from denial of the flesh that makes us temporal but also makes us human; at the end, she is like the anatomy chart which diagrams the physical body but is powerless to show the invisible soul. But if there is no integration of body and spirit for Alma, there is a sympathy reserved for her which is not proffered to Myrtle in *Earth.* Williams rewards Alma with a bottle of pills; she thinks of the prescription number "as the telephone number of God," one of the *"little* mercies" that allows her "to keep on going. She is not totally corrupted because she is not self-seeking and has not corrupted others. Life is not evil for her as it is for Myrtle, and so mercy still exists.

Williams also employs the morality pattern in *The Milk Train Doesn't Stop Here Anymore* (1965), a modern "Death of Everywoman." Like so many of Williams' characters, the faded stage queen, Flora "Sissy" Goforth, is afraid; she is "scared to death of dying." Though Sissy accepts the fact of man's mortality, she is determined not to "go forth till she's ready...." Once before she claims to have been given back life through a lover—her fourth husband Alex, a poet—and now she again thinks that what she most wants and needs is another lover. But time has happened to Sissy Goforth, just as it has to the Princess Kosmonopolis in *Sweet Bird of Youth* (1959). The Princess also desires life and discovers that she can forget decaying beauty and a film comeback she believes was disastrous through the act of lovemaking. Like Sissy, the Princess has a calcified and hardened heart, but through wanting to help Chance Wayne she experiences a miraculous, albeit temporary, rejuvenation of feeling for someone other than herself: "That's a miracle....That means my heart's still alive, at least some part of it is, not all of my heart is dead yet." But in a moment of selfishness upon learning that her comeback was indeed immensely successful, she turns Chance away. They go full cycle in their relationship, from using one another, through momentarily reaching out and helping the other, only to end by turning away from communion with each other. The miracle affects only themselves, and then only for a short time, unlike the miracle at the end of *Camino Real* when *"The violets in the mountains have broken the rocks!"* after the reconciliation between Jacques Casanova and Marguerite Gautier.

In *Milktrain*, Christopher Flanders, the Angel of Death, echoes Hannah's words from *Iguana* when he tells Sissy "that finally, sooner or later, you need somebody or something to mean God to you. ...." Chris tries to convince Sissy that she suffers not from a malady of the body but from an emptiness of the spirit that no physical lover can assuage. In this *momento mori* play, he teaches her the acceptance of the mystery of life *and* death, that death is interwoven with the fabric of life and is indeed the culmination of the pattern. He teaches her "how to live and to die in a way that's more dignified than most of us know how to do it. And of how not to be frightened of not knowing what isn't meant to be known, acceptance of not knowing *anything* but the moment of still existing, until we stop existing—and acceptance of that moment, too." Sissy, in turn, who "get[s] panicky when [she's] not cared for by somebody" fulfills Chris' "need [of] somebody to care for." Though she asserts at first her determination to face death and "go forth alone," she finally admits she "can't make it alone" and needs Chris there with her. Chris' presence at her deathbed is a mercy not unlike Alma's little pills.

Earlier Sissy wonders, when Chris first tells her of his mission, how somebody can mean God to somebody else: "Well, *bring* Him, I'm ready to lay out a red carpet for Him, but how do you bring Him? Whistle? Ring a bell for Him? Huh? How? What?" With a providential, beneficent God receding from the universe (Sissy sees God as the sun which has calcified her heart, while Chris gives her a mobile he has constructed entitled "The Earth Is a Wheel in a Great Big Gambling Casino"), any glimmer of the godly is truly a miraculous act of grace, as it is for Celeste and Trinket in *The Mutilated*, one of two plays produced together under the title *Slapstick Tragedy* (1966). In the Williams encomium, to be mutilated is the human condition; it is only the exceptional person who has totally escaped all traces of some moral or psychological or physical mutilation. But as the Carollers in *The Mutilated* sing on Christmas Eve, "A miracle," some "love unknown," may possibly come to alleviate the misery of "the strange, the crazed, the queer"; "At last for each someone may come/ And even though he may not stay,/ It may be softer where he was,/ It may be sweeter where he lay." The someone who comes to Celeste and Trinket is the Virgin Mary herself.

Trinket has lived for three years, what "seemed like...a *death* time," without physical love since undergoing a partial mastectomy, a mutilation which Celeste has made public. So like the Princess and Sissy, Trinket needs a "kind" lover, but when she finally gathers the courage to invite Slim into her room on Christmas Eve, he rejects her when he discovers her mutilation. Trinket has a strong maternal instinct which has always gone unfulfilled. She sees motherhood as a life-giving religious ritual in which she is denied participation, and daydreams sentimentally about the Blessed Mother and Child: "His sweet, hungry lips are at her rose-petal nipple.—Oh, such *wanting* things lips are, and such *giving* things breasts!" Now Trinket is suffering from a pain in her other breast, but after she and Celeste forgive one another for their cruelties and reconcile themselves to each other, they experience a vision of the Virgin, and Trinket's pain miraculously disappears.

Other Williams heroines share with Trinket the maternal instinct and her faith in its regenerative powers: Maggie in *Cat*, Serafina delle Rose in *Rose Tattoo*, and Lady Myra Torrance in *Orpheus Descending* (1958). Serafina, who knew the wonder of having two lives within her body after conceiving with her husband Rosario, again rejoices in that same wonder after she satisfies Alvaro's need for love. In *Orpheus*, Lady feels as if her heart were cut out of her years before when she had a child cut out of her body. She needs Val Xavier to redeem her from death-in-life existence, and after conceiving a child with him feels *"great—joy!"* over being alive once more: "I have life in my body, this dead tree, my body, has burst in flowers! You've given me life. ..."

Trinket will never experience this joy of motherhood, and the surcease of her pain may be only temporary, for "Jack In Black, who stacks the deck,/ Who loads the dice and tricks the wheel," is there to remind her and us that "the tolling of a ghostly bell" will someday summon all to death. There is no such darkening shadow cast over the "miracle" performed solely by human hands, with no supernatural intervention, at the end of *Night of the Iguana*, Williams' most profound play and his fullest exploration of "person-to-person god-ness." Shannon, the defrocked Episcopalian minister, is, like the captured iguana tied beneath the verandah, at the end of his rope; haunted by his *"spook"* again, he is undergoing a dark night of the soul, hollering out for help. He realizes that "People need human contact," yet he sees that the human condition often keeps man apart from his fellow-men, in isolated "cubicle bedrooms" like those in the stage setting. And so the usual means of contact is "tapping on walls like convicts in separate cells communicate with each other." As Val says in *Orpheus:* "Nobody ever gets to know *no body!* We're all of us sentenced to solitary confinement within our own skins, for life!" It is this "solitary confinement" that Shannon escapes from through his providential encounter with Hannah.

Shannon's crisis in faith springs from his conception of God as a vengeful God who denies man his pleasure, for Shannon has always felt a compulsion to sin—especially to sins of the flesh, like Chicken in *Earth*—followed immediately by guilt and remorse and the need to be punished. Shannon's God is not unlike Sebastian's in *Summer:* He is an "angry, petulant old man....a cruel, senile delinquent, blaming the world and brutally punishing all he created for his own faults in construction...." Again like Sebastian, Shannon is too preoccupied with his own evil and guilt, and thus too obsessed with a sense of his failure in life. He does not realize that to be human *is* to be sinful, but not so flawed as to despair. But fortunately, Shannon has just enough emotional reserve left to muster some sympathy for someone outside of himself. Hannah calls him "a man of God, on vacation," and recognizes, as the stage direction suggests, that her infirm grandfather Nonno, "ninety-seven years *young"* and "the oldest living and practicing poet," "touches something in [Shannon] outside of his concern with himself." Hannah helps Shannon to gain a renewed belief in his own goodness and kindness by prompting him to perform the "little act of grace" of setting the iguana free; as Shannon says, "God won't do it and we are going to play God here." Like Coleridge's Ancient Mariner who "blessed [the water-snakes] unaware" and then saw the albatross fall from off his neck, Shannon rips his own albatross—the gold cross which symbolizes a perverted system of religion by which he feels condemned rather than redeemed—from around his neck. Only after Shannon has freed the iguana, "one of God's creatures," is Nonno able to finish his last and "loveliest poem," whose subject is that man cannot live in a perfect, uncorrupted world, but must have the courage to endure in the face of evil and suffering, without ignoring the good or despairing over the human condition. Since such courage can come only by recognizing the possibility of "broken gates between people so they can reach each other" and by accepting the interdependence of all creatures, Williams gives to Shannon a name containing the alphabet letters needed to spell out "Nonno" and "Hannah."

In an early one-act play, "The Lady of Larkspur Lotion" (1945), one of Williams' characters asks: "Is there no mercy left in the world anymore?/ What has become of passion and understanding?/ Where have they all gone to? Where's God?/ Where's Christ?" Williams' own answer given throughout his major plays is simple without being simplistic. It is given in the form of a challenge which must not frighten: We must be like God to the other, and the other must be like God to us.

Tennessee Williams' Lives of the Saints:
A Playwright's Obliquity

by Gilbert Debusscher

The elucidation of Christian symbolism is a commonplace of contemporary criticism. Naturally commentators have also scrutinized Tennessee Williams' work and have managed to make almost each play yield its Christ figure. It has thus been repeatedly empahsized that a significant proportion of Williams' plays occur around or lead up to the liturgical feasts of Good Friday and Easter.[1] When the time of the play is not near Easter, the plot reproduces more or less faithfully and noticeably some of the Easter week events.[2] In all of these plays the playwright links his principal male character by personal attribute or by action, to Christ. Val's second name "Xavier" in *Battle of Angels* is meant to evoke "Savior"; Jim O'Connor in *The Glass Menagerie* is associated with the unicorn, a traditional Christ symbol; Kilroy goes through the painful blocks of the *Camino Real* that might represent the stations of Calvary; Sebastian in *Suddenly Last Summer* is reported to have ascended a Golgotha-like mountain; Chance in *Sweet Bird of Youth* expects his "resurrection" in Saint-Cloud on Easter Sunday; Shannon in *The Night of the Iguana* is seen bringing a heavy load up a mountain where he is about to be "crucified"; Christopher, in *The Milktrain Doesn't Stop Here Anymore,* whose name—most often shortened to "Chris"—already spells his relationship with Christ, similarly climbs Mrs. Goforth's mountain, in the heat of the afternoon, pursued by the

[1]*Battle of Angels* and *Orpheus Descending, Sweet Bird of Youth.*

[2]*The Glass Menagerie, Camino Real, Suddenly Last Summer, The Night of the Iguana, The Milktrain Doesn't Stop Here Anymore.*

clamour of the pack. Through the actions of these characters
elements of Christ's Passion are reflected in the respective plays
in which they appear. Sometimes the critics' attention is drawn
to this pattern of symbolism rather clumsily as the "God-I, Lady-
You" stammering of Val Xavier or in Flora Goforth's question
to Christopher "Can you walk on water?", sometimes more subtly
as when Jim O'Connor offers Laura "Life-Savers."[3]

Although the signposts are sometimes as evident as those that
point to a Christ archetype, the critics have so far had very little
to say about Williams' references to the lives of the saints. Yet
these appear in his plays as early as *Battle of Angels* (1940) and
provide in later plays dramatic justification for actions, speeches
or scenes that otherwise appear obscure or gratuitous.

It has been pointed out that the name of Val (for Valentine)
Xavier in *Battle of Angels*, suggested "the martyred Saint Valentine as 'love-saviour'."[4] The interpretation of Xavier as Saviour
is warranted by the play's insistence that "Xavier" be pronounced
as if spelled with an initial "s."[5] The allusion to St. Valentine is
equally clear: the play takes place early in February and the
Temple Sisters, a pair of unattractive old maids report on their
receiving a malicious Valentine card (42). This cursory reference
brings to mind, however fleetingly, the custom of choosing a
Valentine on the 14th of February—which the women in the play
actually do as they all settle for Val!—and beyond that to the
legend of the martyred saint with whom the practice of sending
valentines is connected.

We thus get an indication that early in his career Williams was
aware of the possibility of prolonging the meaning of his characters and of making his particulars resonate with broader overtones. That he did not pursue the device further in this particular
instance is probably due to his tyro's inability to control his
referential method properly, an inability which manifests itself
in the confusing tangle of Christian and mythical echoes that
reverberate through this first full-length play.

Eighteen years and seven plays later, in *Suddenly Last Sum-*

[3] *The Glass Menagerie* in *The Theatre of Tennessee Williams*, I, New Directions, New York, 1971. p. 229.

[4] QUIRINO (Leonard): Tennessee Williams' Persistent *Battle of Angels*.
Modern Drama, XI, 1, 1968. p. 31.

[5] *Battle of Angels* in *The Theatre of Tennessee Williams*, I, New Directions,
New York, 1971. p. 18. The first citation from each play will be in a footnote.
Subsequent citations will be identified in the text by page number.

mer (1958), Williams appears in full command of his craft and in this instance the indications of partial identification of Sebastian Venable with his patron saint are more systematic and varied.

As in the earlier example, it is a seemingly incidental mention in Catharine Holly's report that brings the figure of St. Sebastian into the picture. Says Catharine:

> "In Cabeza de Lobo there is a beach that's named for Sebastian's name saint, it's known as La Playa San Sebastian, and that's where we started spending all afternoon, every day."[6]

Williams' familiarity with the circumstances of the martyr's legend is evidenced in a 1948 poem titled "San Sebastiano de Sodoma."[7] The playwright is obviously aware that St. Sebastian was a Roman martyr[8] traditionally considered the lover of Emperor Diocletian (Williams refers to him in the poem as "an emperor's concubine"). After bitterly reproaching him with his conversion to Christianity, the Emperor is reported to have "delivered him over to certain archers of Mauritania to be shot to death" because of his new faith. The handsome youth survived and was nursed back to health by a pious widow. After recovering from his wounds, Sebastian returned to Diocletian to plead the cause of the Christians. "Recovering from his surprise, he (the emperor) gave orders for him to be seized and beaten to death with cudgels and his body thrown into the common sewer." This time Sebastian dies and again a woman appears but now to bury him.

The critics have been prompt to trace the references to the saint's legend in Williams' play. Sebastian Venable possesses the good looks generally attributed to his patron saint. In this connection, William E. Taylor quotes the *Encyclopedia Britannica* according to which "St. Sebastian is a favorite subject of sacred art, being most generally represented undraped, and severely though not mortally wounded with arrows."[9] It is interesting to note that a French erotologist, Raymond De Becker, would com-

[6]*Suddenly Last Summer* in *The Theatre of Tennessee Williams*, III, New Directions, New York, 1971, p. 410.

[7]In *In the Winter of Cities*, New Directions, New York, 1964, p. 112.

[8]Cf. Butler's *Lives of the Saints*. Edited, revised and supplemented by Herbert Thurston, S.J. and Donald Attwater, London, Burns and Oates. 1956, I. pp. 128-130.

[9]TAYLOR (W.E.): Tennessee Williams: Academia on Broadway, in Richard E. Langford, ed., *Essays in Modern American Literature*, Deland, Florida. Stetson University Press, 1963, p. 95.

ment that the representation of St. Sebastian pierced with arrows, i.e. the scene of his life made famous through the plastic arts, is the "sujet privilégié des peintres homoérotiques de la Chrétienté."[10] Williams suggests an unmistakable homosexual reference in the title of his poem "San Sebastiano de Sodoma" and makes his Sebastian character also into a homosexual.

The stories of the two characters also present important points of contact. Both heroes are connected with two women. They are represented in the modern version by Mrs. Venable and Catharine. The first helps Sebastian survive a particularly painful experience: the "pious widow" nurses the Roman character back to life after the torture by the archers; Mrs. Venable tears her son away from the Buddhist monks (358). The second contributes to celebrating the last rites for the dead: the Roman matron buries the saint's bodily remains; the American girl figuratively inters her cousin's usurped reputation. Even more immediately reminiscent of the saint's legend are the circumstances of Sebastian's death. As the Japanese critic Tatsumi Funatsu[11] pointed out, the description by Catharine of Sebastian's assailants is carefully worded so as to remind us of the arrows with which St. Sebastian is almost struck to death:

> "There were naked children along the beach, a band of frightfully thin and dark naked children that looked like a flock of plucked birds, and they would come *darting up* (...)" (415) (...) "Sebastian started to run and they all screamed at once and seemed to *fly in the air* (...) (421) (Italics added)

The context of the play allows us to endow the arrow with sexual symbolism and thus to view the young phallus bearers who pursue Sebastian up the mountain as corresponding to the instruments of torture of the legend.

As appears from the number of commentators I quoted, Williams' echoing the story of St. Sebastian in that of Sebastian Venable has received its share of critical attention. It has generally been interpreted as a straight ironic comment, an unambiguous disparagement of Sebastian through contrast with the early martyr. Thus Paul J. Hurley says:

[10]DE BECKER (Raymond): *L'Erotisme d'En Face*, Pauvert, Paris, 1964, p. 141.

[11]FUNATSU (Tatsumi): A Study of *Suddenly Last Summer. Fukuoka University Review of Literature and Science*, VII, March 1963, p. 359.

"Christian martyrs suffer death to repeat, symbolically, Christ's act of love on the Cross. Their martyrdom is not only an act of faith in God, it is a proof of their love of man. Sebastian's death is a result of his hatred and contempt."[12]

The subsequent examples may indicate that this judgment needs qualification.

No critic has commented so far on a "martyrdom" allusion in *The Night of the Iguana* probably because this play, unlike its predecessor, does not contain an explicit textual reference to a martyred saint. Yet an incident in Act III suggests that the Reverend Lawrence T. Shannon, like Val and Sebastian before him, is to be gauged against his patron, St. Laurence. In this instance again Williams chose to integrate into his play, this time through scenic action rather than textual reference, the scene of the saint's life that has been most often represented in the plastic arts.

St. Laurence is reported to have been one of the seven deacons of the Roman church whose function it was to administer the goods of the Church and to distribute its alms among the poor. For his refusal to reveal to the prefect of the city the place where the wealth in his charge was kept Laurence was put on a big gridiron with glowing coals under it, "that he might be slowly burnt."[13] St. Ambrose, a later commentator, "observes that whilst his body burned in the material flames, the fire of divine love was far more active within his breast and made him regardless of pain so much that when the executioner had turned him over, he said: "It is cooked enough, you may eat!""

The play's scenic allusions to this martyrdom are concentrated in the pivotal scene of Act III in which the Reverend Lawrence Shannon is tied in the hammock, partly as a result of his refusal to surrender the ignition key to the bus, and is burnt by the cigarette butt he drops under him. The idea of being devoured is also present since Shannon is symbolically identified with the captive iguana about to be cooked and eaten by Maxine and the Mexican boys.

In *The Night of the Iguana* again Williams' use of elements from the story of St. Laurence might be interpreted as an ironic comment on the modern hero. The play provides a few opposi-

[12]HURLEY (Paul): *Suddenly Last Summer* as Morality Play. *Modern Drama*, VIII, 4, 1966, p. 401.

[13]Butler's *Lives of the Saints*, III, pp. 296-299.

tions between the two characters that leave little doubt as to the
author's disparaging intentions. Instead of doling out his money,
Shannon is accused—and he only feebly counters the attack—
of having spent a young girl's money during their Mexico City
spree,[14] of having made a profit on the Enteroviaform he sold
to the ladies in his group (275) and of trying "to make a deal" with
Maxine on their hotel fees (265). The comment implied by the
substitution of the comfortable hammock for the awe-inspiring
gridiron is compounded by the irony conveyed in the opposition
between the saint's disregard for intense physical pain and Shannon's disproportionate reaction to the cigarette butt incident:

> (...) (Shannon chokes and the cigarette is expelled.)
> Hannah: You've dropped it on you—where is it?
> Shannon (twisting and lunging about in the hammock):
> It's under me, under me, burning. Untie me, for God's sake,
> will you—it's burning me through my pants!
> Hannah: Riase your hips so I can—
> Shannon: I can't, the ropes are too tight. Untie me, Untieeeee
> meeeeee!   (348)

Finally observe that although both stories mention, the fact that
the martyr might be eaten, in the modern version this is only
conveyed by symbolically identifying Shannon with the iguana;
the suggestion thereby loses a good deal of the gruesome im-
mediacy of the original. By suggesting the St. Laurence pattern
of martyrdom and simultaneously introducing significant variations on it, Williams asks the reader and spectator to understand
the real suffering of the character but only to the extent that it is
genuine; he is at the same time warned *not* to consider it an
extremity of human suffering of which he is given, by means of
the submerged allusion, a far more authentic example.

In the last "hagiographic" instance, Williams does not explicitly refer nor allude to a martyrdom scene. In *The Milktrain
Doesn't Stop Here Anymore,* Christopher Flanders momentarily becomes a modern version of his patron saint for re-enacting
some of the important events of St. Christopher's career. According to legendary tradition, St. Christopher was a giant who had
devoted himself after his conversion to carrying travellers across
a river. One day the burden seemed intolerably heavy although
he was only carrying a child. When inquiring about the unusual

---

[14]*The Night of the Iguana in The Theatre of Tennessee Williams,* IV, New
Directions, New York, 1972, p. 335.

phenomenon Christopher was told by the child: "Christopher, marvel thee nothing, for thou has not only borne all the world upon thee, but thou has borne Him that created and made all the world, upon thy shoulders."[15]

The Christopher of this play recalls his patron saint in many ways. As he comes up the hill in the beginning of the play, he is dragging a heavy sack slung over his shoulder. One of the servants exclaims in lifting the bag: "Pesante—Dio..."[16] which might well be understood as "a heavy God." In fact, the sack contains a mobile symbolizing the earth and the surrounding universe as its mystifying title seems to indicate—"The Earth Is a Wheel in a Great Big Gambling Casino." (29)

Later in the play, Christopher reports on his experience with an old gentleman; the scene recaptures some of the essentials of the legendary Christopher's experience with the infant Christ:

> Christopher: There was a very old gentleman on (the beach). He called "Help!" to me, as if he was in the water drowning and I was on the shore. I swam in and asked him how I could help him and he said this, he said: "Help me out there! I can't make it alone, I've gone past pain I can bear!" (...) I gave him the help he wanted, I led him out in the water, it wasn't easy. Once he started to panic; I had to hold onto him tight as a lover till he got back his courage and said, "All right." The tide took him as light as a leaf (...) (112)

As in the case of Sebastian and Lawrence, Christopher's identification with his namesake is here at the same time established and debunked. The modern character's story exhibits once again revealing contrasts with the legend. In the play, Christopher does not carry the infant Christ but an elderly man; and his destination is not safety on the opposite bank of a river but death in the waves of the sea. Moreover, Christopher's self-appointed task of helping old people, preferably dying women, through the last few of their existence i.e. helping them across to death for a not altogether symbolic reward, prolongs the contrast embedded in the St. Christopher parallel.

Through explicit verbal reference (Sebastian) or through actions, actual (Shannon) or reported (Christopher), Williams suggests parallels between his characters' careers, and the lives of

---

[15]Butler's *Lives of the Saints*, III, p. 185.

[16]*The Milktrain Doesn't Stop Here Anymore*, New Directions, New York, 1964, p. 19.

their patron saints. In so doing he indicates his desire to lift the
events of the play from the realistic to the mythical, from the
straightforward to the oblique.[17] The hagiographic references are
part of a set of devices intended to draw the readers' and specta-
tors' attention away from the surface of the play. They bring to the
action the suggestion that the events occurring on the stage are
merely the limited, contemporary reflection of an original, time-
honoured pattern of larger significance. They are signposts to
the deeper and broader resonances of plays that have too often
been approached as flatly realistic.

Like so many aspects of his playwriting, Williams' hagiography
remains ambiguous. The presence of saintly figures in the play's
texture indicates that the playwright conceives of his central
characters' predicament as somehow comparable to that of their
patron saints. By scenically integrating or verbally recalling the
central scene of their martyrdom, Williams emphasizes through
comparison less the sanctity of his characters than their scapegoat
overtones.[18] Sebastian and Shannon sacrifice themselves or fall
victims to a God whose repellent, savage features they have
found reflected in the outside world. Sebastian identifies God
with his Galapagos vision of newly hatched turtles torn apart and
devoured by birds of prey. For Shannon the world is a dungheap
and for Christopher, it is a nest of vipers.

Some critics like Paul J. Hurley have contended that these
conceptions of God and the world through which He is revealed
were in fact subjective, nightmarish visions imposed by the
characters. Yet nowhere do the plays suggest that they are
merely that. In fact the world of *Suddenly* appears like a vin-
dication of Sebastian's views: devouring is the all-pervading
impulse, the prime mover of the universe. In the same way the
worlds of *Iguana* and *Milktrain* correspond to a great extent
to the conceptions of Shannon and Christopher. The hagiographic parallelism then emphasizes that if these characters appear twisted or depraved and if the suggestion that they might
be saints seems to verge on the sacrilegious, the distortion is

---

[17]In *The Playwrights Speak* (ed. by Walter Wager—intro. by John Russell
Taylor—London, 1969, p. 183). Williams himself suggests the word to describe
his method: "I always try to write obliquely (...) I am not a direct writer; I am
always an oblique writer, if I can be; I want to be allusive; I do not want to be
one of these people who hit the nail on the head all the time."

[18] A feature already discussed in connection with Christian symbolism by
Quirino in the article on *Battle of Angels* quoted above.

not theirs, but that of our world—the savage grin on the face of God—in which they become representative martyrs.

The significant variations from and contrasts with the original patterns do not therefore point up the moral shortcomings of the moderns as compared to their patron saints; much more broadly they emphasize the difference between a mythical world of moral order, in which God was the ultimate source and aim, and the chaotic universe, in which Sebastian, Shannon and Christopher look for Him but are confronted with hideous distortions.

Thus, *Suddenly Last Summer, The Night of the Iguana,* and *The Milktrain Doesn't Stop Here Anymore* prolong, through the hagiographic references, a familiar Williams theme that appeared more clearly in the "Southern" plays, viz. the opposition between the grandeur of the past and the shabbiness of the present. In these three plays in which Williams' metaphysical preoccupations gradually claim precedence over his other concerns, the portrait of the playwright as a modern Southern artist pining away over an image of the Old South is progressively overshadowed by that of a nostalgic Puritan desperately haunted by the security of his former faith and frightened at the metaphysical void to which his quest seems to lead him.

The Distorted Mirror:
Tennessee Williams' Self-Portraits

by Nancy M. Tischler

Tennessee Williams, like any talented playwright, has written a number of bad plays. The most interesting of these is his first major play and the one he continues to love best—variously named *Battle of Angels, Orpheus Descending, The Fugitive Kind, Something Wild in the Country,* etc. The endless revisions with their repeated, repaired, and fresh flaws reveal Williams' blindness to his own strengths and weaknesses. The much simpler and much greater plays that have served as interludes between the revisions of his perennial play contrast sharply with the grandiose failure of his favorite. Many of the same characters, the same themes, and the same images are used to much better advantage in *The Glass Menagerie* or *A Streetcar Named Desire,* but Williams' talent is apparently sufficiently unconscious that he cannot see why his story sometimes succeeds and sometimes fails. He is reported to have commented that *The Glass Menagerie* was better received than *Battle of Angels* because it is safer to write about mothers than about sex. Such a theory could hardly explain *A Streetcar Named Desire.* In all of his revisions of *Battle of Angels,* because of his limited capacity in self-criticism, he has perpetuated the same flaw—a flaw that is instructive in an analysis of Williams' other failures, of his successes, and of that form of Romanticism he so clearly exemplifies. He is in love with an idealized self-portrait, which he understandably continues to garb more elaborately while failing to comprehend more fully. So long as he allows the self-portrait to reveal himself without authorial interference, he succeeds; whenever he tries to intellectualize and explain and universalize that portrait, he fails.

The first version of *Battle of Angels,* written when he was still

"The Distorted Mirror: Tennessee Williams' Self-Portraits" by Nancy M. Tischler. From *Mississippi Quarterly*, 25 (Fall 1972), 389-403. Copyright © 1972 by *Mississippi Quarterly*. Reprinted by permission of the author and publisher.

an unknown, itinerant youth, living the bohemian life, supported by occasional odd jobs and stipends from home, won him a Rockefeller Grant of $1000 and brought him to the attention of John Gassner. With the help of Gassner and Theresa Helburn, he polished the play for presentation as the first play of the Theatre Guild's 1940 season. The play's hero, Valentine Xavier, is an adolescent vision of the artist in the modern world, a compendium of Williams' own brief life and that of those alienated young artists he had come to know in his travels. Val is a young author whose single volume comprehends both his thought and his life, but is too sacred to share until it is complete. In his early days, Williams frequently followed the Romantic creed that equates art and life, insisting that Truth is more valuable than art and there is no truth except that a man experiences for himself. Like Williams, Val elevates the rights of the individual above the demands of society, but also like Williams, he is defensive about his lack of roots or responsibility. Insisting that a man can fulfill himself only when unencumbered, he wrenches free of the clutching hands that try to retain him and the proffered love that would entrap him. There is a price implied in the nomadic life: Val says, "I was tired of moving around and being lonesome and only meeting with strangers. I wanted to feel like I belonged somewhere and lived like regular people." But an inner need to discover what he labels "the secret of life" drives him from job to job and place to place. His real need is for self-fulfillment, not for love or security. Even the desert, he tells the hysterical heroine as she tries to hold him, would be crowded should he share it with her.

The theme is recurrent in Williams' work. His archetypal artist (in "The Poet," a short story, for example) is a solitary wanderer, a Pied Piper who appeals to children and those who can come to him as little children, and who is a threat to the adults. He rejects home, family, job, and organizations for freedom. Always Williams' sympathy and admiration go out to the "lonely exiles" of Greenwich Village or the Vieux Carré. The portrait is clearly an apology for his own rootless life. His background and his strong emotional ties with his home make this justification essential. As a result, there is no solution for Val any more than there is later any clear solution for Tom. To fall in love or to accept the role imposed by society is to die. But to cut the vital cords that bind man to his society and his family is to destroy something in himself. Myra, love, biology, conscience, and society all conspire to murder the nonconformist, disengaged poet.

Val Xavier, the saint of the tale, is thus the modern poet in the typical Romantic fusion of art and religion. Aping Williams' personal poet-hero, Hart Crane, he rejects the middleclass American dream while he fixes his vision on the Holy Grail of pure art and intense experience. Like both Crane and Williams, he has arrived at the threshold of middle-age (thirty in Williams' world), when he appears less the youthful rebel than the aging ne'er-do-well. With blasted dreams and unfinished manuscript, he contemplates a return to the world and momentarily replaces his snake-skin jacket with the blue serge suit of the conformist and finally the white coat of the servant. But at the end of the story, he makes Williams' own decision: he must remain a solitary wanderer and must consequently continue to appear an enemy of the people. He may even—and usually does in Williams' stories—become their victim. (It is, of course, the portrait we see again as Chance Wayne in *Sweet Bird of Youth.*) In a sense, Val insures his own sacrificial death by rejecting the safe exit for the more perilous but more honest one. It is for Williams a satsifying approximation of the Hart Crane image.

In these points, the play closely parallels *The Glass Menagerie*, where the author is again the hero. Here also love and societal pressures are the enemies of art. To leave home and Amanda is to insure self-preservation, but at the same time to kill something vital within the self. It is when Williams extends the poet image that he destroys credibility. Rather than being satisfied with a fairly obvious justification of bohemia, he insists on giving his poet a mysterious origin and a visionary capacity so that he becomes more of a prophet-hero and less of a modern dislocated artist. This pattern is accentuated in later revisions of the play so that he is transformed into the archetypal hero in search of truth and beauty.

In *Orpheus Descending*, a play some seventeen years later than *Battle of Angels*, Val is nearing thirty and has exchanged his boyish charm for a weary disgust at his own corruption. Instead of the bright young animal who seeks an epic answer to his epic questions, we see a tired roué suffering from the effects of the endless party. (In this much of the portrait, Williams is apparently chronicling his disillusionment with bohemia as a post-adolescent way of life, but is still too distressed with the alternative path to reject it outright.)

Although disgusted with the flesh and the world, Val has found in art a means of cleansing and sanctification. His guitar is his sacred symbol, evidence of an immortality and a transcendence of the flesh achievable in art. (Curiously, it also seems to be a phallic symbol, clutched at by sexually undernourished wives of "small planters," stroked by the doomed aristocrat seeking death through sex, and threatened by the penis-envying husbands of the community.) Now Val is Orpheus with his magic lyre, able to charm even Death for a moment. The harpies appear to be those malevolent women who pursue him after he has lost Eurydice and who destroy him in a Bacchic orgy. Thus, he is the archetypal artist in search of truth and beauty, hoping to bring life back to the sterile land (the dry-goods store). He does briefly cause a false Spring—an orchard blooms in the confectionary and life stirs in Lady's womb—but Pluto comes to reclaim his wife and to destroy human happiness.

Val or Orpheus is sacrificed as a scapegoat, cleaning the town of its anger and guilt, but the death seems to be the result more directly of his sexuality than of his artistry. Certainly his occasional renditions of "Heavenly Grass" on the guitar are not adequate motivation for lynching. Williams undoubtedly feels that the artist suffers for his break with social codes of behavior and thought, but he fails here to convince the audience that Val is much of an artist. Undoubtedly too Williams believes that art has had the effect of cleansing and justifying his life: he has used writing as a Catholic uses confession. But in Val's case, it is his capacity for compassion rather than his ability with the guitar that brings Lady's rebirth.

Tennessee Williams, in fact, runs into untold confusions as he continues to rewrite this painfully overwrought play. Seldom does his vagrant hero justify the grandiose claims the playwright makes for him: his life is hardly an idealized quest, an engraved guitar is at best an inadequate symbol for art that justifies all aberrations and all irresponsibilities, and foxes do not make good scapegoats.

The repeated appearance of the fox image (fox and hounds, fox in the henhouse) is the clue to another flaw in this play which is a characteristic flaw of this playwright. The image is D. H. Lawrence's and is characteristically the manner in which Williams refers to Lawrence and the Lawrence hero. Lawrence's effect on Tennessee Williams is at least as important as Hart Crane's, and much less natural. To the rebel in a Puritan family, Lawrence served as a symbol of freedom. In *The Glass Menagerie*, the mother would censor Tom's reading if she could, and underlines this by returning the D. H. Lawrence book to the public library before her son has read it. In *I Rise in Flame, Cried the Phoenix,* the play that dramatizes Lawrence's death, the hero is seen as the foe of all petty feminine restrictions and demands, the old, primitive, independent male principle. The play that was to follow *Battle of Angels,* an adaptation of a Lawrence short story entitled *You Touched Me!,* included much of the same enthusiastic endorsement of fleshly, sexual love. But in the later play, the mood is more clearly Lawrence's, for sex proves indeed to be a cosmic solution. Williams has several times toyed with this notion—notably in *The Rose Tattoo.* Even so late a play as *The Night of the Iguana* continues to use Lawrence (now a decadent, defrocked Christ figure) as muddling along toward a sexual salvation while simultaneously coveting a "voluptuous crucifixion" in much the same manner as the old D. H. Lawrence dies in *I Rise in Flame.* Clearly, Williams has not relinquished the idea that sex is the path to salvation, at least for a few people. Myrtle keeps descending to the kingdom of earth to find her happiness among the lusty living, just as Myra did in that first Lawrencian vision of the sexual Beatrice.

Williams makes the Lawrence figure very clear in *Orpheus Descending,* even to the point of using the trail of sexual salvations as the reason for the crucifixion. Sexuality is equated with vitality and identified with art in its capacity for enriching, sensitizing, and fertilizing human life. Val is a kind of Prince Charming in snake-skin jacket who awakens the Sleeping Beauties, but does not linger to live happily ever after with them. Val certainly brings life back to Lady, who blossoms and prepares to bear fruit like the little fig tree she describes. And the sexual envy by the sterile residents of this wasteland community is adequate motive for watering the soil with Val's blood. But this excessively sexual prowess (idealized as is his poetic sensitivity) draws the attention away from the real question and brings an almost irrelevant death. Williams' hero is more honestly sacrificed for nonconformity than for animal vigor.

Williams is consistently more effective when he develops his natural images rather than combining all possible ideals to make his hero a man for all seasons. The characters that are the more successful self-portraits incline toward but eventually reject sexual solutions. Tom in *The Glass Menagerie,* Brick in *Cat on a Hot Tin Roof,* and Shannon in *The Night of the Iguana* all find sex appealing, but nothing more than a temporary narcotic for forgetting the real anguish of existence. The women who also appear in some way to be self-portraits personify the same tensions. Even the nymphomaniacs (Cassandra in *Battle of Angels* and Blanche of *A Streetcar Named Desire*) realize that sex is little more than a way of forgetting about death. Val says that he once believed people could communicate through touch, but he has come to reject this answer. So do most of Williams' more sensitive people.

His real poet is an asexual wanderer, like Hannah Jelkes in *The Night of the Iguana,* who has learned to rise above the human condition and tolerate the awful solitude of the solitary imprisonment that is life. In fact, Williams' most sincerely felt ideal is the homosexual poet, finding rare moments of love in a world that sees him as an anarchist and an outcast. Thus, the Lawrencian image (no matter how intensely affirmed intellectually) is not germane to Williams' psyche. Norman Mailer may believe that happiness is one great heterosexual bed, but Tennessee Williams merely wishes he believes it. The play is thus, in part, a failure because Williams insists on listening to his conscious rather than his unconscious mind, to other men's answers rather than to his own—a cardinal sin for the Romantic iconoclast.

Among those portions of his world he tried to put behind him in his journey from the St. Louis apartment to the New Orleans flop house was that form of Puritanical Christianity he had assimilated in his youth and hated in his adolescence. Thus Christianity, along with the Puritan sexual ethic and the legalistic behavioral code, became a primary villain in his early plays. His pastors are fools and his church pillars are hypocrites. The honestly religious people in his stories are frustrated by the fare they find at the church social and end by painting red church steeples or running off for a life of prostitution. Vee in *Battle of Angels* offers us a foretaste of the extremes to which the rebellious Puritan will be driven in *Summer and Smoke* and *The Night of the Iguana.* But the more sinister religious figure in *Battle of Angels* is Jabe, the cancer-stricken husband whose rot has gone too deep for the knife and who is doomed. This death-in-life figure, surrounded by his symbols of impotence, sits like the dead hand of historical Christianity, warping the human life below his death bed. This super-annuated Jehovah thumps his cane in fury at the forbidden vitality flowering on the earth below his sterile heaven. When he fails to thwart the love of the rebellious angels, he casts them out of the world that he still controls—murdering one and causing the lynching of the other. This cruel God is a heartfelt part of Williams' visceral philosophy. He puts people into this jungle world, afflicts them with loneliness, decay, and the awareness of impending death, and allows pleasure only to make that death more bitter by contrast with life. Williams may have chosen to reject Christianity in his flight from his youthful world, but he found he could not escape it. This venomous old Jehovah continues to be an underlying theme in play after play.

His natural response was to construct an alternative in his "savior," a god-man who is the very anthithesis of the dying God he hated. Thus Val is by contrast the symbol of human compassion, in love with life and with all things human. His name relates him to the Christ symbol, but his actions equate him more with Lucifer, the rebellious angel. Like many an author, Williams finds it far easier to record the philosophy that has blighted his life than to construct the ideal that would save it. While Jabe can be a fairly consistent symbolic presentation, Val must represent a cluster of values that appear here and there in Williams' personal religious, literary, and psychological history. As a result, he becomes more of a pastiche than a character.

In the more drastic revision of the play, he becomes Orpheus to Jabe's Pluto. But Williams could not resist holding onto the Christian mythology as well, so that the Orphic dimension served only to complicate further the already fantastic symbolism. In addition, the author found that he had to telescope the Orpheus myth so that the later death scene overlaps the Eurydice story. Actually, using either Christian or Greek mythology involved Williams in deep trouble. On the one hand, the story alienated those few who followed its Freudian study of Christian symbolism; and on the other it failed to make sense of the vestiges of the Christian story when translated into a Greek context. As he continues to clutter his play more and more in hopes of salvaging it, he makes it increasingly fascinating to the psychologist and the anthropologist, and diminishes by each stroke that much of its tragic stature. His first audience in Boston was outraged by the play, his more recent audiences have been amused.

All that is wrong with *Battle of Angels* makes increasingly obvious all that is right with *The Glass Menagerie*. In Williams' own terms, he is now being honest instead of artificial, writing from his heart rather than his head, using his own life as his book. Again basing the story on a self-portrait, he is this time less mythic and intellectual and defensive and pretentious. Instead of Valentine Xavier, he is simple Tom Wingfield, hardly an elaborate mask for Tom Williams. The problem basic to the play is again the hesitation to cross a threshold—this time between adolescence and youth, dependence and independence. The trap of love is again sprung by an older woman, but this time she is honestly the mother, not Venus, the Virgin Mary, Proserpine, and Eurydice. Again the young man escapes and must escape from the tender trap in order to live. But this time all of the social world need not lumber after him to destroy him for his apostasy. The punishment lies not in a lynch mob but in the pain of his memories. The love Tom feels for his mother and his sister is much more real and much more demanding than the combination of sex and compassion Val feels for Lady and the other lost females. The simple tale of a supper for a gentleman caller and an anguished leap for freedom needs no mythic undergirding because it is true and natural and universal. Amanda is by her very nature not merely Tom's mother: she is everyone's mother.

The circumstances are much less disguised and idealized than in *Battle of Angels*. The apartment parallels Williams' sombre memories of St. Louis, the girl polishing her glass animals closely follows his portraits of his sister Rose before her mental breakdown, and the mother is clearly Williams' own mother with her memories of Mississippi and of youth and springtime and happiness. The major change is his removal of his hated father, who is now but a smiling picture symbolic of the love of long distance. But this change is useful in allowing Williams to avoid a portrayal he was not yet prepared to encounter, to simplify the story, and to intensify Amanda's demands, her paranoia, and to help explain Tom's guilt. The alteration of Rose's infirmity to a physical one does not change her role drastically from that she has played in his life; and she still retains some of that withdrawal from reality that was the clue to her increasing schizophrenia.

Thus, in *The Glass Menagerie*, Tennessee Williams used the very antithesis of the method he had employed for *Battle of Angels*. Instead of constructing this play, he revealed and slightly ordered his own memories. In a sense, he found this easier because he was dealing with his past in *The Glass Menagerie*, while in *Battle of Angels* he had striven to justify and idealize his present and his future. Where he strove to make *Menagerie* more significant by relating it to the Depression and the growing violence abroad, his prose sounds ponderous and irrelevant to the play's tone. His sentimentality at the end is effective enough because it grows out of the deliberately ironic tone Tom has been using as a defense in most of the story. But the excessively arty stage directions reveal the same tendency toward overemphasis so glaringly evident in *Battle of Angels.*

It is far easier to understand Tom's need to escape Amanda and her smothering motherhood than it is to see the archetypal poet's need to escape love and society. The terms of *The Glass Menagerie* are more concretely stated and the conclusions more acceptable: a man of imagination seldom finds fulfillment in a shoe factory; a boy seldom becomes a man under the watchful eye of a domineering mother; the break with the past is always painful for the sensitive man; and there is health in this drive to preserve one's integrity and develop to one's maturity regardless of the demands of the family.

Williams has used the tension between self-fulfillment and contribution to the family as the core of several of his plays. Apparently he has found that a man who loves his family never really escapes it. Bad plays like *Moony's Kid Don't Cry* and *The Rose Tattoo* are built on this theme, but good ones are as well (*A Streetcar Named Desire* and *Cat on a Hot Tin Roof*). He finds a resolution of sorts in *Night of the Iguana,* where the grandfather and the daughter can make a home in one another's hearts without demanding permanence or needing to escape (as he and his grandfather did). But even as late as *The Seven Descents of Myrtle,* the mother continues to rule the son, here to the extent that he becomes a transvestite in his effort to accept her personality.

This eternal struggle to cut the umbilical cord, underlying almost all of Williams' work, explains a number of his related ideas. The separation from the mother-figure parallels the separation from society and its values. Amanda represents the ideals of the Old South, the Puritan tradition, and a kind of meaningless conformity that destroys the individual without the consequence of enriching the world. In seeing Amanda, we understand the real reason for the angry attacks on conformists, church people, and small-town tyrants. Val is obviously the Romantic ideal that Tom pictures as he makes his escape out of ugliness, censorship, repression, and stifling love into a world of adventure, rootlessness, and moral anarchy. The artist, as he perceives him, lives in a world of polarities: masculine and feminine, past and present, conformity and nonconformity, control and chaos. He also discovers his world is full of paradoxes: love is a weapon women use to unman the male; compassion is a virtue but involvement is a peril; freedom demands cruelty. The world comprehends instinctively that the artist, the fanatic, the lover of beauty, the anarchist are its enemies. Thus it must work to control, to pervert, to tame, and to castrate what it senses to be its enemy. *The Glass Menagerie* understates these discoveries, paralleling the covert way in which life itself reveals them. But *Battle of Angels* intensifies them into hyperbole, alienating the sympathetic viewer by the stridency of the complaint and the exaggeration of the terms. Poets may be fired from jobs or manipulated by mothers, but are seldom blow-torched by red-necked mobs.

The generalization that would grow naturally out of this contrasted analysis of two extremely different Williams plays is clearly that Williams should restrict himself to slightly altered reminiscences. However, another powerfully written play suggests more interestingly the boundaries of Tennessee Williams' talents. *A Streetcar Named Desire* uses many of these same materials with astonishing and effective variations. The story is again one of family tensions, the demands of the past impinging on the present, culture facing barbarism, sickness threatening health, man fighting woman. Yet, while it is much more violent than *Glass Menagerie*, *Streetcar* is much more real and much more tragic than *Battle of Angels*.

The wanderer entering alien territory is again sensitive and artistic and morally suspect. But it is a woman who takes the role of guardian of human values this time. Her age, her accent, her memories, and her demands on those who love her remind the reader of Amanda. But Blanche contains within her character much that reminds one of Tom as well. She too finds the past stifles her, she too searches for a new life that has beauty and adventure. And she is more forthright in the admission that one is never free of the past. It is always part of one's luggage. Blanche contains more of Williams' self than does Amanda. While the playwright saw the earlier character with sympathy and irony combined, he more fully identifies with the later character. Critics have frequently noted Williams' remarkable ability to create fully rounded female characters. The reason is largely that it is in the woman or the effeminate man that Williams most often reveals himself. Blanche, like Williams, lives briefly in New Orleans, her accent and her manners contrast grotesquely with those about her, her love of romance seems ludicrous to the world she can never quite bring herself to enter. In the feminine personality, Williams has found his satisfying parallel to the Romantic poet; in our culture, love of beauty is seen as a weakness in a man, excessive sensitivity as a fault.

The antithesis is Stanley Kowalski—all that society worships in the male. He is virile, loud, smart, aggressive, ambitious, and independent. He is in fact the sum total of those characteristics Williams resented in his father, and his portrait explains the omission of the father from *Menagerie.* Stanley's view of Blanche parallels society's view of the artist. He resents the implicit judgment on his own habits of mind and life. He resents the intrusion into his world of this alien voice. And he feels threatened by the strength behind the veneer of weakness. Therefore he attacks her with his natural weapons, stripping her of her illusive surface; he turns the naked bulb on her to reveal her physical weaknesses. He isolates her from her lover and her sister, and then rapes her and sends her off to the madhouse. His role is essentially the same as that of the men in *Battle of Angels.* This time, though, the brutality is more effective because of the difference in sex. Rather than attributing the men's hatred of the Romantic to some mystique of sex envy that forces the actor playing the sensitive poet to flex his muscles and lounge suggestively around the stage while stroking his guitar, Williams allows the more complex antipathy between the lover of the ideal and the lover of the real to be his motive for destruction.

Rape is a more effective image for what society does to the artist than lynching. In *Orpheus Descending,* the characters toy with the idea of castration, and in *Sweet Bird of Youth,* they carry out their threat. Williams here points out that this is what life and time do to all of us, but to the most sensitive first. Rape is an effective term for what the Romantic believes the world does to him and his art. It robs the artist of his dreams and then uses him for its own diversion. In Holden Caulfield's terms, it prostitutes the artist.

Madness is also a good image for Williams' Romantic ideal, for the world must look on the poet's retreat from its vision of reality as madness. It is not surprising that Williams so often cites Don Quixote as one of his literary heroes. Their theories of madness are remarkably similar.

In *Streetcar,* Williams is able to present in Blanche, even more effectively than earlier in Tom, certain features of his self-portrait. The mask releases him from his pugilistic stance and allows him to admit partial acceptance of his mother's values. Now he can show sympathetically the doomed beauty of the past contrasted with the gross vitality of the present, and the baroque rhetoric of the South compared with the grunts of the animalistic realist. He can confess his love of fragility without sounding sentimental. And he can insist (perhaps protesting overmuch) that his moral "corruption" has a reason and a history, and he can show that it carries with it consequent tortures. He can also admit an ambiguity in his relation to Stanley and his virile world of poker, drink, raw meat, and raw sex. Blanche's flirtation is as real as her disgust. She courts her own disaster; the death-wish, a need for punishment, for self-destruction may be a partial explanation. But the later love-hate between Brick and Big Daddy suggests still another: that the artist secretly admires and even loves the caveman who threatens his existence.

The most curious point of all seems to be a confession that Blanche's world and his are doomed. One can escape only into death, madness, or chaos. In *Camino Real,* his heroes are all diminished but still undefeated Romantics—Byron, Don Quixote, Camille—who have found that the Royal Road turns into the Real Road at the border. Like the Princess in *Sweet Bird of Youth,* they are now in Ogre Country, where their defeat, though inevitable, can yet be heroic. Williams clearly damns the real world, but he finds no escape from it that lasts for long.

Blanche's story is less believable than Tom's, but her character is much more fully realized. Williams' real talent lies not in construction, but in understanding, in characterization rather than in plotting. *Streetcar* contains many of the ambiguities discovered in *Battle of Angels,* but a character study needs less consistency and clarity than does a sermon. Blanche is no idealized heroine. Williams allows the real person to carry the burden of the meaning. Her quest is for love and beauty, as was Val's, her weariness with corruption echoes his, but Williams does not outfit her in outlandish mythic garb, idealize her journey, or insist on her apotheosis. As a self-portrait she is more natural, more honest, and more tragic than any Williams character before or since. She embodies his sense of isolation, his concern for cruelty, his dread of death, and his disgust with his own flesh. She may be dypsomaniac and nymphomaniac and psychotic; she may be as defensive as he is and as full of confused drives and self-hatred, but she is also the Romantic in an unromantic land.

The Romantic imagination may construct myths or enlarge

them in the manner of Shelley and Keats, but there is a form of Romanticism which works more effectively within the bounds of its own literal reality—a Wordsworthian pattern. Here the intellect is useful only in analysis and aesthetic formation, not in generalization and extension. Curiously, Williams, like Wordsworth, also seems unable to judge his own capacities. *Battle of Angels* (like *Camino Real*) sums up so much of his thought, brings together so many of his favorite images and myths and heroes and situations that Williams loves it for its portrayal of his conscious art. *The Glass Menagerie* and *A Streetcar Named Desire* are less conscious, less intellectualized portrayals of a deeper, more emotional experience. They are so true and so simple that he is tempted to dismiss them as obvious. But in their composition lies the key to Williams' greatness—nature rather than art. His later plays have proven most effective in those moments of self-revelation: where Hannah and Shannon are portions of his own psyche perceiving their affinity and their inability to live in harmony for long, or where Brick and Big Daddy acknowledge that their anger grows out of a jealous love and a wish that they could understand one another. His moments of self-justification—Chance Wayne insisting that he is in us all or Brick attacking mendacity—are strident and unconvincing by comparison.

Williams is clearly a latter-day Romantic, by nature and by education. He encompasses the typical tensions of this type: love of both the universal and the particular, of art and of naturalness, of anarchy and of order. He is a visceral rather than a cerebral Romantic, gifted with sensitivity rather than with the philosophic mind. It is a tribute to his ingenuity and to his artistry that he has discovered so many powerful dramas to be dredged from his own emotional experience. His worst plays are inclined to be those that are the most self-aware, most defensive, most idealistic. When he drops the mask and the particular for the archetype, his exaggerated lyricism and over-wrought imagery dominate the play. But when he can lose himself in a character and allow Blanche or Brick or Alma to speak his thoughts in their own voices, he is controlled by the demands of the characters and of their situations. When he reveals his truth instead of pronouncing it, letting it evolve rather than constructing it, feeling it rather than thinking it, he is a powerful playwright.

Tennessee Williams:
"What's Left?"

by Catharine Hughes

Although occasional diehards may hold out for Arthur Miller, and particularly for *Death of a Salesman,* there seems these days to be a consensus that Tennessee Williams is the major American playwright to emerge since O'Neill. Beginning with *The Glass Menagerie* in 1945 and following up with the Pulitzer Prize-winning *A Streetcar Named Desire* (1947) and *Cat on a Hot Tin Roof* (1955), he has staked out a virtually unchallengeable position.

Yet, something did somewhere go wrong. *The Glass Menagerie,* arguably his best play, was produced more than 30 years ago, and even *The Night of the Iguana,* his last major success, occurred some 15 years ago. Since then, we have had such works as *The Milk Train Doesn't Stop Here Anymore, Kingdom of Earth, In the Bar of a Tokyo Hotel, Small Craft Warnings* and *Out Cry,* all of which must be ranked as failures, all of which contain some splendid writing. And, although Williams would— and does—dispute it, the critics have not been the reason.

To find out what has happened, Mr. Williams'...*Memoirs*...is not a bad place to start.

In the foreword, the playwright confesses that "I undertook this memoir for mercenary reasons. It is actually the first piece of work, in the line of writing, that I have undertaken for material profit. But I want to tell you, too, that soon after I started upon the work I forgot the financial angle and became more and more pleasurably involved in this new form, undisguised self-revelation."

Mr. Williams may believe the first sentence—he has always seemed a very honest man, so there is no reason not to take him

"Tennessee Williams: 'What's Left?'" by Catharine Hughes. From *America,* 134 (January 10, 1976), 10-11. Copyright © 1976 by *America.* Reprinted by permission of the author and publisher.

at his word—but I don't believe it for a moment. Given the fact that his financial need can hardly have been that great and given also the man himself, it seems at the very least improbable. Obviously, however, he became thoroughly immersed in his "undisguised self-revelation," and to mixed effect.

Frequently reticent in times past, altogether forthcoming in other circumstances, he has now apparently decided to let it all (?) "hang out" in terms of his homosexuality, problems with liquor and drugs and breakdowns. Realizing that many, perhaps most, Americans have by now either experienced or been witness to similar situations within their own circle, he perhaps recognizes the possibility of empathy as he approaches 65. As one of the characters in *Camino Real* insists, men "make voyages, attempt them, there's nothing else."

Early in the memoirs—which he obviously feels a bit awkward about, continually referring to them as this "thing"—Williams acknowledges: "Somehow I cannot adhere as I should to chronology." And, indeed, he does not, quixotically skipping back and forth in time from his Mississippi birth in 1911, his youth in St. Louis and his homosexual "coming out" in New Orleans, to his early Broadway successes and later failures, interspersing often graphic recollections of his loves, fleeting and long-term. It is, as he says, a "chronicle of time present and past," and its principal drawback is that the average reader, or at least the reader in search of a full autobiographical approach, will find numerous frustrations in terms of gaps in the chronology and an excessive attention to the playwright's sex life. One hesitates to suggest that a writer of Mr. Williams' integrity is deliberately attempting to sensationalize or titillate, yet it does at times seem that way.

These unquestionably poignant memoirs were begun in 1972 and completed in 1975, obviously not a happy time for the playwright. His recent plays had failed. He was attempting to keep one afloat—*Small Craft Warnings*—by appearing in it Off Broadway. He was in distress over the fate of *Out Cry,* a play clearly very important to him, and he was hoping for a better reception for *The Red Devil Battery Sign*—which was to close in Boston in the summer of 1975, after this book had been completed. The great love of his life, Frank Merlo, had died of cancer some time before, and he had suffered a serious breakdown. He was institutionalized by his family.

Approaching 65, what was left?

It's always difficult to speculate, of course, but there are some moderately promising signs. Although ultimately disappointing, Mr. Williams' first full-length novel, *Moise and the World of Reason,* published in early 1975, contained any number of passages on a par with the best he has ever written. At present, there have just been or there soon will be New York revivals of *The Glass Menagerie, Summer and Smoke, Sweet Bird of Youth* and *27 Wagons Full of Cotton,* and a musical version of *Camino Real,* for which he has written the book, is in the works. By several accounts, the out-of-town flop, *Red Devil Battery Sign,* may be one of the best plays he has written, though apparently in need of considerable reworking in order to achieve its potential. The *Memoirs,* I suspect, are more catharsis than anything else, Book-of-the-Month Club alternate selection though they be.

Toward the end of the book, Williams writes that he has "made a covenant with myself to continue to write, since I have no choice, it is so deeply rooted as a way of existence and a form of flight." He has, over the past three decades, provided the American theatre with some of its richest moments (and not a few frustrations), and it is to be hoped that the crepe-hangers may yet have their comeuppance.

The Red Devil Battery Sign:
A First Impression

by Sy M. Kahn

Tennessee Williams' *The Red Devil Battery Sign* had its official world premiere on January 17, 1976 in Vienna's English Theatre. The occasion was preceded by several weeks of preview performances which were well heralded, well received and well attended in Vienna. Although the play had appeared in Boston during the previous year, the Vienna run was advertised as a "world premiere" on the strength of the play having been revised for new production. I must evaluate the play as a reviewer rather than as a critic, with only the single impression of a preview performance (now three months old) and without the advantage of having a script in hand. The script is not available at this writing because Williams is expected to make further revisions for a possible Broadway opening. Consquently, I am writing about a work that has been and still is in progress.

Despite certain flaws of pacing and tempo which I felt were more problems of direction than of the script, and the unsuitability of some accents (from a largely English rather than American cast), certain themes clearly emerge, and with real, if uneven, power. These themes will be familiar to readers of Williams' plays of the 1940s and 1950s who remember those characters so often victimized by both natural and human malevolence. Common calamity, or impersonal victimization by disease, for example, or the natural cannibalism of nature are intimidating enough in themselves in Williams' world, but there is a special viciousness in human actions intentionally cruel, mendacious, and vengeful. Often the events of the calamitous natural world become the large symbols for the depravities of the human heart.

Whether victims of irrational nature or man, Williams' sympathetic characters respond with courage and dignity, and are defeated with grace. To a great extent, the two leading characters in *Red Devil* are cast from this old Williams mold. Presented on the whole realistically, the heroine, called the "Woman Downtown," reminds one, in her distraught, pressed condition of the famous Blanche DuBois of *A Streetcar Named Desire;* her lover, the Mexican band leader called King, dying of a brain tumor as a result of a car accident, reminds one of other sympathetic male characters, such as Kilroy in *Camino Real,* brought down from heights of personal vigor.

In *Red Devil,* Southern evil, cosmic evil, human malevolence of the earlier plays have been translated into and expressed by the menace of big business and international cartels and connections. Thus the title of the play is a metaphor for international conspiracy which accounts for wars like Viet Nam and political assassinations like those of the 1960s. These implications, though never made explicit in the dialogue, were heavily underscored in the production through the Brechtian technique of side-stage projections of war scenes and American victims of assassination. Whether these were directorial overlays, or demanded by the script, one cannot yet say, and the same is true for the periodic use of pulsating red light to emphasize certain ominous moments. In fact, flatly rendered minor characters and a cold, dehumanized atmosphere provided by a backdrop of neon-lit squares gave a semi-expressionistic tone to the production. Williams is given to writing his stage symbols large—to "dotting [his] i's with pumpkins," as Henry James once observed of the stage in general, but we will have to wait for the script to learn who dotted them, Williams or the director, Franz Schafranek.

We discover the "Woman Downtown" incarcerated in a plush hotel in Dallas. She is the estranged wife of the tycoon who owns the Red Devil Company, as well as the hotel. She has reason to appear intimidated, harried, and paranoiac in that she is under surveillance by certain young men in short hair and neat suits, her husband's agents, because she has stolen certain incriminating company papers that will expose international conspiracies. These papers she has shared with her guardian, an old judge, who has decoded them and now intends to spirit her away to Washington where the intrigue will be aired before a congressional committee. However, he is murdered in this attempt. The perennial Williams theme of sexual frustration also bedevils her, along with the red devils of international business and politics, as we learn when she confesses her sexually repressed girlhood and abused marriage. King, her compassionate defender and passionate lover, brings her some measure of fulfillment before he dies. There are several explicit bedroom scenes.

As his name implies, King is a strong, vital male whose passion is to be reunited with his daughter, Nina, who once sang sweetly with his combo. Now she has fled to a rocky and seedy career in Chicago. She eventually returns with McCabe, who wants to marry her, but must also seek approval from the predictably hostile, machismo King. Supposedly as virile as King before his illness (but inadequately played, and with an accent clearly redolent of London rather than Chicago), McCabe wins acceptance before King is fatally stricken on stage by the brain tumor that has increasingly disabled and paralyzed him. However, before dying, King kills a Red Devil Company henchman who has raped the Woman, and she flees the hotel to join the expiring King.

In counterpoint to the menacing and ominous world in which she finds herself is the savage world of street gangs that surround King's house. During the play we hear periodic, off-stage explosions as the gangs contest for power and territory in the slums of the city. Having lost King, the "Woman Downtown" becomes consort of a gang leader, Wolf; she unites rival gangs who, with their slogan of "Burn, Burn, Burn," will attack a corrupt civilization. The play ends with the bleak scene of soiled and tattered gangs dominated by Wolf and the Woman, who respond to the mesmerizing call of revolution in a brutal world.

Williams offers us in *Red Devil* a grim parable of the contemporary world divided into two sets of menacing images: the slick and powerful conspiracies, with the red devil sign as cosmic symbol of hex and hell, and the alternate savagery of fugitive and warring street gangs. King, a temporary savior, dies, as does the Woman's guardian; the brutalized Woman and a ravaging Wolf stand triumphant over slag heaps. Between these alternatives there is no crevice of escape for the individual. In earlier plays, and even as late as *Kingdom of Earth,* psychologically uncomplicated sex offers some defense against, or recompense for, the natural terrors of the world, as well as a basis for love; in *Red Devil* sex is debased and love doomed. Violence and revolution are the final response to a civilization beyond redemption. Always given to a rather paranoiac and pessimistic view of the world,

Williams in this play gives full expression to his feelings of oppression, alienation and inevitable defeat, even though King maintains a certain dignity until his death. Without him, the "Woman Downtown" becomes the Woman Underground in a darkening, cataclysmic landscape, but with the seed of revolution quickened within her. Though the play sprawls, is scenically choppy, and obviously needs the revision Williams is attending to, the Vienna version generates power—and, as I witnessed, sent at least one Vienna lady howling from the theatre into the night.

The Countess:
Center of *This Is (An Entertainment)*

by Judith Hersh Clark

This Is (An Entertainment), given a lavish premiere production, which opened January 20, 1976, by San Francisco's American Conservatory Theatre (and was poorly received by the critics), is regarded by Tennessee Williams as a work in progress, and, as written and revised for ACT, the play shows Williams' concern with characterization, particularly as an outgrowth of characters he explored in two earlier plays: *In the Bar of a Tokyo Hotel* (1969) and *The Two-Character Play* (1976).[1] He calls it a delicate combination of the lyric and the farcical, and indeed both plot and characterization contain a strong element of the fantastic. The Countess, the central character of *This Is*, seems to be compounded of elements of character pairs in these plays: Miriam and Mark of *Tokyo Hotel* and Clare and Felice of *The Two-Character Play*.

The plot itself is complicated and confusing. Set in the Grande Hotel Splendide, located in a small European country, the action alternates between the hotel's opulent lobby and the Count and Countess's separate suites. The hotel is invaded first by the Countess, whose entourage includes her chauffeur-lover and her literally horned husband. The second invasion, midway in the play, is that of a revolutionary army, led by General Eros, who later becomes the Countess's second lover. The simplest plot

[1]Published as *Out Cry* by New Directions in 1973, this second edition, considerably revised and retaining the play's original title, is in *The Theatre of Tennessee Williams* (New York: New Directions, 1976), Vol. 5, which also contains a note on the four productions to date. A quotation from this edition is identified in the text by page number. [See also Footnote 2 to Thomas P. Adler's "The Dialogue of Incompletion..." and *Chronology of Important Dates* in this volume.—Ed.]

thread concerns the Countess's destruction of her husband and her two lovers (both played by the same actor), amidst a revolution, in itself corruptible. The play also contains several dream-like visions of the Countess's dead mother, as well as illusion-breaking scenes where the Countess, the Count, and Eros step out of their roles. This chaotic plot reflects a near schizophrenia within the Countess herself.

The very first scene of *This Is* plunges us into the three personalities of the Countess which vie for dominance and which derive from the earlier plays. Most vividly she is a time-defying sensualist, scorning her husband, commanding her chauffeur-lover, tossing diamonds to servants. At the sound of her dead mother's soprano voice, however, she subsides into the gentle wistfulness of her second personality. Her third personality was added only in revision; stepping back from her role as Countess, she assumes the role of actress and declares that her part is a mockery of a human being, but she nevertheless re-enters the illusion of the play.

The time-defying sensualist, in the very extravagance of her actions, recalls Miriam of *Tokyo Hotel*. Domineering and selfish, Miriam has contempt for Mark's weakness; she is, in his words, a "bitch." She wants to have Mark drugged and bundled and shipped to the States, perhaps to an insane asylum; this is less farcical than the Countess threatening her husband with an elephant gun, but the husbands' humiliations are similar.

Time-defying in words, the Countess also shares with Miriam a fear of the dark, which may be interpreted as a fear of aging and death. The "circle of light" that bounds Miriam is a defense against the dark, and she can remain in it only by "Animation, Liveliness." In Scene 7 of *This Is*, the Countess is afraid of a shadow; it causes her to lose momentum in her race to outrun the moment, and it reminds her of Isadora Duncan's death by strangulation. In Scene 10, the shadow again shakes the Countess's confidence; she sees it as a premonition, perhaps of her guilt in the downfall of General Eros, perhaps of loss of control over her own character.

Paradoxically, the Countess also resembles Mark, the artist-victim of *Tokyo Hotel*, and Miriam's foil. Mark has images that "flash in his brain"; the Countess sees events before they occur. The Countess rushes to greet the revolution, despite sniper fire. Mark describes his work as "adventuring into a jungle country with wild men crouching in bushes...with poison arrows too."

Most important, Mark the artist and Miriam the "bitch" are, as Miriam sums them up, "Two sides of!... One! An artist inhabiting the body of a compulsive—" Mark: "Bitch!" Miriam's description fits the Countess as well.

The Countess, an extravagant sensualist one moment, becomes a sad romantic the next. This abrupt change echoes Williams' note on Clare in *The Two-Character Play: "the grand and the vulgar disappear entirely from the part of Clare in 'The Performance,' when she will have a childlike simplicity...pure and sad..."* (310) Further, the Countess's wistful dependence on a past that takes the form of her mother's ghost recalls the passivity of Clare and Felice in "The Two-Character Play."[2] Just as the sister and brother are unwilling to leave the security of the house, to face the staring people in the street, the Countess is unwilling to have her mother's spell end, to face an awakened lover.

Least emphasized by Williams—apparently an afterthought— is the aspect of the Countess which breaks theatrical illusion. Nevertheless, it is important since it severely threatens the existence of the other two parts of her personality. Like Clare, who sees doing "The Two-Character Play" as "insane," the Countess calls her play a joke-book. Like "The Two-Character Play" for Clare, *This Is* becomes a prison for the Countess-as-actress. Like Clare, she struggles to be rather than to play a part. In vain. Clare's part is a role in her own past, and the Countess's is the role of an increasingly conventional, romantic heroine.

At the center of *This Is (An Entertainment)* is the Countess— three separate personalities. In the play's present form, the Countess finally leaves the revolution-torn country, contentedly bearing the seed of her condemned lover. *Tokyo Hotel* and *The Two-Character Play* end with some connection established between the pairs of opposing characters; no such harmonizing of roles occurs for the Countess in *This Is*. Since Williams still considers *This Is* a work in progress, he may yet resolve the conflicting personalities of the Countess.

---

[2]"The Two-Character Play," within the play of the same title, has no direct parallel in *This Is*. While the shift of the Countess into her passive role is a drawing back from the play's surface, the surface is broken only in the few, brief moments when the Countess-as-actress comments on her play. In those moments, the rest of *This Is* is the play-within-the-play.

Notes on the Editor and Contributors

STEPHEN S. STANTON, Professor of English (department of humanities) at the University of Michigan, has edited *Camille and Other Plays* (with an "Introduction to the Well-Made Play") and *A Casebook on Candida.* Formerly bibliographer for *The Shaw Review,* he has contributed articles on American and European drama to *PMLA, Modern Drama, The Reader's Encyclopedia of World Drama,* and other publications.

THOMAS P. ADLER teaches dramatic literature and film at Purdue University, where he is Associate Professor of English. He has published widely on modern British and American drama, as well as Victorian poetry. His book on *Robert Anderson* will appear soon, and he is currently at work on a critical study of the Pulitzer plays.

LOUISE BLACKWELL is Professor of English and Director of the honors program at Florida A. & M. University. Author of a book of short stories, *The Men Around Hurley,* and co-author (with Frances Clay) of *Lillian Smith,* a critical-analytical study, she was a Fulbright lecturer in American literature in 1972-73 at the University of Sao Paulo in Brazil.

JUDITH HERSH CLARK, Associate in English at the University of California, Davis, is writing a book on Tennessee Williams.

HAROLD CLURMAN, co-founder in 1931 of the famous Group Theatre, is drama critic of *The Nation* and has directed plays internationally, including many Broadway productions. Also a professor at Hunter College, New York, he is presently writing *Ibsen's Plays: An Interpretation* and has published many books on the theatre, including *The Fervent Years, The Divine Pastime,* and *On Directing.* His reviews have been collected in *Lies Like Truth* and *The Naked Image.*

RUBY COHN, who has taught at the University of California, Santa Cruz and the California Institute of the Arts, is Professor of comparative drama at the University of California, Davis. Her books include *Samuel Beckett: the Comic Gamut, Currents in Contemporary Drama, Dialogue in American Drama, Back to Beckett,* and *Modern Shakespeare Offshoots.* She has also published numerous articles and is an editor of *Modern Drama.*

DONALD P. COSTELLO, Professor of English at the University of Notre Dame, has published criticism on Graham Greene, J. D. Salinger, Henry James, LeRoi Jones, Edward Albee, as well as Tennessee Williams. His book, *The Serpent's Eye: Shaw and the Cinema*, was published in 1965.

GILBERT DEBUSSCHER teaches English and American literature at the Free University, Brussels, Belgium. He is the author of *Edward Albee: Tradition and Renewal* (the first study of the playwright) and several articles on contemporary American drama. He is presently Chairman of the Belgian-Luxembourg American Studies Association.

ARTHUR GANZ, who teaches English at the City College of the City University of New York, is the editor of the volume on Pinter in the *Twentieth Century Views* series, the co-author of *Literary Terms: A Dictionary*, and the author of numerous articles on such modern playwrights as Chekhov, Shaw, and Giraudoux.

ROBERT BECHTOLD HEILMAN, scholar and critic, is known for *The Ghost on the Ramparts, Magic in the Web: Action and Language in Othello, This Great Stage: Image and Structure in King Lear,* and other books. Recipient of a D.H.L. from Kenyon College, he is currently in England on a Guggenheim fellowship, writing a book on comedy. He was Chairman of the English department at the University of Washington from 1948 to 1971.

CATHERINE R. HUGHES is drama critic for *America.* The author of *Plays, Politics, and Polemics* and *American Playwrights: 1945-75,* she is currently writing *Tennessee Williams: A Biography.* Formerly a theatre consultant for the New York State Council on the Arts, she has contributed theatre reviews to *Christian Century, Saturday Review, Antioch Review,* and many other journals. Her historical drama, *Madame Lafayette,* had a successful Off Broadway run.

ESTHER MERLE JACKSON, author of the well-known study, *The Broken World of Tennessee Williams,* is Professor of theatre and drama at the University of Wisconsin, Madison. She has published studies of dramatic form in the works of other American playwrights, including Maxwell Anderson and Imamu Amiri Baraka (LeRoi Jones).

SY M. KAHN is Professor of English and drama and Chairman of the drama department at the University of the Pacific. Since 1949 he has directed plays of Tennessee Williams and has lectured abroad on Williams' work. A contributor to *Tennessee Williams: A Tribute,* he has published articles on literature and several volumes of poetry.

ROGER B. STEIN now writes and teaches primarily on the relation between American literature and the visual arts, for which work he has held both Guggenheim and Fulbright fellowships. He is Associate Professor of English at the State University of New York, Binghamton.

NANCY M. TISCHLER is Professor of English and head of humanities, Pennsylvania State University, Middletown. Author of the early study, *Tennessee Williams: Rebellious Puritan*, she has also published *Black Masks: Negro Characters in Modern Southern Fiction* and articles on drama, religion, and fiction in many periodicals including several devoted to Southern literature. She has contributed to *Tennessee Williams: A Tribute*.

GERALD WEALES, Professor of English at the University of Pennsylvania, is the author of *American Drama Since World War II, Tennessee Williams*, and *Clifford Odets, Playwright* and the editor of critical editions of two Arthur Miller plays, *Death of a Salesman* and *The Crucible*. He has contributed theatre reviews to *The Reporter* and other publications. He is presently at work on a book on American film comedy in the 1930s.

Chronology of Important Dates

1911	March 26: Born Thomas Lanier Williams in Columbus, Mississippi.
1918	Family moved to St. Louis, Missouri.
1927	First work published: an essay, "Can a Good Wife Be A Good Sport?" in *Smart Set* magazine.
1928	First story published in *Weird Tales*.
1929	Entered University of Missouri. Received small prizes for prose and poetry.
1931	Withdrawn by father for flunking ROTC and put to work in International Shoe Co. warehouse. Spent long nights writing at home.
1935	After nervous breakdown, spent a year recuperating at home of grandparents in Memphis. First play, *Cairo! Shanghai! Bombay!* produced.
1936	Entered Washington University, St. Louis. *Candles in the Sun* and *Fugitive Kind* (not the later film script) produced.
1937	Entered University of Iowa. Sister Rose underwent prefrontal lobotomy.
1938	Graduated from Iowa.
1939	Itinerant writer, wandering from Chicago to St. Louis, to New Orleans, to California, to New Mexico. Won Group Theatre prize of $100 for *American Blues*. Awarded $1000 Rockefeller grant.
1940	Entered John Gassner's advanced playwriting seminar at New School, New York City. Failure of *Battle of Angels* in Boston.
1941-44	Lived and wrote in New Orleans and New York and worked as waiter-entertainer, elevator operator, and theatre usher in New York, and as MGM script-writer in California.
1944	*The Glass Menagerie* opened in Chicago, December 26.

1945   *The Glass Menagerie* produced at the Playhouse, New York; directed by Eddie Dowling and Margo Jones. Won New York Critics' Circle Award. Published by Random House. Fourth unsuccessful operation for cataract on left eye.

1946   *27 Wagons Full of Cotton and Other Plays* published.

1947   *A Streetcar Named Desire* produced at the Barrymore Theatre, New York; directed by Elia Kazan. Won second New York Critics' Circle Award and Pulitzer Prize. Published by New Directions.

1948   *Summer and Smoke* produced at Music Box Theatre, New York; directed by Margo Jones. (Revived Off Broadway under Jose Quintero's direction in 1952.) *American Blues: Five Short Plays* published. *One Arm and Other Stories* published.

1950   Novel, *The Roman Spring of Mrs. Stone* published.

1951   *The Rose Tattoo* produced at Martin Beck Theatre, New York; directed by Daniel Mann. *I Rise in Flame, Cried the Phoenix* published.

1953   *Camino Real* produced at National Theatre, New York; directed by Elia Kazan. (Revived under José Quintero's direction in 1960.)

1954   *Hard Candy: A Book of Stories* published.

1955   *Cat on a Hot Tin Roof* produced at Morosco Theatre, New York; directed by Elia Kazan. Won third New York Critics' Circle Award and second Pulitzer Prize.

1956   Film, *Baby Doll*, opened in New York. Poems, *In the Winter of Cities*, published.

1957   *Orpheus Descending* produced at Martin Beck Theatre, New York; directed by Harold Clurman. Began psychoanalysis.

1958   *Garden District (Something Unspoken and Suddenly Last Summer)* produced Off Broadway; directed by Herbert Machiz.

1959   *Sweet Bird of Youth* produced at Martin Beck Theatre, New York; directed by Elia Kazan.

1960   *Period of Adjustment* produced at Helen Hayes Theatre,

New York; directed by George Roy Hill. Film, *Fugitive Kind* (screen version of *Orpheus Descending*) opened in New York.

1961 *The Night of the Iguana* produced at Royale Theatre, New York; directed by Frank Corsaro. Won fourth New York Critics' Circle Award.

1962 First version of *The Milk Train Doesn't Stop Here Anymore* produced in Spoleto, Italy.

1963 Second version of *Milk Train* produced at Morosco Theatre, New York; directed by Herbert Machiz. Entered period of depression over death of intimate friend, Frank Merlo.

1964 First version of *The Eccentricities of a Nightingale* tried out in summer stock.

1966 *Slapstick Tragedy (The Mutilated* and *The Gnädiges Fräulein)*, produced at Longacre Theatre, New York, and directed by Alan Schneider, closed after seven performances.

1967 First version of *The Two-Character Play* produced at Hampstead Theatre Club, London. *The Knightly Quest: A Novella and Four Short Stories* published.

1968 *Kingdom of Earth (The Seven Descents of Myrtle)* produced at Ethel Barrymore Theatre, New York; directed by José Quintero.

1969 *In the Bar of a Tokyo Hotel*, produced Off Broadway and directed by Herbert Machiz, closed after twenty-five performances. Converted to Roman Catholicism. Admitted to St. Louis hospital after nervous collapse in Key West. Released three months later.

1970 *Dragon Country: A Book of Plays* published.

1971 First volume of *The Theatre of Tennessee Williams* published by New Directions.
      Second version of *Two-Character Play* (titled *Out Cry*) produced at Ivanhoe Theatre, Chicago.

1972 *Small Craft Warnings*, produced Off-Off-Broadway and directed by Richard Altman, was first commercial success since *Iguana*.

1973   Third version of *Two-Character Play* (titled *Out Cry*), pro-
            duced at Lyceum Theatre, New York, and directed by Peter
            Glenville, closed after twelve performances.

1974   *Eight Mortal Ladies Possessed: A Book of Stories* published.

1975   First version of *The Red Devil Battery Sign* closed in Boston
            and New York opening postponed. Second version of *King-
            dom of Earth* produced in Princeton, N.J. Fourth version of
            Two-Character Play produced Off-Off Broadway. Novel,
            Moise and the World of Reason published. *Memoirs* published.

1976   Second version of *Red Devil* produced in Vienna; directed
            by Franz Schafranek. *This Is (An Entertainment)* produced in
            San Francisco; directed by Allen Fletcher. Fifth volume of
            The Theatre of Tennessee Williams published. Second ver-
            sion of *The Eccentricities of a Nightingale* produced in
            Buffalo, New York, and at Morosco Theatre, New York;
            directed by Edwin Sherin.

1977   *Vieux Carré* produced at St. James Theatre, New York; di-
            rected by Arthur Allan Seidelman.

Selected Bibliography

*I. Articles and Interviews About Williams' Life
and Approach to Writing*

Williams' publisher in America is New Directions; Secker and Warburg Ltd. publishes his plays in Great Britain. He has written prefaces to many of his plays, and in this country these are usually printed in the single play editions (New Directions, New American Library, and Signet).

Barton, Lee. "Why Do Homosexual Playwrights Hide Their Homosexuality?" *The New York Times*, January 23, 1972: II, 1, 3.

Bentley, Eric. Letter in "Drama Mailbag," *The New York Times*, February 13, 1972: II, 5. Replay to Barton.

Buckley, Tom. "Tennessee Williams Survives." *The Atlantic*, 226 (November 1970), 98-108.

Funke, Lewis and John E. Booth. "Williams on Williams." *Theatre Arts*, 46 (January 1962), 16-19, 72-73.

Gaines, Jim. "A Talk About Life and Style with Tennessee Williams." *Saturday Review*, 55 (April 29, 1972), 25-29.

Gussow, Mel. "Tennessee Williams on Art and Sex." *The New York Times*, November 3, 1975, p. 49. Interview on *Memoirs*.

"Playboy Interview: Tennessee Williams—A Candid Conversation." *Playboy*, 20 (April 1973), 69-84.

Reck, Tom S. "The First Cat on a Hot Tin Roof," *The University Review* (University of Missouri at Kansas City), 34 (Spring 1968), 187-92.

_____. "The Short Stories of Tennessee Williams: Nucleus for His Drama." *Tennessee Studies in Literature*, 16 (1971), 141-54.

Waters, Arthur B. "Tennessee Williams: Ten Years Later." *Theatre Arts,* 139 (July 1955), 73.

Wenning, T. H. "Unbeastly Williams." *Newsweek,* June 27, 1960, p. 96.

Williams, Tennessee. "On a Streetcar Named Success." *The New York Times,* November 30, 1947. Reprinted in *American Playwrights on Drama,* edited by Horst Frenz. New York: Hill and Wang, Inc., 1965.

――――. "The Timeless World of a Play, introduction to *The Rose Tattoo.*" New York: New Directions Publishing Corp., 1950. Reprinted in *American Playwrights on Drama,* edited by Horst Frenz. New York: Hill and Wang, Inc., 1965.

――――. "Tennessee Williams Presents His P. O. V." *The New York Times Magazine,* June 12, 1960, pp. 19, 78.

――――. "Survival Notes: A Journal." *Esquire,* 78 (September 1972), 130-34, 166, 168.

――――. "Let Me Hang It All Out." *The New York Times,* March 4, 1973, II, pp. 1-3.

II. *Works on Tennessee Williams*

USEFUL BIBLIOGRAPHIES

Carpenter, Charles A. "Modern Drama Studies: An Annual Bibliography." *Modern Drama,* 17 (March 1974), 80-81; 18 (March 1975), 72; 19 (June 1976), 185-86.

Chesler, S. Alan. "*A Streetcar Named Desire:* Twenty-Five Years of Criticism." *Notes on Mississippi Writers,* 7, 44-53.

Eddleman, Floyd E., ed. *American Drama Criticism,* Supplement II. Hamden, Conn.: The Shoe String Press, Inc., 1976. Pages 178-83. (See also base volume and Supplement I.)

Presley, Delma E. "Tennessee Williams: Twenty-Five Years of Criticism," *Bulletin of Bibliography,* 30 (March 1973), 21-29.

Robbins, J. A., ed. *American Literary Scholarship.* 11 vols. to date. Durham, N.C.: Duke University Press, 1964-74.

CRITICAL BOOKS, ARTICLES, AND SOME REVIEWS

Asselineau, Roger. "Tennessee Williams on la nostalgie de la Pureté." In *Das Amerikanische Drama von den Anfangen zur Gegenwart,* ed. Hans Itschert, pp. 276-92. Darmstadt: Wissenschaftliche, 1972.

Bentley, Eric. *In Search of Theater.* New York: Vintage Books, 1954, pp. 84-86. Review of *Streetcar.*

_____. *What Is Theatre? Incorporating "The Dramatic Event" and Other Reviews:* 1944-1967. New York: Atheneum, 1968. Reviews of *Camino Real* and *Cat.*

Brooks, Charles B. "The Comic Tennessee Williams," *The Quarterly Journal of Speech,* 44 (October 1958), 275-81.

Callaghan, Barry. "Tennessee Williams and the Cocaloony Birds." *Tamarack Review* (Toronto), 39 (Spring 1966), 52-58. Review of *Gnädiges Fräulein.*

Casty, Alan. "Tennessee Williams and the Small Hands of the Rain." *Mad River Review,* 1 (Fall-Winter 1965), 27-43. Religious interpretation of early plays.

Clurman, Harold. "Theatre." *The Nation,* 214 (April 24, 1972), 540-41. Review of *Small Craft Warnings.*

_____. "Theatre." *The Nation,* 216 (March 19, 1973), 380. Review of *Out Cry.*

Debusscher, Gilbert. "Tennessee Williams' Unicorn Broken Again." *Revue belge de Philologie et d'Histoire* (Brussels), 49 (1971), 875-85. Discussion of *Glass Menagerie.*

Dickenson, Hugh. "Tennessee Williams: Orpheus as Savior." In *Myth on the Modern Stage,* pp. 278-309. Urbana: University of Illinois Press, 1969. Discussion of *Orpheus Descending.*

Dukore, Bernard F. "The Cat Has Nine Lives." *Tulane Drama Review,* 8 (Fall 1963), 95-100. Discussion of Animal Imagery in *Cat on a Hot Tin Roof.*

Durham, Frank. "Tennessee Williams: Theatre Poet in Prose." *South Atlantic Bulletin,* 36 (March 1971), 3-16. Discussion of *Glass Menagerie.*

Falk, Signi Lenea. *Tennessee Williams.* New York: Twayne, 1961.

Fritscher, John J. "Some Attitudes and a Posture: Religious Metaphor and Ritual in Tennessee Williams' Query of God." *Modern Drama,* 13 (September 1970).

Gelb, Arthur. "Williams and Kazan and the Big Walk-Out." *The New York Times,* May 1, 1960, II, pp. 1, 3.

Gussow, Mel. "Catharsis for Tennessee Williams?" *The New York Times,* March 11, 1973, II, pp. 1, 5. Review of *Out Cry.*

Hagopian, John V. "Cat on a Hot Tin Roof." In *Insight IV: Analyses of Modern British and American Drama,* edited by Hermann J. Weiand, pp. 269-75. Frankfurt: Hirschgraben, 1975.

Hirsch, Foster. "Sexual Imagery in Tennessee Williams' *Kingdom of Earth.*" *Notes on Contemporary Literature,* (Carrollton, Ga.: West Georgia College), 1, No. 2 (1971), 10-13.

Hughes, Catharine R. *Tennessee Williams: A Biography.* Englewood Cliffs, N.J.: Prentice-Hall, Inc., forthcoming in 1978.

Hurley, Paul J. "Tennessee Williams: The Playwright as Social Critic." *The Theatre Annual,* 21 (1964), 40-56. Discussion of *Cat on a Hot Tin Roof.*

———. "*Suddenly Last Summer* as Morality Play." *Modern Drama,* 8 (February 1966), 392-402.

Hyman, Stanley Edgar. "Some Trends in the Novel." *College English,* 20 (October 1958), 2-9.

Isaac, Dan. "Big Daddy's Dramatic Word Strings." *American Speech,* 40 (December 1965), 272-78.

Jackson, Esther Merle. "Tennessee Williams." In *The American Theater Today,* edited by Alan S. Downer, pp. 73-84. New York: Basic Books, Inc., 1967.

———. "Elements of Form in the Drama of Tennessee Williams." In *Das Amerikanische Drama von den Anfängen zur Gegenwart,* edited by Hans Itschert, pp. 265-75. Darmstadt: Wissenschaftliche, 1972.

Kahn, Sy M. "Through a Glass Menagerie Darkly: The World of Tennessee Williams." In *Modern American Drama: Essays in Criticism,* edited by William E. Taylor, Deland, Florida: Everett/ Edwards, 1968. Discussion of some central themes in Williams' work.

Kalson, Albert E. "Tennessee Williams' *Kingdom of Earth:* A Sterile Promontory." *Drama and Theatre,* 8 (Winter 1969-70), 90-93.

_____. "Tennessee Williams Enters *Dragon Country.*" *Modern Drama,* 16 (June 1973), 61-67.

Kernan, Alvin B. "Truth and Dramatic Mode in the Modern Theatre: Chekhov, Pirandello, and Williams." *Modern Drama,* 1 (September 1958), 101-14.

King, Thomas L. "Irony and Distance in *The Glass Menagerie.*" *Educational Theatre Journal,* 25 (May 1973), 207-14.

Link, Franz H. *Tennessee Williams' Dramen: Einsamkeit und Liebe.* Darmstadt: Thesen Verlag. 1974. Discussion of the major plays.

Miller, Arthur. "The Shadows of the Gods: A Critical View of the American Theatre." *Harper's,* 217 (August 1958), 35-43. Reprinted in *American Playwrights on Drama,* edited by Horst Frenz. New York: Hill and Wang, Inc., 1965. Contains discussion of *Cat on a Hot Tin Roof.*

Miller, Jordan Y., ed. *Twentieth Century Interpretations of A Streetcar Named Desire.* Englewood Cliffs, N.J.: Prentice-Hall, Inc., 1971.

Nelson, Benjamin. *Tennessee Williams: The Man and His Work.* New York: Obolensky, 1961.

Novick, Julius. "Honest or Merely Disarming?" *The Village Voice,* March 8, 1973, p. 58. Review of *Out Cry.*

Performing Arts (San Francisco), 10 (February 1976). Premiere cast and notes on *This Is (An Entertainment).*

Petersen, Carol. *Tennessee Williams.* Berlin: Colloquium Verlag, 1975.

Peterson, William. "Williams, Kazan, and the Two Cats." *New Theatre Magazine* (University of Bristol, England), 7 (Summer 1967), 14-19. Comparison of the two endings of *Cat on a Hot Tin Roof.*

Popkin, Henry. "The Plays of Tennessee Williams. *Tulane Drama Review,* 4 (March 1960), 45-64.

_____. "Tennessee Williams Reexamined." *Arts in Virginia,* 11 (Spring 1971), 2-5.

Presley, Delma E. "The Search for Hope in the Plays of Tennessee Williams." *Mississippi Quarterly,* 25 (Winter 1971-72), 31-43.

Rogoff, Gordon. "The Restless Intelligence of Tennessee Williams." *Tulane Drama Review,* 10 (Summer 1966), 78-92.

Rorem, Ned. "Tennessee Now and Then." *London Magazine,* new series,

15 (June-July 1975), 68-74. Review of *Eight Mortal Ladies Possessed: A Book of Stories.*

Sacksteder, William. "The Three Cats: A Study in Dramatic Structure." *Drama Survey,* 5 (Winter 1966-67), 252-66.

Starnes, Leland. "The Grotesque Children of *The Rose Tattoo."Modern Drama,* 12 (February 1970), 357-69.

Tharpe, Jac L., ed. *Tennessee Williams: A Tribute.* Jackson: University Press of Mississippi, 1977. A volume of critical essays.

Tischler, Nancy M. *Tennessee Williams: Rebellious Puritan.* New York: Citadel Press, 1961.

————. "Tennessee Williams' Bohemian Revision of Christianity." *Susquehanna University Studies,* 7 (June 1963), 103-8.

Traubitz, Nancy B. "Myth as a Basis of Dramatic Structure." *Modern Drama,* 19 (March 1976), 57-66. Discussion of *Orpheus Descending.*

Vidal, Gore. "Selected Memories of the Glorious Bird and the Golden Age." *The New York Review of Books,* February 5, 1976, pp. 13-18.

Vowles, Richard B. "Tennessee Williams: The World of His Imagery." *Tulane Drama Review,* 3 (December 1958), 51-56.

Weales, Gerald. *Tennessee Williams.* Minneapolis: University of Minnesota Press. 1965.

Weiner, Bernard. "New Dramatic Territory." *San Francisco Chronicle,* January 22, 1976. Review of *This Is (An Entertainment).*

Weissman, Philip. "A Trio of Tennessee Williams' Heroines: The Psychology of Prostitution." In *Creativity in the Theater.* New York: Basic Books, Inc., 1965. Reprinted in *Twentieth Century Interpretations of A Streetcar Named Desire,* edited by J. Y. Miller. Englewood Cliffs, N.J.: Prentice-Hall, Inc., 1971.